mindfire
dialogues in the other future

ALEXANDER BLAIR-EWART

A Patrick Crean Book

SOMERVILLE HOUSE PUBLISHING
Toronto

Canadian Cataloguing in Publication Data

Mindfire

"A Patrick Crean Book"
ISBN 1-895897-43-2

1. Forecasting. 2. Civilization, Modern - 1950-   .
3. Social prediction. I. Blair-Ewart, Alexander, 1947-   .

CB161.M55 1995   303.49   C95-931535-7

Edited by: Harry Posner
Interior design: Brenda van Ginkel
Jacket design: Alexander Blair-Ewart
Jacket portrait photograph: Andrew "Woody" Stewart
Jacket digital illustration: Ron Giddings
Author photograph: Gerry Riley

Printed in Canada

A Patrick Crean Book

Published by
Somerville House Publishing
a division of Somerville House Books Limited,
3080 Yonge Street, Suite 5000, Toronto, Ontario M4N 3N1

Somerville House Publishing acknowledges the financial assistance of the Ontario Publishing Centre, the Ontario Arts Council, the Ontario Development Corporation, and the Department of Communications.

For my three sons, Justin, Damon, Christian.

Thanks are due to the several people who contributed in their various ways to the process that led to this book.

Praise and thanks to Harry Posner (a.k.a Ace Osmer) who managed to be all things to all people at *Dimensions* magazine and who never once complained or lost his composure amid the daunting task of transcribing and retranscribing my near endless editings of these interviews. And for his attention to detail as he diligently gathered all of the pieces of this book together and created the index in record time. Included also is his fine interview with Dr. Graham Farrant.

Special thanks to Ero Talvila who played the role of the original winged messenger to the new spiritual community in Toronto. And who seeded the inner life network and *Dimensions* long before it had a name.

Thanks to Valerie Elia who generously volunteered to interview Marion Woodman and Elizabeth Kübler-Ross.

Thanks also to Debra and Jessica Earhart, Linda Steeves, Wendy Fredericks and Robert Stocks.

To Patrick Crean for fostering this undertaking.

contents

why you are reading this book

THE FUTURE WE WANT is the one with a united world community of free peoples. This new world federation will take the necessary steps to save the Earth from the looming ecological crisis, weapons of mass destruction, overpopulation, and the inequities of poverty, ignorance, and the oppression of minorities and women.

This future has floated into planetary focus for a brief moment a few times this century. The last time was during the heady days of the revolution in Eastern Europe and Russia. The first time was at the end of the "war to end all wars." When most people think about the future now, it seems filled with trouble and frightening changes. Yet the future is being sold to us as never before.

In a world of futurehype, apart from the frenetic people involved in producing technology, almost no one is looking forward to the future. We stand at a juncture in time where technology has already succeeded in defining the future for the whole human race. We have rubrics such as "free-market democracy," "democratic competitiveness," "technological efficiency," "downsizing," "new world order," and most lately "internet" and "cyberspace."

All of these buzzwords and slogans add up to the fact that the world is going through a cataclysmic change, a change in governance, a change in economic values, social values, a change in everything that we mean by culture. And the one thing that characterizes all of this change is that it is occurring as the outreach of technology into society.

It is obvious that whatever our current mainstream view of the future may be, the vast majority of people don't believe in it. If young people believed in their future, they probably wouldn't be killing each other in significant numbers, they probably wouldn't be addicted to crack and crime in large numbers, they probably wouldn't be committing suicide in such alarming numbers. It's clear the future isn't working in the form that we now think of it. And the strident voices that clamor for a return to so-called traditional values sound both naive and sinister.

Technology is a fixed prophecy of the future: because it is the nature of technology to always know in advance how it is going to make its own prophecies come true, it carries an overwhelming power of conviction. A technological future is a future defined by elitist minorities — the transnational corporations involved in technological research — who decide what the breakthroughs are, with everybody else driven by market forces to go along with them. In the technological future the only contribution you can make is with your pocketbook. And in many areas of life new technology is compulsory. You are being directly affected whether you like it or not.

In this *other future* everybody who cares to be involved is shaping it. So it's not as if this book is telling you about another future that's going to happen to you. This book is saying to you, "Here is a way of thinking about the other future that involves and includes you, and to which you should make your contribution, because this is where you can begin anew to exercise your freedom and make a contribution that will have meaning for you and your community."

Technology wears many masks, and one of the masks that technology has adopted is the mask of the "new age" movement, where we hear so much about "reprogramming your subconscious mind," "seminars for success," and "stress management," as opposed to the realization of your spiritual being and what it would mean to realize the true nature of yourself as a spiritual human being instead of trying to improve it within the paradigm of technology. Yet the real meaning of the new spirituality is that it balances and tempers the influence of technology. Many ill-informed people imagine that the new spirituality is some modern exotic but deranged version of the old spiritualities. Some kind of flaky flight into reality. Nothing could be further from the truth as this book will make clear.

It is undeniably true that technology has made the world in many respects a very small place. There's hardly anyone alive now who is not aware that there's actually a planet out there beyond the borders of our own continent and country. There is a multicultural universal humanity on Earth. Technology has brought this awareness to everyone. The Gaia image of the Earth from space is the most universal symbol of our time. But where is there a universal, human, spiritual vision of this new global humanity?

This unfortunately is still missing from the international conferences and forums. Still not on the agenda along with NAFTA, World Free Trade, GATT, and the power strategies to bring about new world order. It is precisely because of the absence of a universal spiritual vision of global humanity that all of these economic and technological power mergers will lead to ever greater chaos and interethnic wars.

A universal spiritual vision of global humanity is the most urgent issue of our world-changing time. Without it none of these new world order strategies stand the slightest chance of success. We don't have this vision yet and this book isn't claiming to have it. Yet there is here a highly developed beginning, an exploration well under way. Vast numbers of people all over the world are still held captive by various forms of propaganda and corruption, and so must wait for a future when they can freely participate in global humanity. In the meantime, what these dialogues are about is how that new humanity can come into being. And as the dialogue is still open and must always remain open, that means that everyone is included.

All of the people in this book are talking in one way or another about the new community, and everyone who is aware of what's going on sees that that's the one thing that is collapsing in the face of globalized economic technology. Rabbis and priests decry its loss; popes come out in support of it; swamis suggest meditation techniques to protect it. Everybody is aware that community is the ultimate endangered species on planet Earth, and it is because we're having a crisis in community that all the other communities of creatures on this planet are also having a crisis. It's all part of the same thing.

The one thing that all of the people in this book share in common is that they are capable of imagining a future other than the mainstream version. They are capable of looking at themselves and the people around them, looking at humanity and the planet, looking into the future and saying, "It could be different, it could be like this." And the "this" they're talking about is not something technological. On the other hand, it's not something Luddite either. The people in this book aren't saying let's throw a clog into the machine, smash all the computers, and return to some imaginary Garden of Eden. All of them know that there's no going back for us. Part of what they're saying is that we can use what communications technology has done to the world as a springboard into a future beyond technology itself. So it's not cyberspace but real alternative reality space.

The time will come when we're living in the post-technological era. How far away that is comes down to this — whether we suffer from a poverty of imagination and cannot yet imagine any alternative future to the future as technology, or whether we are creative enough to give birth to a culture and a future that's capable of creatively and spiritually balancing the overwhelming impact of technology.

In order to discover a new community we have to be prepared to think about it, talk about it, and be prepared to take the risk, a risk beyond the safety of know-it-all cynicism, acknowledging what our heartfelt longings are towards family, community, and the emerging global culture. If people aren't involved, then corporate entities and corporate governments are going to decide for them what their lives are going to be like. Now that political democracy has disappeared from the planet and been replaced by free trade areas and world economic considerations, the imaginative creation of new community becomes the next revolution of freedom.

Here in this book we have a group of highly diversified individuals who've dreamed another future, who've thought another future, who think of the world not just in abstract terms, but actually think of the whole of the presence of life, and think of all of the beings involved in that presence simultaneously. We've always had a word in the West for this way of looking at things. We've always called this "metaphysics." A metaphysical view of life deals with what is at the heart and core of human beings, of beings collectively, and of life as a whole. All of us are inevitably part of that. Now in this post-metaphysical era we no longer seek to once and for all define human beings or the world. Our gift and challenge is that as yet there is no final vision for this other future. So it's something that we have to create and invent and get involved in. This book is about that involvement.

Alexander Blair-Ewart

1

thinkers
on the edge

FRITJOF CAPRA

GRAHAM FARRANT

MICHAEL MURPHY

mindwalk
into the
new rising
culture

FRITJOF CAPRA
in converstaion with
ALEXANDER BLAIR-EWART

Fritjof Capra is a physicist and best-selling author of The Tao of
Physics *(1975),* The Turning Point: Science, Society and the
Rising Culture *(1984),* Uncommon Wisdom: Conversations with
Remarkable People *(1989), and coauthor with Brother David
Steindl-Rast and Thomas Matus of* Belonging to the Universe:
Explorations of the Frontiers of Science and Spirituality *(1991).*
*He is currently the director of the Elmwood Institute, an
ecological think tank located in Berkeley, California, that
sponsors educational conferences, lectures, and seminars within
the framework of the new paradigm. We reached him in
Washington, D.C., just prior to the North American release of
the movie* Mindwalk, *a screen adaptation of* The Turning Point.

ABE: Do you see the new paradigm breaking through, or is it still an
underground phenomenon?

FRITJOF C: I work within an institutional framework that I have created called the Elmwood Institute, which is an ecological think tank located in Berkeley, California. I organize conferences and lectures, seminars and workshops within that framework. And what we have been doing, especially over the last couple of years, is talk to corporations, and I think this is where the ecological paradigm is now having one of its most effective impacts. More and more corporations, especially small and medium-size companies, have recognized that they need to manage their affairs in an ecologically responsible way, to be aware of the environmental impact of their operations. So there's a whole school of ecologically conscious management that is emerging, and we are very much working with those pioneer managers. I think that's one of the more interesting and important areas where the new paradigm is emerging.

ABE: In *The Turning Point*, and also in *Mindwalk*, there is discussion about new macroeconomic patterns and how they demand the awareness of social costs in economic planning. Can you talk about how this inclusion of social costs actually works in practice for corporations?

FRITJOF C: Well, what works in practice is that you tackle the principle stumbling block to sane ecologically and socially responsible work. And that's the notion of unlimited growth. Economists, businessmen, and politicians are obsessed by the notion of unrestricted, unlimited economic growth. That notion of growth is the major driving force behind economic policy-making, both in business and politics, and at the same time, tragically, it's the main driving force behind the environmental destruction, and also the social destruction that we can see around us. So, what you need to do is to ask, "Which enterprises should be allowed to grow and which shouldn't?" And there the idea of sustainability has come to the fore as the key concept or criterion. What it means is that a sustainable society is one that can satisfy its needs without diminishing the chances of survival for future generations, that is, without diminishing the planet's resources, without destroying our life-support systems.

ABE: Now it's interesting that the term "sustainable growth" or "sustainable development" has a very different meaning coming out of the mouths of ecologically conscious people on the one hand, and politicians on the other. Do you think the politicians actually understand what it means?

FRITJOF C: Well, some do and some don't. Most of them use the term as a buzzword and end up distorting it.

ABE: A lot of them sound as if they're just using a new term for old-style growth.

FRITJOF C: There's a confusion between sustainable and sustained. You see, sustained growth is growth that goes on and on. Sustainable refers to the whole system, actually to the whole planet and society.

ABE: In *The Turning Point* you talk about the "entropy state" of most economies in connection with the second law of thermodynamics. Do you have any ideas about how we might resolve that particular difficulty?

FRITJOF C: This is a difficult question. We need to develop technologies that exemplify a certain simplicity and a certain elegance, rather than ever more complication. And so we need to ask, what really are the human needs? I think it is related to the question of sustainability. Yes, we need to create technologies and administer these structures that satisfy our needs. But we also must ask, do we really need cars? Are trains and buses better than cars to get from here to there? What about walking or cycling? And is it always necessary to go from one place to another? If we change our housing patterns, our work patterns, the whole commuter traffic pattern, maybe we wouldn't need to travel so much. And if we change the patterns of production, maybe we wouldn't need to ship goods around from one place to the other and back. So, there is a certain simplicity which then brings with it a certain elegance that we need to acquire. And we can look into nature and see how the technologies of natural systems work, because there we see the simplicity and elegance very beautifully. That's a difficult task, but certainly one we need to pursue.

ABE: One of the underlying thoughts here is what you call—you quote Bateson—"systemic wisdom."

FRITJOF C: Yes, and Schumacher also made that point, to move from complicated to simple systems, which are not necessarily less complex or less sophisticated, but show that kind of natural elegance you see in the "systemic wisdom" of nature.

ABE: I guess a lot of corporations are beginning to understand that natural elegance through the concept of downsizing.

FRITJOF C: Yes, and decentralizing.

ABE: One of the things that comes through very strongly in your writings and also in the movie *Mindwalk* is Gaia ecology. Could you talk about Gaia ecology in relation to transpersonal ecology?

FRITJOF C: I think the philosophical thought that ties those areas together is that of deep ecology. When you take ecological awareness at its deepest level, you become aware of the fundamental interconnectedness and interdependence of all phenomena. You become aware that we are embedded in larger systems and in the cyclical processes of nature, as individuals and as societies. This sense of being embedded, of belonging, then becomes a sense of the spiritual. And then you belong, as Gary Snyder says, to the earth's household, and that's the best translation I know of the Greek word *oikos* from which the word ecology comes. Brother David Steindl-Rast develops this thought in the book *Belonging to the Universe* which we created together. When you belong to the earth's household, you belong to a community, therefore you behave in a certain way, and that becomes the basis of an ecological ethic. Then you ask yourself, to develop this ecological ethic as a society, what is the basis? I just said that when you belong to a community you behave in a certain way. But this cannot be derived in a scientific or logical manner. This is a psychologically motivated impulse, and the psychological motivation of belonging is a transpersonal motivation. That's how I understand the term "transpersonal"—you go beyond the individual person and you connect the individual person, namely yourself, with the whole.

ABE: The character Sonya (played by Liv Ullman) in *Mindwalk*, in response to someone's question, says, "Yes, ultimately, whether we like it or not, we're all part of one inseparable web of relationships."

FRITJOF C: The film was created and directed by my brother. For me the film is one more tool in an educational campaign that the world now so urgently needs, to promote this shift of thinking and of values. The character Sonya obviously represents me in terms of ideas, and she gives voice to these ideas that were explored in *The Turning Point.*

ABE: The movie points at certain spiritual concepts such as karma, and the idea of being individually responsible to this new sense of community. The idea of karma can be understood in an esoteric, mystical way. But how does that concept become real now in this new sense?

FRITJOF C: An ecological interpretation of karma would be that the universe is nonlinearly interconnected. So whatever you put out eventually will come back, because all ecological processes are cyclical. We're all embedded in these cycles. So when you throw something away, there is no "away" you can throw it to. It's all part of a cycle which will come back. And if that something which you throw away is toxic, it will come back to haunt you, or it will come back to haunt your children in future generations. That, to me, is the idea of karma.

ABE: Can we hope now, because of the change in the power structure in the United Nations, that we might be able to move away from the imperialistic model and towards something that's more holistic?

FRITJOF C: Well, that's certainly the hope, but how long this will take I have no idea. The United Nations has a very important role to play because we don't want a world government. The world has become much smaller, much more interconnected. But we don't want a world government. We want a coordinating body, a body that coordinates individual, national, and regional development. And that's the role that the U.N. should play. I think what we need is decentralization and cultural pluralism, to have different cultures in different parts of the world being autonomous, but to have them coordinate their efforts. The most serious problems we are facing today are global problems. No country alone, for example, can hope to solve the problem of global warming, or ozone depletion.

ABE: Could you talk a little bit about what the movie is about?

FRITJOF C: *Mindwalk* is a dialogue involving three people. We don't talk about spirituality directly, because in my experience it's much better to imply it and to live it, rather than to talk about it endlessly. The place where this dialogue unfolds is a holy place, Mont Saint-Michel, which is a Christian sacred site, and was a Druidic sacred site before that. It's filmed in such a way that the wholeness and holiness, the sanity and beauty of the place, shine through in every part of the film. And that was our way to include spirituality.

ABE: So you were working with a symbolic model there?

FRITJOF C: Yes, very much so. See, the film is a dialogue and it addresses the conscious mind through the dialogue. But at each stage the ideas in the dialogue are associated with metaphors, very powerful visual metaphors. And so the subconscious is addressed through the metaphors and through the scenery. The whole of Mont Saint-Michel is the central metaphor of the film. And so we address the conscious mind and the subconscious at the same time.

ABE: I see. Part of what is being dealt with there is the idea that physicists don't have a language or a way of exploring these ideas. Does the film provide that kind of language, a basis from which people can discuss these things?

FRITJOF C: Yes, it does so in a language that is even simpler than the one I use in my books. And that, of course, was a big challenge. Many people who saw the film told us that for the first time they had understood what matter is made of, and what the essence of the new science of matter is. So I'm very excited by that.

ABE: Here you are defying the whole Hollywood movie concept. The one thing a scriptwriter is not allowed to do is create "talking heads."

FRITJOF C: This was my brother's basic idea, to have the dialogue be the basic structure, the center of the film, and then to string these visual metaphors along the dialogue. He sometimes says it's an antifilm, because it's so much against the Hollywood recipe. I also work a lot with dialogue in the book *Belonging to the Universe*, and also at the Elmwood Institute where we sponsor a lot of public dialogues. Because what we need is to explore ideas. I always think of dialoguing as walking around an idea together, looking at it from different sides. And when you have an audience, they can really experience the thinking process.

ABE: This whole idea goes back, doesn't it, to ancient Greece, where the *dialogos* meant people speaking the "Word" in a sacred sense.

FRITJOF C: And in particular the dialogue format has been used repeatedly in the history of Western culture at turning points or crucial junctures, such as the Socratic dialogues at the dawn of philosophy, or the

Galilean dialogue after which *Mindwalk* is actually patterned. Galileo wrote his famous book about the Copernican system as a fictitious dialogue involving three people. And so dialogue has been used again and again to explore new ideas in the history of science and philosophy.

The way Galileo set it up is that one person represents the new paradigm. His historic book is called *Dialogue Between the Two Principle World Systems,* which are the Aristotelian/Ptolomeic on the one hand, the old paradigm, and the Copernican/Galilean as the new paradigm. So one of those Renaissance speakers in Galileo's book represents the author's ideas, the new paradigm; the other one represents the Aristotelian, old paradigm ideas; and the third one is a neutral bystander who hosts the whole event. When my brother wrote the story for the film, he transposed this into our time. So there is the physicist, Liv Ullman, representing my ideas, and there's a conservative politician representing the old paradigm because we wanted this film to have a political impact. And the third person, the host, is a poet, and he's very eccentric, because we work a lot with humor and eccentricity, to avoid the feeling of a lecture. The really new and radical thing about this recreation of the Galilean dialogue is that the new paradigm is presented by a woman. And that's our feminist statement in the film.

ABE: That's really a deep signature for our time, with the reemergence of the goddesses. Coming back to your book *Belonging to the Universe* with Brother David Steindl-Rast, what led you to create a book with him?

FRITJOF C: He is a Benedictine monk, Austrian born like myself, living at Big Sur in California in a monastery. The way it happened was that in 1985 we had an Elmwood symposium, which was our first invitational symposium. We had founded the institute just a few months earlier, and we invited the country's leading new paradigm thinkers to ask critical questions about new paradigm thinking. We wanted to define our baseline, to see where we start from, scientifically and philosophically. Brother David was in that group. At that symposium I presented five criteria for the new paradigm in science, and then he and a colleague, another monk at the monastery, a little bit tongue in cheek, presented five parallel criteria for the paradigm shift in theology. And we found it so interesting that we started exploring this in conversations and finally began to tape the conversations, which eventually evolved into the book. Everything is spoken and transcribed. We didn't write anything. The book is the Western equivalent of the *Tao of Physics,* because it compares the new thinking in science with Christian theology.

ABE: What's the main thesis of that? How do those things compare?

FRITJOF C: The main thesis is that both science and theology are based on human experience, and that the ecological paradigm, which is now emerging in science, is based on the human experience of a sense of belonging. That's why we chose the title *Belonging to the Universe*. And this is also the very essence of religious experience, which is then interpreted and analyzed by theology. So, what we do is we relate the statements of science and theology to this basic human experience of belonging, and we reinterpret, or rather Brother David does, the basic concepts of Christian theology from that ecological point of view. You could say it's an ecologizing of Christianity.

ABE: How would that compare to what Matthew Fox is doing?

FRITJOF C: I think it's pretty close.

ABE: Does it go deeper?

FRITJOF C: Well, it has science in it. And so, because it's a dialogue, we constantly shift back and forth from science to theology. I would say that it's also more socially and politically oriented. We talk about the political implications of this ecological way of seeing the world.

ABE: Can you bring those five criteria to mind?

FRITJOF C: Each one is a shift from the old way of thinking to the new. The first is the shift from the parts to the whole. The second is the shift from structure to process. The third is the shift from the notion of an objective science to what I call an epistemic science, a science in which epistemology, the process of knowledge, plays a central role. You cannot talk about reality without talking about how you know reality. The fourth criterion is a shift away from the metaphor of architecture in relation to knowledge, as when we say "the basic building blocks of matter," etc., and a shift towards the network as a central metaphor. And the fifth is the shift from truth to approximation—the notion that we cannot know the truth rationally, ever. We can only approximate it.

ABE: And what was your Benedictine monk's response to that?

FRITJOF C : Well it was pretty much the same criteria applied to Revelations and the various concepts in theology. This list is actually at the beginning of the book. That's how we start off our dialogue.

ABE : So, from his point of view, then, as a Christian, he's obviously living in this new paradigm. Does Brother David have anything to say about how Christianity really works in this new paradigm?

FRITJOF C : Yes. We started out talking about religious experience and the interpretation of religious experience in theology—the notion of God and the notion of sin, all these basic concepts and ideas. And we talked about paradigms and paradigm shifts. And I asked him, "What is specific about the Christian paradigm? What is specific about Christianity?" And he said—and this to me is one of the most beautiful parts of the book—he said, "The specific role of redemption in the Christian sense, and the specific teaching of Jesus Christ, is a transition from alienation to community." Sin is alienation, and Christianity has to be understood in terms of community. So when we say in science "ecological," he says "ecumenical." He draws that parallel.

ABE : That's elegant and profound.

the revolution of cellular conciousness

DR. GRAHAM FARRANT

in conversation with

ACE OSMER

Dr. Graham Farrant is an eminent psychiatrist and a pioneer in the field of cellular consciousness. He conducts lectures and experiential workshops in Australia, the United States, and Canada. Dr. Farrant is internationally renowned for his healing approach to the variety of human issues related to prebirth and birth. He specializes in assisting people in accessing organic memories from as early as conception.

ACE OSMER: The work that you've been doing for the past twenty years, utilizing the tool of primal therapy to get to this place where you can talk about cellular consciousness, the actual memory of being the sperm and the egg, the experience of conception, all of this spells revolution from the point of view of the prevailing psychotherapeutic paradigms. And I'm surprised that there isn't an incredible fervor around that one notion alone.

DR. GRAHAM FARRANT: Well, in a sense there is, at a grassroots level. I mean, I do workshops in nine countries, and they're always full. And so in a slow but evolving way it is growing, it is snowballing, perhaps not in the establishment academia, but I never expect them to respond quickly, quite frankly.

ACE: Can you talk a little about your background and how you came to these discoveries?

GRAHAM F: I have a degree from Harvard and one from McGill, one from England and one from Australia, and I had university and hospital appointments, as well as senior consultant positions in Australia. But I gave them away because my five years of classic Freudian analysis hadn't helped two particular symptoms that were evolving by the time I was forty. So I came back to America with four children, my family, to embark on this whole approach of deep regressive psychotherapy in the hope of personally finding a solution to something that the classic myelinated memory idea hadn't resolved. And lo and behold, I had discovered the key to my whole problem, which was that my mother had tried to abort me at six weeks. I retrieved the memory of that so accurately that I knew how she did it. And when I told her, she confirmed it, having never told anybody, not even my father.

Truthfully, she didn't like being pregnant. She didn't enjoy sex, so it was not something she was interested in. When the attempted abortion didn't succeed, of course, she had a great concern that she may have brain damaged me. So when I did arrive, she was very concerned that I be quite "perfect" and reared me that way, obsessively. I ended up being punctual and fastidiously tidy, exceptionally neat, to the point of being rigidly concerned about everything. I changed that with analysis, but didn't quite understand what I came to call my social paranoia, the ridiculous irrational feeling that when I arrived at a new situation, like a cocktail party, I would shortly be asked to leave, because they wouldn't like me. Now I've always been gregarious and outgoing, enjoyed people, so this was out of place. But when it was linked to the attempted abortion, it made sense. Once I'd made that profound connection through a premyelinated memory, the symptoms disappeared. I therefore knew that there had to be a memory of a kind that predated the central nervous system. I began to pursue the whole concept that there was a way of retrieving early memories.

ACE: So you changed your way of working with people?

GRAHAM F: Yes. I suitably prepared my consulting rooms and I allowed people to journey, to go wherever they wanted to go with their body, through movement and sound, the preverbal expressions of our lives. And lo and behold, the unbelievable happened, that even earlier memories came back.

Movements began to appear in different people that were reported as meaning the same thing, like implantation in the womb wall, or descent in the fallopian tube, and then the actual conception, and then the egg and sperm. These were the years 1976-79, and fortunately I made a video of myself regressed, doing these movements, but I didn't show anybody until the *Miracle of Life* film came out in 1983. It's from the Karolinska Institute in Stockholm, Lennart Nilsson's pioneering work. He managed to film actual conception in a human body for the first time, and he noticed two things then that I had relived four or five years earlier that ought not to have been true, because it wasn't medical wisdom of the day, namely that the sperm *did not* penetrate into the egg to fertilize it. The egg sent out little arms that went round the back of the sperm and gently brought it into its substance. And the movements of my hands in the regression were like this [*makes circular inward movements with his arms and hands*]... extended arms with the wrists doing this "come here" movement.

The other point is that I was taught that the egg sped up as it multiplied and divided and there was constant action and movement. But in my regression experience as a fertilized egg I stopped twice, and in *The Miracle of Life* they noticed that it seemed as if the cell took rest breaks. I actually remember the night I burst into tears recalling my experiences of four years previous, in a sense, for me, validating what I'd been experiencing with clients. These people had done their work; they'd been to talking therapists, like I had, and they hadn't resolved significant problems or conditions which were still a mystery to them.

ACE: Can you talk a little bit about the vanishing twin syndrome that you've researched?

GRAHAM F: That's a study that was ongoing in Pennsylvania, where, with the advent of ultrasound, we were able to tell that a larger than expected number of pregnancies start off as twins. Elizabeth Noble, at the Pre- and Perinatal Congress in Amherst in 1989, presented a paper on "The Surviving Twin." She felt that it could be as high as 80%. I think probably 20% at least, and the research shows that it's at least 5–7%, that within the first month, one of the twins is absorbed. Mother doesn't have a bleed or a pain. She doesn't know she's having twins. But the one that survives, grows up, comes to see me, and reports things like, "I have this expensive compulsion when I go shopping to buy two pairs of everything. I never wear the other one, I put it in a closet, and I do wish you'd tell me why I do this because my husband's getting angry." [*laughter*]

Another woman could only live in duplexes. She would get erratic and scatty if she had to live in a flat that wasn't attached to another building next door. One wealthy man actually owned a duplex and had the other one empty. He needed the rental, but he had it empty because he had this delusion, this feeling, that the other person would come back. And they always feel that they are not meant to be alone, and when they are obliged to be alone they get very uncomfortable inside, because many of them feel guilty about the death of their twin, as if they somehow were greedy or hungry or demanding and caused the twin to expire. Twins that actually survive through to birth can present with symptoms of compulsive eating or narcolepsy, which is a syndrome in which you can fall asleep for no apparent reason. Nilsson in his work noticed that twins who share blood vessels can actually kink each other's cords and stop the supply coming through to each other, resulting in this "I need more," an oral hunger, or they end up going to sleep.

ACE: Aside from the clinical applications of these discoveries, there are some deeper metaphysical questions which your work raises. You speak about a triune consciousness at conception—the egg, the sperm, and the soul. Where is the "I," the ego, the individuality of the human being in all this?

GRAHAM F: If I understand that by "I" you mean the sophisticated consequence of the union of the egg and the sperm, then the spirit, the soul is, in my opinion, the ultimate essence of our human nature. And when the I/ego dominates or is only cognizant or present as the driving, motivating force of existence, then we get enmeshed in duality and materialism and attachment. In solving the deficiencies in either the egg or sperm that were existent at conception, one of the pathological clinical identities that I think I've identified over the last twenty years is that we don't realize that the deepest and most profound truth of our human nature is the soul aspect. We have to be *in*formed, we have to be in human existence to be in this particular dimension. When my clients regress back and resolve the issues of the "I" and the Maya, as it's called in the Indian culture, the veil of darkness is thinned out, and what we get in touch with is the soul, the feeling of spirit; it's the wholesomeness and completeness of the state of unconditional love. Some people call it bliss or ecstasy or divinity, cosmic consciousness. These words describe the feeling of being attached and connected to humanity, the awareness of the planet as a cell, as a global village, concern about the environment, concern about the starving people of Africa, at whatever level it takes your interest, a feeling of being involved in something other than the very personal interpsychic ego or I.

ACE: There's a certain Buddhistic quality to the way in which you're describing this work, especially in relation to the individualization, or lack of it, of the "I" as it passes from one incarnation to another.

GRAHAM F: I go along with that to an extent. I suppose I've still got enough "I" left to feel that any work I haven't finished in this lifetime I've got to finish in the next. [*laughter*] So almost regrettably I take a little bit of my karmic work with me into the next experience. I'm a devotee of Sai Baba, and he says you're all waves in my sea of love. And you rise up and have an existence and then you die down and fade and join again with the sea. But you're made of the same essence, and the purpose of my mission and your life is to become aware of your own divinity. I like that picture. So that, I suppose, with my physical death I do fuse again with the sea, and then I'll come again as another wave. But then I've got to take into account what I just said, that somehow I've got that remnant work to do that I didn't do in this karmic lifetime.

ACE: You also talk about prezygote, pregamete memories that in your opinion are memories of the spiritual world out of which we emerge.

GRAHAM F: There is something that I call the "Reluctant Soul Syndrome." There's a very definite group of people who don't want to be here. They have been yearning to go back from whence they came. They have this definite feeling that life was very much purer and more fine and complete and whole there. They live alone; their occupations are lonely—they process films in darkrooms, or they're librarians in small chambers; they're test tube scientists in small rooms; they're nuns in cells, or they live in religious communities of like-minded people. They don't have a social life; they don't have a sexual life particularly; they don't feel comfortable relating to people, and it's very hard for them to come out into the world. They're philosophical; they spend a lot of time reading; they're often out of their bodies; they're dreamers. They're lovely folk, but they have this whole drive to go back. Now sometimes it reaches into depressive suicidal rumination, but they rarely ever do it.

ACE: Are there a lot of people in the field working the way you're working and replicating your findings in a clinical setting?

GRAHAM F : Yes. In Australia there are four psychiatrists who worked and trained under me who are doing their own work in this area. There are several in Switzerland who sponsor the workshops for me there, who are very on track in this respect. Also in southern Germany, Belgium, and around the United States. So yes, there are people who are finding it valid, effective, efficient. It doesn't take years and years; it's a natural process.

If you have a trauma after the age of language, talking about it with someone will resolve it. If it happened before language, say from prebirth to twenty months, bioenergetics, or some form of Gestalt, physical approach will probably be necessary. But it could happen right back at conception—rape, incest, threatened abortions, twinning, manipulative conceptions, the AIDS babies—there are a million Americans who will never know their father because of the anonymous sperm bank situation, etc. These folk are going to have significant cellular trauma. They'll never know who their fathers are.

ACE : The implications of this are really extraordinary for the way that society is to understand the whole nature of what we're doing here, how we get here, and how conscious we have to be of the process.

GRAHAM F : There's the point I'd love to emphasize. Out of it, for me, comes the constructive preventative suggestion of conscious conception. I don't want to get into the abortion row that is rampant in North America at the moment, and you'd think I'd be interested because I survived my own. But I went through the phase of feeling depressively that I wished my mother had been successful in her abortion attempt, because until I solved the mystery, the returning depression and paranoia was miserable, and I didn't understand it. And of course now I'm glad she wasn't successful. There was a reason why, I guess karmically, I had to go through all that, otherwise this would never have come about. I don't think I would have journeyed into this area unless I had to. We do what we need to learn.

But it is important that young people be taught during preadolescent schooling that there is a cellular memory, that it does make a difference if you conceive a child consciously, as opposed to it being a mistake in a car, on drugs. It is also now understood that when young people commit suicide, the way they do it pertains to the way they were born: if they had the cord around their neck, they hang themselves; if they were a forceps birth, they shoot themselves in the forehead; if they were drugged at birth, they take an overdose; if they are a cesarean, they cut their wrists.

ACE: What are some of the longer term effects of prenatal experience?

GRAHAM F: We're getting solid scientific proof now of the long-term consequences of events that happen before birth. Candice Pert, a brilliant scientist, with all her work on neuropeptides, has come to express the idea that the mind is in every cell of the body, not just confined to the brain. So she talks about body/mind and soul, rather than the more usual body, mind, and soul, that the mind is everywhere and every cell has intelligence, every cell has receptors that can give and take information, and that basically we human beings are a bundle of information flow and memory. And she doesn't feel uncomfortable any longer with the idea of reincarnation, because matter can neither be created nor destroyed. So what does happen when this physical body demises? What happens to the information flow that is probably going through our bodies at the speed of light? If one cell hurts here, then every cell knows it immediately, and maybe it's transmitted through wave impulses or sound that we can't hear. She feels that it's transmuted into some other form, that it doesn't actually disappear.

ACE: This is similar to the notion of the akashic records.

GRAHAM F: Absolutely. So here's a pure scientist talking like this. Are you aware of Deepak Chopra's work?

ACE: Yes, I interviewed him several years ago.

GRAHAM F: Well now, he said a very powerful thing when he described the whole possibility of cellular intelligence. I think the sentence goes something like, "With the return of the memory of health, enough energy comes with it to last a lifetime." So he's talking about healing cancer and AIDS and serious chronic degenerative illness, that if we human beings can use our memory to get back to health, to the time when we had health, then the wholeness and energy that comes with that is profound and available for use.

ACE: When Deepak Chopra talks about cellular intelligence and memory, is that the same kind of memory that you're talking about when you speak of the memory of the sperm or egg? Is it the same pool of awareness that both of you are talking about?

GRAHAM F: I believe it is. And what I really appreciated and enjoyed about his comment was that it reminded me of an added dimension. My work has consciously been focused on pain, in the sense that I encourage, allow, permit, want people to come to me to find the courage and the strength to go back in time and face the pain, the trauma, the incident that happened somewhere back in historical time that caused them to stop being whole, that broke their heart, that split them asunder, the rape or incest or the abortion, or father attacking mother while you were in the womb, etc. And out of that wholeness comes a unique type of strength, optimism, confidence, and courage. I guess you might say the "I-ness," or even the awareness of divinity, carries you back into the present-day life equipped with the wherewithal to be fully your genetic potential, not split into anger and terror, or love and hate, wish and fear, wanting to have love combined with fear of relationship. But more a wholeness and wanting to relate to another person who is as whole as they can be.

ACE: How do you distinguish between someone who is connecting to actual prebirth memories, and someone who is dipping into the world of archetypal or genetic memories, memories of previous lifetimes, etc.?

GRAHAM F: As an example, if you remember that a woman is born with all the eggs she's ever going to have, fully grown, and that they were there four months after conception in the womb, so that when your mother was a fetus in your grandmother's body, you as an egg were in your mother's ovary, and if something profound happened to grandmother that affected her pregnancy with your mother—the most profound that I've seen clinically is the death of your great-grandmother—then that really makes grandmother depressed and makes fetal mother contract. Something has happened. There's not enough love or nutrition or health, and that's maybe transferred down to the egg, which is the biggest cell in the body. And that can be so unpleasant that it is spun off as a past life or archetypal memory, rather than felt as a biological physical phenomenon in this sequential lifetime. It seems to especially affect women more than men.

Breech birth with cord and forceps, etc., is a very dangerous, life-threatening, difficult, potentially tragic birth for a fetus. I've seen them again and again split off parts of it into past life, archetypal memory, all sorts of things, rather than to persevere, feel it all for what it was, a horrendous physical experience of this lifetime. So I really surround my clients with a great deal of support and nurturance while they courageously get the fragrance back. Then some of the archetypal, past-life stuff diminishes in the material. But anything is okay along the journey to find the truth. I don't impose. I never interpret anything for anybody. I always let them tell me what they think it is. But I say something like, "Well, would you keep your options open, that there may be other aspects or other explanations?"

Let me just spin back to the point of emphasizing possible advantages to the society of this kind of work: conscious conception, sound antenatal care, the mother and father becoming as aware as possible of their own births, their own conceptions, and how that can unconsciously play out in the way that they create their child, contemplating gentle childbirth as opposed to hospital births (not that they're not appropriate in certain circumstances); good bonding, breast-feeding, enough family support; governments agreeing to maternal vacation, and giving father some time off.

ACE: Not to harp on the abortion issue, but it's obviously an interactive thing, conception and birth. We're talking about spiritual essence, ensouling, the egg resting and deciding whether to complete the process of incarnation, and you have the mother's consciousness bearing on that as well. It seems to me the whole nature of the way we understand abortion might need to be readdressed in the light of the work that you're doing.

GRAHAM F: Well, let me just mention an unusual clinical syndrome that I see time and time again, which is what I understand as a compulsive aborter, a woman who unconsciously gets pregnant only so that she can have an abortion. Now when these women come into therapy they discover that they themselves were in fact unplanned and unwanted, and actually survived an abortion, or certainly survived a mental abortion, e.g., a Catholic or other religious mother who couldn't have an abortion for religious reasons, but wished that she'd had. So they are in fact acting out some generational intent or wish on the mother's part. Strange, unusual suggestion, but it fits for them. Or they feel their life is so miserable that they wish their life had been aborted, so they do it to some other human being. We need to have lateral thinking on this abortion problem.

Young girls particularly, or young men who create their share of the fetus that is to be aborted, are looking and yearning and wanting something, certainly not wanting a pregnancy, but wanting something from each other that they feel isn't there within themselves. If we can raise their consciousness to what that might be—and I certainly feel it's the yearning to be in touch with their divinity—then that's the key. If they were in touch with that, the lustre and power and magnificence, the beauty and contentment and wholeness that exists in that state would mitigate against the need to "screw" each other as a magical way of getting that something, that spark that they feel they're not in touch with. And this involves education from a very early age to do with desires. Swami Sai Baba talks about the ceiling on desires, that desires anchor us into misery, and we'll never get satiated if we have endless desires for objects or wealth or power. Don't repress them, but add something else that has the brilliance and lustre and completeness, and the desires will fade away. This has to do with spiritual aspects, not religious, not in that dogmatic sense.

ACE: It seems that, with the triune consciousness which your cellular work implies, i.e., that we are conscious of being the egg, the sperm, and the soul incarnating, the left brain/right brain dichotomy falls flat, and indeed it has been increasingly undermined as a valid paradigm.

GRAHAM F: Well, for one thing, the mind is not in the brain. We now know from Candice Pert's work that it's everywhere, so let's stop this emphasis on left and right. We're everywhere, we're a wholeness, the total organism is the answer, and we're a repetition of the macrocosm. I mean, the salt content of the sea is the same as the salt content of every cell in our body.

ACE: What your work seems to be pointing to, as well, is that there is an innate desire in every human being to recall themselves to themselves in a total way.

GRAHAM F: That's the absolute truth.

ACE: How do you work with clients to enable them to do that?

GRAHAM F: People take their time, on the floor, in a soundproof, padded space to use movement and sound, and get back to the lost truth of what actually happened, and then find a way through intense expression to release the trapped pain of it, to integrate, to incorporate, and to end up with that whole feeling of pretrauma health that Chopra talks about. And then to use that to come forward into the here and now, use that strength to either say no to people who push you around, or yes to life if you're contracted and withdrawn. And it works.

ACE: Which is the main thing.

GRAHAM F: Well, for me, it is, you see. Press reporters often will ask me, "Well, where's your scientific proof?" I'm tired of that kind of demand on me, when I'm not Candice Pert, I'm not Deepak Chopra, I'm not a molecular biologist or a nuclear physicist. Refer to those people, they've written it all up. David Chamberlain in his book *Babies Remember Birth* has the largest bibliography and references that you could possibly need. And there's Tom Verny right here in Toronto who has been engaged in similar work. I'm a clinician and I work extremely well with people, and I have this capacity, having been there, to allow others to go there with a lot of love and support. That's my contribution.

the future of the body

MICHAEL MURPHY

in conversation with

ALEXANDER BLAIR-EWART

Michael Murphy cofounded Esalen Institute, the world's premiere human potential center, and has authored numerous books, including Golf in the Kingdom *(1973),* Jacob Atabet, An End to Ordinary History, *and the acclaimed* The Future of the Body: Explorations into the Further Evolution of Human Nature *(1992), in which he presents evidence for metanormal perception, cognition, movement, vitality, and spiritual development from more than three thousand sources.*

ALEXANDER BLAIR-EWART: Everybody now thinks that they know what "human potential" means, and everybody has a very subjective idea of what it would it mean if they fulfilled their "potential." I'm wondering if I can get you to talk about what the human being is?

MICHAEL MURPHY: I think, first, there is a lot of language that I do not find highly useful anymore. For example, simple dichotomies between, say, spirit and matter, or that the aim of our growth is something called "enlightenment." I don't use the term enlightenment in my books. I don't use that clean, clear distinction of spirit and matter. I chose twelve sets of human attributes to begin to suggest the complexity of human nature. They include our ability to perceive what's outside of us; our bodily awareness— and remember, each of these can be deepened, extended and elaborated— our communication abilities, our vitality, our movement abilities—and that includes both the movement of the physical body and a spirit body (if indeed there is one, as all the near-death experiences, out-of-body experiences, various kinds of psychedelic experiences, and a whole range of human experiences indicate)—abilities to manipulate the environment, cognitive abilities—some of them on the analytic side, some on the imaginative side, some on the gestalt making and synthesizing side. Then we have volition, that whole range of experience we relate to self and individuation; our relation to pain and pleasure, delight. Then we have the gamut of our emotional life, culminating in love, and then the bodily structures themselves. Now, all of these are part of the human potential because each of them gives rise to the extraordinary.

We can also talk about our capacity for relationships with the world and with others, and our ability to create institutions such as marriage, parenting and schooling, institutions of worship, of inquiry such a universities, and so forth. So any definition of the human potential has to include that wide array. If I was going to talk in simple metaphysical terms, the human potential includes this latent divinity typically perceived to be both within us and outside of us.

ABE: Let me just try to connect with that on a deeper level. I would agree with you, obviously, that there is this divine capacity in all human beings, and we've understood that divinity for millenia, as either being a goddess figure or a god figure, or in the Vedantic/Buddhist experience, something which is ineffable and attributeless. And one of the things that we've been exploring in the last several years here within the new consciousness movement is the extent to which it is a deeply philosophical, metaphysical movement, and the extent to which it is actually a religious movement. When you talk about the human being discovering this divine essence in themselves, are they going to discover something god- or goddess-like, or is it something that is beyond that?

MICHAEL M: For me, both approaches have their deep value, if I understand you correctly. To talk in personal metaphors, God, as a person or superperson, corresponds to an objective reality, and mystics and philosophers have spoken in this language from time immemorial both East and West. By the way, the Buddha himself refused to say anything metaphysical, and the great dominant traditions of Buddhist philosophy don't talk about a personal god. But within the larger Buddhism, it's very personal. The personal apprehension of the personal divinity, the person-to-person aspect of the human/divine contact, has appeared in every single religious tradition. It will not be repressed. To use Freud's metaphor, the repressed will return. The personal dimension of contact with the divine will always return in every tradition. Nevertheless, the language of the impersonal is also useful, I think. It's been stupendously important in my own life to keep reminding us that there is a divinity beyond any name we can come up with, or any emotion we can feel, or any marker we can assign to that divinity. What's the line from the Upanishads? "One unmoving that is swifter than mind, that the Gods reach not, for it passes ever in front, that standing passes beyond others as they run." In other words, it is ultimately ineffable, ultimately unmarkable, ultimately uncapturable. It is the ultimate "more," you see. And the impersonal metaphors are useful in reminding us of this and orienting us towards this radically transcendent other.

But then we turn again to this personal divinity. Both sides of the equation have been very important for me, and both of them keep rising up in every tradition. By the way, in the traditions in which the dominant metaphors are of a personal divinity, a Judeo-Christian-Islamic tradition, there you have the Jewish mysticism of the Kabbalah and the Zohar which says the ultimate ground is Ainsoph—it's beyond all markers. Or you have Meister Eckhart saying beyond God there is the Godhead, the Urgrund. Or you have in Islam the Fana, which means annihilation; it is beyond any self and beyond any god. And you read Rumi or you read Avicenna, or even Rabi'a, and there it comes up again. In the traditions of Vedanta and Buddhism and Taoism in which the primary metaphors seem to be impersonal, the personal rises up. In the Western religions where the dominant metaphors are personal, the impersonal appears among the greatest philosophers and mystics, saints and sages. So you cannot finally escape those two aspects of divinity or those two significations of divinity in human consciousness.

ABE: Is this ineffable, absolute something, the unnameable, in any way interested in humanity directly?

MICHAEL M: Well, not only is it interested, it is immanent in humanity. I take completely seriously the testimony, not only of the great philosophers, mystics, saints, and sages, but of all the common folk, if you will, who feel a close kinship. And as a person pursues this passionate quest to know, that kinship grows into knowledge by identity—"*tat svam asi*" in the Upanishads, "Thou *art* that." See, you *are* that. Atman *is* Brahman. Meister Eckhart said, "Those who say that God and I are two, that God is there and I am here, make a great mistake. The ground of God and the ground of the human soul are one." All of these great mystics and mystical philosophers who are honored in the Christian tradition keep saying that. And Islamic mysticism is shot through with that. So, that speaks of a divine immanence.

ABE: That relationship, then, is not extrinsic, it is something that is discoverable by human beings as their inherent nature.

MICHAEL M: Yes, absolutely.

ABE: So the interesting aspect of it may in fact be its human part, which is us.

MICHAEL M: Yes, you can say that, but realizing that we are self-transcending creatures. So, it's which part of us? A thought comes in and it passes, or you deliberately suppress it, or you stand back from it. Now, is that thought part of yourself? You have some sensation from some body part, and you consciously or unconsciously—this is now well established with many kinds of research—modify that feedback from that body part. You are standing back from yourself. In other words, we are constantly engaged in transcending ourselves. You know, we can't get up in the morning without transcending ourselves. Okay, so then, when you get into this more intense experience that typically arises out of a deep commitment to something, such as being in love, or a deep involvement in a transformative practice, you then encounter parts that really have to supervene upon other parts. I would say we're self-transcending creatures, and so, just as to the cosmos as a whole there is a transcendent as well as an immanent dimension, so in the human individual, this principle of transcendence is constantly at work. And then, of course, there is the whole question of evil.

ABE: Would you like to talk about that? *[laughter]* Step right off a cliff here?

MICHAEL M: Well, it's the toughest problem in philosophy. It's so big, I don't know how to start. Esalen has always been engaged at an immediate level with practical problems of evil. But there's also a sense in which that kind of work, while it's fundamentally necessary, often gets at the symptoms and not the cause. And part of the cause is that humanity has not yet fully embraced its deepest or greatest destiny. It doesn't have a vision and theory adequate to it. We don't have practices adequate to it; we do not have institutions that adequately support it. We have to get down to the root causes, and I want Esalen also to be devoted to helping out on getting to the root causes. We don't need to be alcoholic or drug addicted, etc. You can trace, I believe, every affliction, to some extent, to a failure to embrace this larger destiny.

It seems that built into life is the dynamic of "grow or die." Norman Mailer claims we pay more and more for staying where we are. So this is the second way to address the evils. Now, I'm talking at a practical level about what to do about evil. Frankly, at this stage, I feel vastly incompetent in dealing with why there is evil in the first place. I have just never read an argument that satisfies me, and I've read a lot of them, you know, justifying God's ways to man. Take, for example, *The Odyssey*—pain is the "hammer of the gods to break a dead resistance in the mortal heart. If he were not forced to want and weep, his soul would have laid down at ease and never thought to climb towards the sun." In other words, the justification for pain and suffering is that it's this hammer of the gods to break the dead resistance in the mortal heart. Now certainly that is a function of pain and suffering. There's no doubt about it. But why did God have to do it that way in the first place?

ABE: Can I offer you my definition of evil?

MICHAEL M: Great.

ABE: My definition of evil is that it's the necessary concomitant result of consciousness passing from instinct to full awareness, and that in the process you're going to get experimentation from whatever level of ignorance the human being happens to be at at the time. That experimentation will produce the side effect of evil, from which the human being will then be forced to learn and transcend.

MICHAEL M: Well, that's a good one. What you're saying certainly rings true. But a person could come back, like Ivan Karamazov, who says, "To enter a world where helpless children suffer..." You know, that story in *The Brothers Karamazov*— "I decline the ticket of admission." And you know, that's a deep response in a lot of people. It's at that level that they just cannot believe that God is good. And the only response basically that Alyosha gives in *The Brothers Karamazov* is a leap of faith, it's to love God in spite of the obvious monstrousness of the world. In other words, that our feelings finally are not reliable indicators of truth, that it's some deeper faith that reaches towards God and says, "I love God in spite of this. It's a mystery. It's finally just a mystery." That's where I end up, intellectually. And then, when it comes to the question of the why, I'm open to any new good attack on that. *[laughter]* I just don't think it can be justified intellectually. I think it has to be answered practically by what we do in life, by either practical immediate deeds—helping somebody who is sick, environmental action, whatever—and what I would call "going to the roots of it" with deep philosophical envisioning of the good. That's actually where Dostoevsky ends up in *The Brothers Karamazov.*

ABE: In your book *The Future of the Body* you actually raise the issue: what are good transformative practices and what are not good transformative practices?

MICHAEL M: In chapter twenty-five I give four fundamental ways in which transformative practices fail. First, if they reinforce particular beliefs which are limiting, which they can do; if they develop particular virtues at the expense of others—for example, like some of the psychological work we did at Esalen in the sixties, where there was a tremendous premium put upon openness and honesty and it often overrode empathy and kindness. Not only beliefs, not only virtues, but basic human capacities or attributes, where some are developed at the expense of others. For example, a person who is quite shy about people goes to a highly ascetic, contemplative ashram, develops a tremendous capacity for contemplative meditation, and becomes severely withdrawn from interpersonal relationships, or indeed masks certain aspects of himself which then erupt in group destructiveness, say, in power needs and sexual needs, etc. And we see this in many cults. Then, a fourth dynamic that comes into play is when a practice—and this is particularly true of contemplative, shamanic, religious practices—opens up a particular aspect of transcendent reality which is real, and it becomes dominant to the exclusion of others and leads to or reinforces either a limiting trait or a limiting belief system. And this interlocks with the first three. When transformative practices, by their very success, reinforce limiting traits, and an inadequate set of virtues, narrow belief systems, people's difficulties not only are not cured, sometimes they're actually made worse. I have observed this in many, many cults, and I've seen it in particular schools of psychotherapy. I think there's a growing wisdom about this.

ABE: There seem to be a lot of new therapies and techniques being developed. What value do you think they have?

MICHAEL M: We've never invented more practices than now. I mean, the Ford Foundation asked Esalen in 1967 to do an inventory of ways of growth or transformative practices, and we identified about ten thousand techniques clustered into two hundred major approaches. And we estimated at that time that probably one major approach was being invented every week. So there's this very often constant reinvention of the wheel happening. A lot of people will shop around; they'll go from one to another, and much of that is dilettantism. Yet much that is criticized as dilettantism, I feel, is a genuine drive in humans for wholeness. I list ways in my book in which these practices complement one another, ways in which we can build up a unified curriculum. This is a very old idea. You find it in the Bhagavad Gita, the triple path of the bhakti, jnana, and karma yoga, and you find it in ancient Greece— "A sane mind and a healthy body." In our time it's still in the works, but what you have is people learning by experience that certain things are too narrow. Woody Allen said in one of his movies that he had been in psychoanalysis for twenty years, and that he was going to give it one more year and then go to Lourdes. Well, you see, I've seen people in Gestalt therapy for ten, fifteen years, reworking the same trauma, this obsessional concern with small corners of the self. And finally, it doesn't work, and it becomes evident, if not to them, then to others around them.

ABE: To what extent do you think people in narrow practices are realizing the need for greater balance?

MICHAEL M: You see so many people who come to Esalen who have been in very strict meditation practice, and they come looking for something like Reichian therapy or Gestalt therapy to release their emotional and physical armor. Certain practices are designed to do a particular job, but they are then made to carry the load of a whole integral practice. In other words, you cannot finally make psychoanalysis a complete transformative practice. Some of my friends are in psychoanalysis three or five times a week, and after twenty years, you just wonder. It just doesn't seem to be working that well. So some practices are not designed to be a complete curriculum of transformation. And then, other practices, even those which are more holistic and have a broader scope to them, can, for the reasons I mentioned earlier, by reinforcing a limited set of virtues or belief systems, or reinforcing or masking a destructive trait, also fail. I think we're in a period now where we have to assess these practices. That assessment is going on. But we have to continue, I think, searching for new ways to create integral practices.

ABE: Where would you position the value of transpersonal psychology, say the work of Ken Wilber and Dick Anthony and people like that?

MICHAEL M: They have certainly made a very good start in joining contemplative traditions or knowledge with the discoveries of modern depth psychology. But I believe it's only a start. We have a lot more work to do along that line. Now, most of the transpersonal psychologists have had very little to say about the somatic disciplines and the role of the body. You know, I'm very interested in the transformation of the body itself, and I think that's an idea that's still coming on-line. Now, this is a more radical side of my beliefs. I think it's part of what's emerging in our time. I believe vision is still dawning; practices are still developing on a great historical scale, and I think we're coming to appreciate the body's capacity for radical change, even for divinization. I was oriented to that through Sri Aurobindo, and confirmed in it by my readings now of many Russian philosophers. By the way, Esalen is publishing a whole thirty volumes of Russian philosophy, you know, prerevolutionary work by people who really believed that the body itself could be radically transformed or resurrected, as they put it, and I miss that in much of the transpersonal writing. But the transpersonal people have certainly made a good beginning in a broad synthesis of religious practice, or contemplative shamanic practice and modern depth psychology.

ABE: So you feel that's a fruitful direction.

MICHAEL M: Oh, absolutely. Ken Wilber is definitely one of the important pioneers, and the *Journal of Transpersonal Psychology* does a lot of good work.

ABE: At one end of the spectrum you have the "traditional psychiatrist's couch," and then at the other end you have cathartic psychotherapeutic practice, an extreme of that being, say, primal screaming or whatever.

MICHAEL M: I have to say this. I think some practices are falling away. For example, the hard encounter type groups of the sixties have to a great degree fallen away, because they just weren't as helpful as people once thought they were. And the same for primal screaming. I think that it has a usefulness for a few people in a few circumstances, but typically there's a huge enthusiasm for some important new approach like that, and then it fades, and it either disappears entirely, or it is useful in particular circumstances for particular people, whereas other things endure. I would argue there's a kind of cultural sorting out of these techniques going on. We've seen a lot of that at Esalen.

ABE: One of the things that you seem to be questioning in what you're saying is the psychologistic approach to the human being altogether.

MICHAEL M: The strictly psychologistic, yes, absolutely. Is this what you mean, psychologistic without any transpersonal orientation?

ABE: Yes. I headed a little column I wrote a while back with "Don't Let Psychology Suck the Magic Right Out of You."

MICHAEL M: Amen! Amen! I am very sympathetic to Jim Hillman's critique of psychologizing. I share that feeling very much.

ABE: So what is it that people have to get hold of as they're "working through their stuff" and losing grip of the vision of themselves as a magical, spiritual, creative entity? How is that to be avoided in an age where, as you say, a new psychotherapeutic approach of some kind or another is being developed every day?

MICHAEL M: Well, again, I would say we need balance here. We have to acknowledge that modern depth psychology since Freud has really taught us a lot about unconscious and dissociative functioning and ways to rid ourselves of certain phobias, anxieties, etc. We have learned from it; it's important, and it's good. But we need a vision of human possibilities way beyond the medically oriented therapies typical of so much psychiatry or psychoanalysis. In other words, we need a larger vision, and we need to get past these obsessions with small corners of the self. Fritz Perls, who invented Gestalt therapy, used to say that the best defense against growth is psychotherapy. Gurdjieff said, "The ultimate defense against the enjoyment of life and personal development was spiritual practice." And Ouspensky said, "Abandon the script." Well, they're all getting at the same thing. You know, humans are habituating creatures, and we can habituate ourselves at any level, and kill the enjoyment of life and kill the possibilities for growth. So we need to be alert to that. We need a large vision of human possibilities; we need to see that we're much more than just our emotions, our problems, our complexes.

ABE: What I like most about *The Future of the Body* is that even though it is not hard science all the way through, what it is saying is something that I agree with absolutely, which is that healthy human reason can chart these waters. And that, if we're prepared to be open-minded and hardheaded at the same time, we can actually do something about our future.

MICHAEL M: That captures the very center of what I intended for that book. Beautiful. Now I do use that fancy phrase "synoptic empiricism," and I make the claim that every type of data in the book is subject to verification by others. In other words, none of it finally depends upon faith. It's all subject to experimental practice. But, you have to broaden out your definition of what empiricism is. By this I just mean that empiricism means the direct apprehension of real things, based on actual human experience, and then communal verification or non-verification of that experience. There's the empiricism of the senses, and there's what Steven Phillips and others have called mystic empiricism. But we need what James called "radical empiricism." I call it "integral" and "synoptic empiricism," or "multidisciplinary empiricism," and it includes different fields of inquiry and different ways of knowing, but all of them, I think, deserve to be called a genuine knowledge quest. So yes, healthy human reason. It's not, on the one hand, the revelation and faith, or fantasy and superstition, nor on the other hand this hard, scientific fundamentalism, which claims that only the empiricism of the senses is valid.

ABE: You are pointing in the direction of a human being that is not fully with us yet. All we know about this future human is that he or she is going to be very different from anything that we know historically. Is it possible to form any impression yet of what that new human is going to be like?

MICHAEL M: In my book I talk about the "prefiguration of the metanormal" in religious doctrine, in science fiction, and in modern literature. I argue that all twelve sets of extraordinary human attributes that we talked about earlier have been pictured already in movies, children's cartoons, or science fiction. One could argue that artists have the freedom to picture our greater possibilities, have more freedom, often, than philosophers and psychologists, and we're getting this now as, let's say, the folk wisdom of the age. My little boy, for example, is full of imagery about this possible future, whether it's from *Star Wars,* or a movie like *Cocoon,* or what have you. In other words, humans are constantly picturing this possible future, and it's far more rich and complex than we commonly want to think. And yes, on the basis of those hints and glimpses, and then by mapping the extraordinary we can begin to get a sense of it.

What I resist, Alexander, is projecting what, for me, seems unwarranted now. The analogy I use is that you're going through a forest and you can see down the trail ahead of you, but you can only see about fifty or sixty feet. And as you walk along, you can see a further fifty or sixty feet. In other words, as we move forward, I think we can picture more. So people ask, "Could the human body, through mental practice alone, become immortal?" And I say, "Well, there's no theoretical reason that I've ever encountered to say it couldn't, but we don't have any evidence yet that it can." I present data in the book in relation to how subject the flesh is to passionate imagery, you know, false pregnancy, religious stigmatics, or even a bodybuilder like Frank Zane who changed himself into three separate bodies in three years. I mean, radically different bodies. So the transformative ability of the flesh is incredible, and not only just in muscular, ordinary terms, but in energetic ways that start to get into dimensions that are more mysterious—that there are energetic fields, or a luminescence of the flesh that develops between lovers and in certain athletes, around certain saints and shamans, where you begin to get into a kind of metaflesh. The Russian philosophers speculated about this. One of them said that lovers are privileged to see the flesh of Heaven in their beloved. Now he wasn't talking a kind of purple metaphor there. He talks as one who is actually seeing something real.

ABE: And we all know these shape-shifting, transformative people.

MICHAEL M: Exactly. There are a lot of hints that we are capable of what I would like to call radical transformation, and certainly we're capable of radical shifts of mind, of heart. I don't think anybody can argue with that. There are types of experiences in which we know things far beyond the ordinary intellect, and I think all of us have occasionally glimpsed this, some of us more than others. So people with good healthy reason, as you put it, who aren't dogmatic about these things, have to agree that consciousness can alter to an amazing degree. And now I think we can see a lot of evidence that the flesh can alter, too.

2
journeys
into gaia

PAUL WATSON

JANE GOODALL

TERENCE McKENNA

archangel
of the sea

PAUL WATSON

in conversation with

ALEXANDER BLAIR-EWART

Captain Paul Watson is director of the Sea Shepherd Conservation Society and the world's most widely recognized and controversial ecology activist. One of the founders of Greenpeace, he is famous for the sinking of two Icelandic whaling ships in the early eighties and has continued since that time to fiercely oppose all those who would annihilate endangered marine species for profit. Paul Watson is truly an archangel of the sea. Arrested many times, he has never been convicted, and continues to hold the philosophy that all species on planet Earth deserve our respect and protection. He is the author (with Warren Rogers and Joseph Newman) of Sea Shepherd: My Fight for Whales and Seals *(1982), and* Ocean Warrior: My Battle to End the Illegal Slaughter on the High Seas *(1994). Paul's activism carries certain risks. In the spring of 1995 he was attacked and severely beaten by a mob of several hundred sealers in a hotel on the Magdalen Islands, Quebec. He survived the attack and continues to fight for ecological sanity.*

ALEXANDER BLAIR-EWART: Environmental activism has increased dramatically over the last decade. Is that due to the frustration that is felt because people aren't waking up fast enough?

PAUL WATSON: Yes, that's a problem. Things are happening too fast, and education is certainly no longer a viable solution because by the time you educate this generation as to what is happening, it will be too late. For instance, by the time we educate the Japanese to stop killing whales, there will be no more whales left. Lobbying has certainly proven not to work because you can get new rules and regulations, but they're overturned again. For example, environmental groups spent hundreds and thousands of dollars and a lot of energy to get the United States Congress to vote for sanctions on countries that were killing whales illegally, and when a moratorium was set by the International Whaling Commission in 1986, those sanctions could have been applied, thus effectively ending all whaling worldwide, but President Reagan chose to discriminate on the application of those rules and so whaling continued. So all the work to get those rules and regulations were for nought because the president just could not do it.

I look on activism as achieving two objectives. The most satisfying part is that you physically save lives in the moment. So we go in, interfere and harrass, intimidate, halt whaling or sealing operations. And you get an instant gratification in what you are doing. The other objective is that it's the best form of education, because we use the drama of the situation to publicize the issue, so that, for instance, the sinking of the ships in Iceland was a very viable educational program, because what happened there is that you had everybody across this country and throughout most of the Western world talking about the issue. People were in Moose Jaw or Medicine Hat, wherever, in the local bars, talking about Iceland and whaling. They might not have agreed with what we did, but they were talking about the issue.

ABE: How do the people who are the direct object of your activism feel?

PAUL W: When we sunk the *Sierra*, the first mate on board the vessel was interviewed by NBC. They asked him what he thought of it and he said, "Well, it was the only way we could have been stopped." And they asked, "Well, what do you think about it?" and he said, "Before this I never really thought about killing whales, whether it was good or bad or whatever, and then I saw people who were willing to risk their lives and freedom to protect them, and I'll never kill a whale again. In fact, if the *Sea Shepherd* wanted me as a crew member, I would join." So I feel that if we are able to actually convert whalers into anti-whalers, then that proves that we're an effective educational organization.

ABE: At the same time you're sailing close to the wind—pun intended—in relation to the law, nationally and internationally.

PAUL W: Well, the amazing thing about it is that we really have never broken any laws. It's just what people perceive. In the United States and Europe we get a lot of support. In Canada we don't get as much, the reason being that Canadians have this, I think, "healthy respect for law and order." That is, whatever the government tells them to do, they do. And so what Canadians do is perceive that we break the law because we act on our own, independent of any authority.

First of all, everything is well researched in advance. We don't go into anything half-cocked. So in 1985 the first move I made against Iceland was to bring the *Sea Shepherd* into Reykjavik harbor to hold a press conference. We were on our way to the Bear Islands to protect pilot whales at the time. And I told them that we had no intention of taking action against their whaling fleet that summer, but at the moratorium on commercial whaling that had taken effect in 1986, we advised Iceland to abide by the regulations or we would enforce the regulations against them. We don't do anything covertly; we always announce in advance what we are going to do.

ABE: That didn't really get out into the media.

PAUL W: That didn't get out, no. They just want to report what they want to report. We have to live with that and use it to the best of our ability. What happened is that we sailed to the Faeroes, and 1986 came along and Iceland continued whaling. We then moved to the International Whaling Commission. I went so far as to bring the ship right to Malamose Sweep in the harbor to sit outside the hotel where the meeting was to take place, again warning Iceland to abide by the regulations. Iceland applied to the Scientific Committee of the International Whaling Commission to continue killing whales. They were refused. We then waited for the U.S. government to take action under those amendments, the Pelly amendments. That's when President Reagan chose to discriminate on the application of the law, and said, "We will not invoke sanctions against a NATO allied nation." Not only that, but Mr. Reagan sold out the whales by authorizing an okay from the

Department of Commerce for Iceland to continue to actually up the amount of whale meat it could sell to Japan in return for having Reykjavik host the summit conference with Mr. Gorbachev. So the price of the summit conference were the lives of the whales.

So we watched this and we said, "Okay, the lobbying effort didn't work, the law is not being upheld, and that seems to be the end of it." That's when we took action. I sent two engineers to Iceland—Ron Coronado and David Howan— and they infiltrated. They were there all through the summit in October and into November, and they got jobs in the whale meat processing plant, because Iceland has more jobs than people and it's a very healthy economy in that respect. It's not that they need to kill whales. But what happened was that Ron and David spent that time doing reconnaissance and planning.

ABE: Does your organization have any rules of conduct during these kinds of operations?

PAUL W: All *Sea Shepherd* agents in the field are free to make whatever decisions they want to make, as long as they abide by our five guidelines for operation. First, no *Sea Shepherd* crewman can carry or use a firearm. Second, we cannot use explosives. Third, no action can be taken where there is a possibility of an injury to the opposition. Fourth, we have to accept responsibility for what we do. And five, we have to accept whatever moral or legal consequences will befall. So as a result, Ron and David checked over everything they could possibly do, and then on Sunday, November 9th, they gained access to the whale processing plant and totally destroyed it using sledgehammers, monkey wrenches, and whatever other implements of destruction were lying around. And also exposing $4 million worth of whale meat by opening and destroying the refrigerator systems. Although it was wasteful, tactically we felt we had to deal them as much economic damage as we possibly could.

And then Ron and David moved to Reykjavik harbor fifty kilometers away, boarded and searched the three vessels, and found watchmen sleeping on the third one. They cut that ship loose and let it drift into the harbor, and then, and only then, went down into the engine rooms of the other ships, opened up the sea valves to flood the engines, and sank them. Then they went to the airport. Now, the reason they didn't turn themselves in is that they had two briefcases full of evidence from the whaling station on illegal takes, and so they had to get that stuff out to us first. We turned that over to the International Whaling Commission, which was embarrassing to Iceland.

Now, immediately we were accused, especially by Greenpeace, of being a terrorist organization, and also by Iceland.

ABE : I found that totally incomprehensible at the time, that the term terrorist and Sea Shepherd and Watson were being linked. I wondered whose agenda it was, attaching the term terrorist to what you were doing, because it was absurd. There was no terror involved.

PAUL W : Actually, the first such accusation came from Greenpeace. It was picked up by Iceland and then it was picked up by Canada. But we tried to defend ourselves on the grounds that no terrorist organization operates under those rules and guidelines. It was a police action, really, arresting an illegal operation. Then what we did was we accepted responsibility for the sinkings and made ourselves available. I wrote three letters to Iceland that went unanswered over the next year, saying we would be prepared to answer any charges Iceland wanted to bring against us. They wouldn't answer the letters. Instead they just kept throwing out accusations.

So on January 20th of 1988, I flew to Iceland to demand an apology or an arrest. I was met at the airport by 150 police officers and it was actually quite funny because they held me for twenty-four hours and deported me the next day, refusing to lay charges. Not only that, but during the interrogation, I was interrogating them, they weren't interrogating me. I said, yes, we sank those ships and not only that, we'll sink the other two at the first opportunity unless Iceland abides by the law. And they refused to charge me. They said, "We want to get the other guys, not you." And I said, "Well, I'll put them on a plane and bring them here if you want them. They're standing by ready to answer." You see, to put us on trial would be to put themselves on trial, so we were deported. Now, the only legal case that has come out of this entire incident is my lawsuit against the government of Iceland for illegal deportation because they had no legitimate right to do that.

ABE : Why do you think Greenpeace felt that it was necessary to speak of terrorism and start a propaganda campaign?

PAUL W : We have a very strange relationship with Greenpeace, being that the Sea Shepherd Conservation Society is composed of some of the founding members of Greenpeace. A lot of our people left Greenpeace out of disillusionment.

ABE: They seem to be doing quite well from the point of view of collecting funds. It's a vast operation with lots of publicity.

PAUL W: There's both positive and negative about it. The positive part of Greenpeace is that it is able to reach a lot of people and therefore stands as a symbol of an environmental movement. And just its name sometimes can sway a lot of opinions. The negative part is that it has become a multinational ecocorporation. One year it brought in $94 million in donations. That's way up there as far as organizations and businesses are concerned. The problem is that it has become so bureaucratic that they can't make a decision.

They find themselves often in a bind on issues because when it conflicts with natural or cultural considerations, the people in that regional area won't support it and so their hands are tied and they can't do anything. And the organization has become a bureaucratic boondoggle. It's also so heavily involved with internal politicking and infighting over positions, people's vested interest in their jobs, etc. When we set up Sea Shepherd, I took to heart what David Brower said, which is that any organization after ten years is useless, it's become too bureaucratic, and so one must get out of it. He was forced out of Friends of the Earth and subsequently founded Earth Island Institute.

ABE: When you talk about becoming active, are you talking about the individual running the risk of arrest?

PAUL W: No, I don't expect the average person to go out and spike trees or strangle Exxon executives or whatever. What I expect people to do, really, is shift their attitudes so that they're no longer working for themselves, for their own material self-interest; they are now working for the Earth and for the environment, and therefore they should do what they do best. If you're a journalist, if you're a communicator, if you're a teacher, do it for the Earth, not for yourself. That's all you have to do. I really don't think that everybody should be an activist. In fact, I'm working on a book now which is a guide to strategy for the environmental movement, and I divide this into different ways, such as the way of the educator or the communicator, the way of the artist, the way of the infiltrator, someone who infiltrates a government and works for the Earth from there. There is a way of the catalyst which is somebody who can focus on issues, or the way of the warrior, which is a more activist, more militant approach. You have to pick the way that is going to make the best contribution.

The most important thing is to serve the Earth, and to take a biocentric viewpoint, not an anthropocentric viewpoint of things. I think this is the only salvation for the Earth, which involves a complete revolution in consciousness, economically, spiritually, politically, and culturally. Everything has to be shifted from an anthropocentric to a biocentric point of view. If that happens, then I think that there is real hope for our species and for the Earth.

ABE: I gather that you have been an animal lover all your life. Are you a vegetarian?

PAUL W: Yes. I was raised in New Brunswick in a fishing village and I became a member of the Kindness Club which was set up by Ida Fleming, the wife of Hugh Armstrong, who was the Conservative premier in New Brunswick in the fifties. But when I was nine to twelve, my brothers and I became hit men for the Kindness Club. That is, we would disrupt trap lines and duck hunts, that sort of thing. And later when I ran off to sea I was in the Merchant Marines and in the Coast Guard and then got involved with Greenpeace. This gave me an opportunity to put maritime skills together with what I really wanted to do, which is protect wildlife, in this instance to protect marine wildlife. I'm first and foremost a wildlife conservationist.

ABE: Are we close yet to a place where the politicians and the system as a whole are going to wake up?

PAUL W: No, we're in a situation right now where politicians and the system are still co-opting the movement.

ABE: I'm very concerned about that because there's a "resource ecology" lie that I hear all over the place, which means "business as usual." And we recognize this attitude when we hear the words "resource ecology" and hear talk about "sustainable growth," whatever growth is supposed to mean in this situation. How can we avoid having environmentalists co-opted by politicians?

PAUL W: I don't know if it can be avoided because they have the power and they have the influence. I think that that's where the activities of a small active organization come in, which is to constantly rock the boat and yell out that "We're mad as hell and we're not going to take it anymore!" As long as there are people making waves then people can be shifted away from that pie-in-the-sky attitude adopted by these corporations. I find it amazing that there are environmental organizations supporting "ecologically positive" disposable diapers. No disposable diapers are ecologically positive. After all, you're putting raw human sewage into dump sites, which is illegal. With my daughter, we went to the trouble of finding—and it worked out brilliantly— these diaper services. They take the real cloth diapers, wash them, and return them to you so you don't have to clean them yourself, which is probably a better alternative.

ABE: How is it that these illegal activities are abided?

PAUL W: Somehow or other the entire society looks the other way because of the multimillions of dollars made with the sale of disposable diapers. It's almost like we've developed a schizoid attitude towards things, where we can, as environmentalists say, "You shouldn't do this, this, and this, but really, you know, everything is so big and I'm so small, it really doesn't make much difference." It's a very frustrating thing. The hope that I have is that we will be given a rude swift kick in our collective rear ends by, hopefully, a minor environmental collapse, not a major one. Chernobyl is a good example of that. Chernobyl didn't work because it will in the end kill about a million people, slowly, out of sight and out of mind. If it had left a million radioactive, bloated bodies on the streets of Kiev, that would have been the end of nuclear industry. But it didn't, and it's killing them the way we've come to like it, quietly and out of sight. And never mind that the reindeer population was totally destroyed, that 74% of the lamb population in Scotland had to be destroyed, that there is a shortage of birds in Europe. Never mind that. That seems to have been totally glossed over, and it's business as usual.

ABE: You are doing the utmost that you possibly can to wake people up. I'm doing what I can. It seems like a drop in the bucket, though. What is it that we're not doing? What is it that we haven't understood about collective psychology here in this crisis?

PAUL W: How do you sway a runaway train if what is tempting people onto the track is material wealth, short-term satisfaction? I think Leonard Cohen actually put it best in one of his songs: "We're locked into our suffering and our pleasures are the seal." And we can't throw off the pleasures, even though we know it's leading us at one hundred miles an hour into a stone wall. We can't get rid of this because it's so momentarily gratifying. I don't know if that's even possible, to get people deflected away.

ABE: It's like we've all got addictive psychologies at every level of society, and we're not able to break these lifestyle habits and wake up.

PAUL W: I see that in myself. There are things that I do which are environmentally unsound, but I do them. For instance, I fly in airplanes. It's almost like you're locked into the structure and you can't even function if you don't drive a car or don't do such and such. So I don't know if it's possible for us to change unless there is an environmental motivation for us to do it, and what worries me now is people are becoming more and more environmentally aware, and the media is telling them to be more environmentally aware, but it's the politicians and the establishment who are turning that into profit and into power. I'm not that optimistic, but all I do know is that as long as there is life, there is hope.

ABE: I go through cycles with it, and lately I've been feeling reasonably positive. On the one hand you have this terrifying and terrible sense of loss for this beautiful thing, the Earth, realizing that it's disappearing and that you feel totally powerless to do anything about it. But at the same time, you feel stupid about feeling grief because you think: Don't do that! Don't hold the funeral before you've done absolutely everything you can possibly think of to avert that disaster.

PAUL W: Yes, I don't allow that to get me down. I take kind of an Eastern view of it, in the sense that you have to do what you're doing because it's the right thing to do, and whether you win or lose, whatever the ultimate end result is, don't be swayed by the way it's going, just fight it right into the ground if you have to. And that way I find that by being detached from it, I don't find myself emotionally drained by the issues that I'm involved in, and also I'm able to function in situations where, for example, whales are being killed in front of me without becoming emotionally traumatized.

ABE: You've worked with people who couldn't handle the emotional impact of watching whales being slaughtered and wildlife being destroyed?

PAUL W: I've known people who have become depressed and have committed suicide. People who can't operate objectively are in serious danger of doing something technically negative. You can't lose your temper, because if you do then you're going to do something that's going to backlash on you. It's very easy to kill people. If you allow that anger to overcome you, somebody could get hurt, and if you kill somebody on the other side, no matter if they deserve it or not, it's going to come back and it's going to hurt you more than ever.

ABE: It seems that outspokenness and directness, particularly in Canada, are almost forbidden in this very apathetic nation. We're so used to being paternalistically watched over by our overlords, but our overlords are leading us horribly astray and it's time for us to wake up.

PAUL W: The authorities aren't used to that attitude.

ABE: Exactly. And people look at you as if you're insane when all you're doing is exercising your rights as an individual.

PAUL W: Actually, after the Iceland campaign I appeared on talk shows where people called up and said, "Who do you think you are? God?" And I'd say, "No, the job's taken. All I'm doing is saving lives by enforcing international regulations. Also, I don't have much use for any government that defends its authority through violence and who maintains an army telling me that I'm violent. What kind of hypocritical stance is that?"

ABE: So you get accused of arrogance?

PAUL W: The human species is incredibly arrogant. When you point out their arrogance you yourself are accused of being the same. You see, we're not here to talk with the opposition. We have nothing to say to them. We're here to give them a swift kick in the ass and then the moderate groups can work out a solution with them. We're the bad guys, we're the unpredictable guys. When we go into a confrontation, they never know what we're going to do. They think we might blow them out of the water. We don't care. They think we're crazy. That works to our advantage. We're really going in as a blitzkreig, and in many ways that has helped to soften up the opposition, and also it can delay things. As a good example, Earth First occupied a forest area in Texas. It took the Sierra Club thirty days to get an injunction, but in the meantime, Earth First's legal victory came through, and that's a good example of the two approaches working very well.

ABE: It sounds as if what we're looking for here at this stage, then, is some sort of coordinated infrastructure.

PAUL W: Yes, but I don't know if it has to be coordinated. It may be even better if it is uncoordinated. The wolf campaign worked beyond my wildest expectations because what happened is that I started it in 1984 at the end of the wolf hunt, and in 1985 it started to expand. By 1987 the wolf campaign was perfect because I had so many groups that were opposing it. I had Friends of the Wolf in Bellingham, Washington, Friends of the Wolf Montana, Friends of the Wolf California, B.C., and Alberta. Totally uncoordinated. One group was occupying the minister's office; another was occupying John Elliott's office, the wildlife office in Prince George. Another group was dropping parachutists into the area. Another group was taking them to court, and everybody was working towards the same objective completely independently and on their own.

ABE: There are people out there who would like to do more but are frightened that they might end up in prison for God knows how long if it went badly. You're involved in educating people how to do it right, not hurting anybody while they're at it, and how to stay free while they're getting on with the job.

PAUL W: It takes calculating your plan in advance and building a strategy before you go into something. Say you've decided to go out and spike trees, for instance. Spiking trees is a very complex operation. We started tree spiking originally in Vancouver, which was the first place it ever happened. But there are things that you have to know first. You find the lots that the trees are going to be on, say Lot 555, which is going to be sold. Then you document exactly what you have got in that lot, so that the loggers know, because you want the spikes there as a deterrent. You're not there to destroy the equipment. You are there as a deterrent. So, for instance, spikes should be put in on a specific angle. If you put them in on a downward angle, moisture then moves down the spike and you could then cause rot inside the tree, which would kill it. The spike should be vertical, at even a slight angle, so that any moisture will roll down the spike and not into the tree. That can protect the tree. There is no sense saving trees by killing them.

So you send off your press release announcing that Lot 555 has got 40 six-inch spikes, 2,003 twist nails, 200 teflon nails which are undetectable through normal means, and 100 ceramic spikes, also undetectable. This way they know what they're dealing with, and then they can compute whether or not it's economically advantageous for them to go ahead. They can actually work out what kind of damage is going to be caused. And that should be enough to stop them from going in. Now, if they escalate, you escalate. For instance, in California, they said, "We're going to cut down all those trees that are spiked just for spite and leave them on the ground." My response to that was to tell the Earth First people, "Fine, tell them to go ahead and do that, but then you're going to spike every log in a log boom heading into the factory." If they want to escalate, you escalate and go right for the equipment. It's not so much the damage that can be caused to the blade as it goes through, it's the downtime which can mean twenty to thirty thousand dollars. Blades are only worth one thousand dollars.

Now, when they try to throw at you that spiking trees is terrorism, you can reply that, first of all, nobody has ever been injured, and the reason nobody is injured is that every chain saw that goes into a tree has a chain guard in it. If the chain breaks, which it can do in normal use, of course, the person is protected. On a sawmill, there's a plexiglass shield between that saw and the people working. It has to be there, and if it isn't there, their union will be asking why it's not there. So it shouldn't cause any injury, and if any injury does result, it's because of irresponsibility on the part of the company that hasn't taken proper precautions. And also, metal things can be found in any tree; it doesn't have to be put there deliberately.

ABE: Where did the idea for tree spiking originate?

PAUL W: I got the idea originally when my father cut down a tree in our backyard when I was a kid and we found it had a horseshoe in it. He broke his chain saw on that horseshoe. And the horseshoe had been nailed in there perhaps one hundred years ago. The other tactic I developed recently for pulp mills is that you get a drill with a 1 1/2" or 1" bore on it, and first of all you knock a cork out of the tree with one of those chisel tools, and then you drill into the tree, pad plastic bags or Styrofoam in there, and then put the cork back in. Now, what happens is that then moves into a pulp mill and the plastic will melt inside the pulp equipment and can bring the whole thing to a halt. Again, that would be a deterrent because you tell them in advance, "You have three hundred trees in there that are stuffed with plastic bags."

Then there are different strategies. On Mere's Island, when the Indians spiked the trees, the loggers came in with metal detectors, found the spikes, and put fluorescent X's on the trees so that they would know which ones were spiked. Well, the next day the Indians went in there and put fluorescent X's on every single tree in the forest. So those are the kinds of tactics used. I think it's really important that you use your imagination. For example, in Seattle somebody finds out that the mayor isn't recycling. Well, how do we focus attention on that? We go get the mayor's garbage and hold a press conference with all his garbage on display. It's a small thing, but it's a media thing and gets people's attention.

ABE: Can you talk about the Japanese situation? Every time they are criticized for their actions they counter with racist propaganda.

PAUL W: I was confronted with this at the International Whaling Commission when I gave a press conference and the Japanese president accused me of racism. In fact, he said, "Anti-whaling is nothing more than a caucasian plot against the yellow peoples of the world." My answer to him was, "My wife is Chinese, and she is part of this, and I don't think she has any plot against the yellow peoples of the world. A lot of our members are Japanese Canadian or American, and the Japanese are the last people to point the finger of racism at anybody." Anybody who refers to the Koreans as garlic eaters and refuses after generations to give them rights in Japan, anybody who can do to the Chinese what the Japanese did to them... and, as a Canadian, I would like to point out that the three hundred Canadians who were marched off the cliffs in Hong Kong in World War II were marched off because they were white, not because they had done anything reprehensible. So I just throw it back in their face.

ABE: How do you get the Japanese to stop killing whales?

PAUL W: The only way to really stop the whaling is to sink their ships, and I've already made it a straightforward promise that if we were to get a million dollars, which unfortunately we don't have, we could end whaling worldwide. All I would need to do is put people in positions to waylay the fleet. What happens is that the ships are irreplaceable. It's economics; there's not enough money in whaling to build new whaling ships. Every whaling ship you sink is a whaling ship permanently out of commission. I asked the Japanese whaling commissioner in 1983 at the conference in Britain, "When are you going to stop whaling?" and he said, "When it is no longer economically viable to continue." I said, "What if that means the extinction of the whale?" And he said, "Well, what good are whales if there is no whaling industry? We'll get the most return out of our original investment in fleets and equipment before we pack it in." So they're looking for the most return. If you wipe out their equipment, just from a purely logistic point of view it's not in their interest to replace it.

ABE: Do people offer financial support to your organization?

PAUL W: Yes they do. But one thing that I discovered when I speak to people who are interested in helping us out financially, is that when they go talk to their lawyers they're often told, "If you give this group money, you're going to be held responsible for their actions," which they're not. It should be pointed out that nobody is. What we are doing is in fact enforcing the law, and none of our supporters have ever suffered because of that.

ABE: What is *Sea Shepherd* engaged in ongoingly these days?

PAUL W: One of our objectives is the seizing of a Japanese/Taiwanese drift net, worth about $1 million each. We'd like to seize one, put it in the hold, bring it back and string it up somewhere so that people can see the immensity of the problem. There are about 1,700 of them in use. Second is to destroy as many nets as possible. All we have to do is take a couple of barrels of concrete, attach it to one part of the net, and throw it down. The concrete brings the net down, and as soon as the net reaches sixty fathoms the floats are crushed by water pressure. On the bottom there are small creatures that can live in and around it, so they don't have to worry about that. It may take something on its way down, but that is preferable to the incredible loss of life on the surface. Two barrels of concrete can take out a $1 million net. Also there are at least fifty pirate ships out there, totally unregistered, totally illegal. Our plan is to take those ships, just seize them and arrest them on the high seas. The difficult task is to come up with a way to do it without carrying weapons. They might have some weapons and although we do have defenses—bullet-proof vests and things like that—we have a record of having never hurt anybody, and we want to keep that record intact.

warrior
of the wild

DR. JANE GOODALL

in conversation with

ACE OSMER

Jane Goodall was a young secretarial school graduate when the legendary Louis Leakey, in a stroke of genius, sent her to Tanzania in 1960 to study chimpanzees. There she has remained off and on for thirty years, in what has become the longest unbroken study of animals in their natural habitat ever conducted. She later completed a Ph.D. at Cambridge University, and has written a number of books, including Innocent Killers *(with Hugo van Lawick),* In the Shadow of Man, Grub the Bush Baby *(with Hugo van Lawick, 1971),* Through a Window: My Thirty Years with the Chimpanzees of Gombe *(1986),* The Chimpanzees of Gombe: Patterns of Behavior *(1987), and* Visions of Caliban: On Chimpanzees and People *(1993). She is often on tour raising awareness and funds for her continued work at Gombe, as well as working for more humane treatment of animals in biomedical research and elsewhere. Dr. Goodall is an untiring fighter for a more human relationship to the natural kingdom, and has become one of the most publicly recognized and respected scientists in the world, receiving many honorary degrees and awards. The Jane Goodall Institute, headquartered in Tucson, Arizona, and with branches worldwide, promotes conservation awareness, education, and research.*

ACE OSMER: Could you talk about the early days, prior to your work at Gombe, when you were with Dr. Louis Leakey? It must have been an incredibly exciting period for you, given that Dr. Leakey was involved at Olduvai Gorge and amazing things were being unearthed there. How did you come to meet?

DR. GOODALL: Well, I'd wanted to go to Africa since I was eight years old. It was impossible; we didn't have any money, and English girls didn't go off and live with animals in those days. *[laughter]* But I fortunately had this wonderful mother who always said to me, "Jane, if you want to do something enough, and you work hard enough, and you take advantage of any opportunity, you'll get there in the end." Well, I received a letter from a school friend whose parents had moved to Kenya, saying "Why don't you come and stay?" So I left my job in London with documentary films, because it paid almost nothing—in those days employers could get away with that—and went and worked as a waitress at home in Bournemouth in order to raise the money for a return fare. My mother insisted that we find a firm with a branch in Kenya so that I would have a job lined up and I wouldn't have to go and sponge on my friend. So I went, and I had a month roaming around with my friend, and then somebody said to me, "If you care about animals, you should meet Louis Leakey."

So I called up the museum and said that I would like to speak to Dr. Leakey, and a voice said, "I'm Leakey—What do you want?," very brusque. *[laughter]* Well, I went to see him and he toured me around the museum, asking lots of questions. He was very impressed that I knew what an ornithologist was, and an ichthyologist. I hadn't read for nothing; I'd read books and books about animals. And so he offered me a job as his secretary—it just happened his secretary was leaving. And I cheekily said, "Well, that would be absolutely fabulous, but I have this tremendous need to get out of town and see what it is like in the bush." And he said, "Well, if my wife likes you, then I'll let you come with one other helper to Olduvai." What was so magical about Olduvai in those days is that it wasn't the famous site that it is today. It was a gorge in the middle of the Serengeti plains. It wasn't even a track in those days; it was just wilderness. So, although the fossil hunting was fun, chipping away in a very old-fashioned manner with dental picks and pickaxes, it was the evenings that excited me, when Gillian and I were allowed to go out with the two dogs that the Leakeys always took with them, and just explore. And there were rhinos; there were lions; it was just magic. It was the Africa I had dreamed about.

ACE: So you were in heaven.

DR. GOODALL: I was absolutely in heaven. And even with the digging, sometimes you'd hold this bone in your hand and you'd think, This was once a living beast and it had a smell and a color and a texture to its skin or its fur. And that was magic, too.

ACE: How did he choose you, then, for the assignment with the chimpanzees?

DR. GOODALL: Well, he began talking about the chimps, but not in terms of my going there. When he realized that I was somebody who truly wanted to learn about animals, somebody who had all my life been learning about animals, writing about animals, and that I truly didn't care about hairdressers and boyfriends and parties, *[laughter]* I think he felt that I was the right person.

ACE: And yet your training really wasn't in that area.

DR. GOODALL: I was totally self-trained, you see, self-motivated, almost self-driven. That was what I *had* to do.

ACE: So you went off to begin this assignment studying the behavior of chimpanzees in the wild on the shores of Lake Tanganyika, and I understand that your mother came with you at the start. Were there many obstacles at the beginning?

DR. GOODALL: Well, the first obstacle was money. I worked for Louis Leakey for a year, and then I went back to England and I worked at the London Zoo, because I thought I'd get near the chimps in that way. And I also spent a bit of time with one of the leading anthropologists in London learning about methods. All that time Louis Leakey was trying to find some money, because people didn't want to give money to an untrained girl. He finally got the money from an amazing man called Leighton Wilkie. In fact, Wilkie is the name given to our current top-ranking male chimp at Gombe.

Anyway, he got us the money to start. The British authorities in what was then Tanganyika (now Tanzania) wouldn't allow a young English girl off into the bush alone—absolutely not. So I had to have a suitable companion, and Mum offered to come.

ACE: That's quite a sacrifice.

DR. GOODALL: She's always been adventurous. She was absolutely invaluable as a companion, but also because she brought a whole lot of simple medical things with her—my uncle was a surgeon—and she set up a clinic. It was that clinic that really started the super relationship that I've always had with the local people.

ACE: I understand it took quite a while to garner the trust of the chimpanzees.

DR. GOODALL: That was the worst practical obstacle that I had to overcome, the fact that the chimps are so very fearful. Well, it took eight months, and even after that there was only a few I could approach. The good thing was that even when they were still being fearful, I was able, from my peak, to see some really exciting things, and that was how we got the National Geographic Society involved.

ACE: What was the response from the scientific community to your discovery that the chimpanzees not only could create and utilize tools, but also were meat eaters, and were even cannibalistic at times?

DR. GOODALL: Well, most people were really very excited. There were one or two people who said I must have taught the chimps how to use tools. [laughter] So it was generally well received, although I think I had to overcome the "National Geographic cover girl" image.

ACE: Well, I do remember, as a teenager, at least twenty-five years ago, seeing these television programs and news articles about your work. In fact, there's been a whole generation that has grown up aware of your work and very sympathetic towards it.

DR. GOODALL: That's right. And you know, the weird thing is that it's all over the world. I mean, I even get letters from a film team wanting to come out to Gombe from Chile. It's absolutely extraordinary. I met somebody in Angola, a Portuguese, who said that his entire life changed as he read one of my books. So, it's really everywhere, and absolutely incredible to me.

ACE: In regards to those two discoveries—the tool-making and meat-eating behaviors amongst the chimpanzees—at the time what did it mean to you in terms of your understanding of human evolution? Did things shift for you in a dramatic way?

DR. GOODALL: Well, yes, I guess it did. It was certainly drummed into me that we were "man the too lmaker," and that is what differentiated us from the rest of the animal kingdom. And I think it was very easy for me, having been at Olduvai and having worked with Louis Leakey, to imagine early humans, Stone Age man, using twigs and grass blades in the same manner that I observed amongst the chimpanzees, and it offered me the realization that behavior doesn't fossilize, that looking at our closest living relatives helps you to imagine what those early people were like.

ACE: And also the distinction between the animal kingdom and the human kingdom really begins to blur.

DR. GOODALL: That's right, and that boundary line is still shifting. Every time somebody produces another way in which one animal or the other does something that only *we* were supposed to do, there's always a furor. *[laughter]* I mean, we hate this continual challenge to our supremacy because we are so arrogant.

ACE: In your books you talk so eloquently about these wonderful chimpanzees, the alpha (dominant) male Figan, the strange and sometimes nasty duo of Passion and her daughter Pom, the sexually arousing Gigi, and you speak of them as if you recognize a soul or spirit there, a uniqueness and individuality. Do you feel that they each are individual spirits in the same sense that you might talk about a human being as an individualized spirit?

DR. GOODALL: Yes, I really do believe that.

ACE: There are people who would say that animals have a kind of group soul, if you like.

DR. GOODALL: I absolutely believe that they're as much individuals as we are. I mean, they are so different from each other. There's no question in my mind—they're as different from each other as we are.

ACE: There's another part of your story which I find really fascinating, and this is the difficult period for you and your companions, which took place from

1974 for about five or six years, during which four of your student assistants were kidnapped for political reasons, and at the same time there was warfare amongst the chimpanzee communities, and even cannibalism. The thing that occurred to me, Dr. Goodall, is that animals are known to be incredibly sensitive to what's happening in their human environment. It occurred to me that there may have been some connection to what was happening in the surrounding human environment near Gombe, or even in a wider sense, in Africa itself, that the Kasakela community of chimpanzees may have been reflecting or responding to in some fashion. Is this too outlandish a thought?

DR. GOODALL: Well I absolutely agree with you that any domestic animal has a tremendous sensitivity to human moods and they know if you're sad or happy, and they respond accordingly. You see, we very deliberately tried not to have that kind of relationship with the chimps, and I would be extremely surprised if they were picking up on anything like that. We're not too sure about movements of people outside the park. It could be that a whole chunk of habitat was removed, and that might have had an influence on the chimps. That is a possibility. Unfortunately we don't know. We tried afterwards to look back over the records when people were having to move from one village to another to cultivate new areas, but there's not a proper record.

ACE: The other aspect to your work that has been fundamental to a kind of revolution that's happening now in terms of our consciousness of the world around us involves the ethics of scientific investigation, and the way you've been a humanizing influence on that. Do you see that as a trend and do you see this trend evolving over the next decade?

DR. GOODALL: Thank God it is. Yes, I truly think it is. I think young people today are adopting a very different approach to using animals in research, for example. Very often there's absolutely no need at all for it, and they realize that. I'll give you a beautiful example. This is one I really love, actually. I went back to my old school in England, and they had just had a new biology mistress. And one of the girls was telling me—it was in the middle of summer—that the previous biology teacher had been teaching them about earthworms. So the new teacher told them all about earthworms and they learned about their mating behavior, etc. And then she asked them all to go out and find an earthworm. Well, for one, she was quite stupid, because it was the middle of summer and the earth was very hard, and the only place they could find earthworms was in the rose bed. [laughter] Well, the gardener was furious because they dug it up! *[laughter]* Then they took all their worms in very proudly. And she gave each of them a razor and said they were to slit up their worms. Well, they were absolutely horrified and one of the girls said, "I'm not going to," and she ran with her worm out the door, and they all followed. Every single child put their earthworm back in the earth and covered it up again. Isn't that a lovely story?

ACE: That's wonderful.

DR. GOODALL: And, you know, when I was two years old, my mother says I used to take earthworms to bed with me to watch them crawl, *[laughter]* and instead of being like most mothers and saying "Yechh," and throwing them out the window, she said, "Jane, if you leave them here, they'll be dead in the morning." And I would run down with them into the garden. So it sort of tied up two parts of my childhood to hear that story. And I think that illustrates the trend you're talking about.

ACE: There must be a balance point there. In the concluding chapters of your book *Through a Window* you talk about biomedical research using chimpanzees, and some of the horrendous conditions that these animals face. At the same time you intimate that there's a place where, as long as there's humane treatment of these animals, it's okay to do research on them if human beings are going to benefit.

DR. GOODALL: I think if you read it more carefully, it's a little different from that. See, the thing is that I'm not a doctor; I'm not a medical researcher. I can't answer questions about the need for animals. I hope and pray the day soon comes when we don't need to use any. I think we should be giving much more money and praise to people who are searching for alternatives. I mean, why aren't *they* getting Nobel Prizes? I don't know if it's going to require legislation or what, but there are so many alternatives to animal testing and animal research already available and approved at a very high level that we don't have to use animals. And yet we're still allowed to continue to torture them. The point is that I personally dislike the use of any animals for research, and I want it stopped. But I appreciate that it can't all suddenly stop. I mean, there's no way that it can.

ACE: I was thinking about some of the more radical animal activists out there who feel it necessary to actually raid clinics . . .

DR. GOODALL: No, that's wrong, and it doesn't help at all. I feel very strongly about this, and we had a big discussion about this yesterday when I was talking to some anthropology and psychology students. The first thing that you have to do, if you want to protest something, is please get your facts straight. Really line up the information. You know, so many animal rights people publish photographs that were taken thirty years ago, and what good is that going to do? It doesn't happen anymore like that. Secondly, if you permit yourself the luxury of getting angry, you can't think straight. There's no way that you can think clearly. Thirdly, the person you're arguing with will immediately become either angry or defensive, or both, and then he can't think straight either, and he doesn't then want to hear what you're saying.

So one tries to be rational about it. I know that, whatever I think, I can't stop animal research just like that. We can work towards changing attitudes, which is why I have to go into the labs, which I hate. But I'll tell you one thing that I think is truly super. The terrible lab that I describe in *Through a Window* where the chimps are in cages of 22" x 22" within metal boxes—well, they've thrown it out; it's gone and they've built a completely new lab, where, although the conditions aren't ideal, the chimps have plenty of space. And you know what's really fascinating? When I first met the director of that lab, he was cold and hostile, and if looks could have killed, I would have been dead. *[laughter]* Well, when I met him again a few months ago, I didn't recognize him. He was smiling, his eyes looked kind, and he said, "Jane, I really do thank you for what you did, because now we've been able to change it." You see, I really feel desperately sorry for a lot of the people in these labs.

ACE: People don't often get that perspective.

DR. GOODALL: No, they don't. I've been into a lab where there was a little chimp that I saw on a previous visit, very outgoing, clearly the leader of this group in the nursery, and he'd been taken out so that he could still see the others, but he was in a tiny cage by himself, depressed and hunched and rocking and miserable. And I said to this woman—they call themselves "technicians"—"How can you bear it?" And her eyes immediately filled with tears, and she said, "Jane, I can't. It's tearing me apart. But I have to stay, so that I can be with him." She said, "If I didn't think that you were fighting for me on the outside, I couldn't take it. None of us could." Well, you see, I'm fighting for the people as well as the chimps. I think I'm at an advantage over many of the animal rights people, because I do like people very much, too. They fascinate me, and I always think it's a challenge to find where the people who seem horrible really aren't horrible at all.

ACE: You talk about the chimpanzee being a kind of bridge from the prehuman to the human. You yourself seem to be a bridge between the old paradigm of scientific reality and the new paradigm which recognizes that we have a definite effect on the subjects we observe, and where we have to recognize the interrelatedness of all things. Do you see yourself consciously in this role or is it something that has just evolved for you organically?

DR. GOODALL: I think it's just something that happened. I suppose that in one's life there's a right time for things, and this was the right time for me. I had gained so much from the chimps by being with them, and that sort of enriched me and made me grow in a certain way. And then I wrote the big book *The Chimps of Gombe*, which meant that I had to go back and do all of the reading I'd missed out on when I went straight into a Ph.D., missing the earlier degree. I always felt a little bit like I had a chip on the shoulder; I didn't feel that I could talk as an equal with other scientists. So to write that big book I had to go back and do it all. I couldn't write about chimpanzee aggression and how it relates to hormones and the brain, and so I went and read it all. I think that book gave me a new credibility in the scientific world. And that was the exact point where I could jump in and try to help in the labs.

ACE: Can you talk about the effects of the vast desertification that is going on across parts of Africa? What effect is that having on the communities of chimpanzees there?

DR. GOODALL: Well, where the desertification is occurring is still mostly where there never were that many chimps. And for the most part, I think, the chimps, if they were there, have already gone before that happened, the problem being the destruction of the habitat. But basically the habitat is being destroyed all over Africa, and the chimps are disappearing equally fast. So, in that the creeping of the desert is destroying habitat, yes, the chimps are affected too. But I haven't worked much in those areas. I've been further south...

ACE: ...where things seem to be a bit more pleasant for those communities.

DR. GOODALL: Well, they're pleasant for the communities that are not being hunted and poached, and they're pleasant for the communities that aren't in the middle of logging, and they're pleasant for the communities that aren't in areas where there are too many people who are always wanting to cut down more and more trees to grow their crop. So it's pleasant for fewer and fewer communities.

ACE: Is the chimpanzee now considered an endangered species?

DR. GOODALL: Yes, absolutely. There's only four countries left where chimps are present in really significant populations, and that's in the central part of the range, which is Congo, Zaire, Gabon, Cameroon.

ACE: If we begin to reclaim, through desalination technologies, etc., some of that desert and reforest it in some fashion, do you think that there's a possibility that these communities can then expand or is there a point beyond which things cannot return to the way they were?

DR. GOODALL: I think the solution lies more in saving what we have, because people need all that land, too. I mean, overpopulation is the big problem. So what we're working very hard on is to work not only with governments, but also with local people, because, if you want to try and save a large piece of forest for the chimps and the other animals there, if there are hunters, what are they going to do? If they traditionally hunted, you have to try and think of alternative ways for them to make a living. And if the government is making money from selling timber, then you have to try and think of alternative ways for them to get foreign exchange. So, I'm becoming involved increasingly in things that are far beyond chimps. I've just come back from a trip through Africa that took six weeks. It took me from Tanzania to Uganda to Burundi to Angola to Congo. And I was taking with me an exhibit called *Understanding Chimpanzees*, which has large photographs, videos; it has objects actually used as tools by chimps from all over Africa, all their different cultures, and various other things, like drawings made by chimps and children's drawings of chimps. And around that exhibit, which we set up for a week in each place, we built whole wildlife awareness weeks with involvement of presidents and prime ministers. Lots and lots of involvement with children. And the impact of those weeks was far more than anything I could possibly have imagined. You know, there's a real interest and desire to help on the part of the children, total understanding on the part of the governments as to the need for conservation. But the countries are so economically poor that you become increasingly aware of the real problems in having any meaningful things done.

ACE: You're also active in monitoring the treatment of zoo animals.

DR. GOODALL: Yes. We have a program where we collect information on zoo chimps. And we have eighteen zoos now involved, using keepers and student volunteers. That's pretty exciting. We're hoping that the zoo community will help us with the pitiful conditions of the chimps and other animals in some of the African zoos. You know, this isn't because the African zoos are particularly cruel. It's just that very often the keepers don't have money even to feed themselves.

ACE: In an early chapter in *Through a Window* there's a beautiful section where you talk about a kind of mystical awareness that one can experience in the wild. I wonder if you could talk a bit about that. Have you had unexplainable experiences in that environment?

DR. GOODALL: Well, I'm not sure I've had them in that environment more than any other. I think that all my life I've had mystical experiences. It's just that the ones out in the forest, where I love to be most in the world, are very special. And it's a question of being able to forget that you exist. I think that's the key to it, which is why I love to be on my own in the forest, and to share the experience afterwards. Because as long as you're aware that you're there as a person, then those kinds of experiences are denied to you, I think.

ACE: And I guess that foundation can help in the way that you're able to attune to all the various species and the chimpanzee communities in particular that you work with.

DR. GOODALL: Yes, I think so. And I know that, as far as interacting with animals, I very often go to visit, say, one of the places where they have chimps who can still be handled, and people say, "Well nobody else who is a stranger has come in and had the chimps trust them like they trust you."

ACE: I suppose you've evolved a nonverbal language that speaks to them.

DR. GOODALL: Yes, it must be. It's sort of automatic. I don't consciously think of what I'm doing. And funnily enough, I don't have this relationship with gorillas at all. It's really funny. I mean, I do with dogs and cats and most animals, but young gorillas are more likely to bite me than anything else. *[laughter]*

ACE: You are considered one of a kind of triumvirate of women warriors of the wild, including the late Dr. Dian Fossey and Dr. Birute Galdikas . . .

DR. GOODALL: Half the time, people say, "How can Jane be lecturing? She's dead!" *[laughter]*

ACE: That's true. I have heard people confuse you with Dian Fossey. There are strong risks involved in your work, and Dian Fossey, in a way, gave her life for her work. I'm wondering what keeps your fires burning for this, that fuels the kind of joy that you feel?

DR. GOODALL: Well, what keeps me burning is that, God, there's such a lot to do. *[laughter]* I mean, I need about twenty lives after I pack as many lives into one day as I can. And I think what keeps me burning, first of all, is going back to Gombe and being in the forest. Although I can only do it now seldom for more than a week, that week is very rich and healing. Secondly, doing a lecture tour like this, okay, it may be exhausting, but yesterday I probably touched about three hundred children who are about fifteen years old. They listened to me for an hour and you could literally hear a pin drop. So I talk about what's happening in Africa and show some slides, and I see tears. That's the payback; that's what keeps me going. It's the feeling I get from people, and their commitment to what I am begging them to do. So it's their response.

ACE: It's actually quite a wonderful circle, because I know that probably millions of people who are aware of your work, and who are cooped up in the concrete jungles far away from the real thing, really do relate to the feeling that you carry towards your work. And that's an amazing thing that you've accomplished, to make that connection for people who aren't anywhere near it.

DR. GOODALL: The other thing that's exciting is, because I travel such a lot and meet these wonderful people along the way, I can sort of perform a networking role and link them up with each other. Such exciting things are happening out there today.

magic plants and the logos

TERENCE MCKENNA

in conversation with

ALEXANDER BLAIR-EWART

Terence McKenna has spent twenty-five years exploring "the ethnopharmacology of spiritual transformation" and is a specialist in the ethnomedicine of the Amazon basin. He is coauthor with his brother Dennis of The Invisible Landscape: Mind, Hallucinogens, and the I Ching, *author of* Food of the Gods *(1993), and* The Archaic Revival *(1992).*

ALEXANDER BLAIR-EWART: You've suggested that the term new age consciousness doesn't really describe what is actually happening. And you've replaced it with the term "archaic revival" or "archaic consciousness." I'm wondering what led you to that.

TERENCE McKENNA: Well, two things. First of all, the realization that there seems to be a dynamic within civilizations such that when a civilization finds itself in trouble, when its first premises no longer seem to make sense, it will search through its past to find a steadying and revivifying model of some sort. We're all familiar with the way in which the Renaissance exhumed classical values, classical aesthetics, legal theory, architecture, theories of polity, etc., even though they had been dead since before the fall of the Roman Empire. And we are the heirs, then, of this classical revival which took place in the fifteenth century. Now our dilemma seems more curious and more global than the dilemma that Europe faced in the early fourteen hundreds, and consequently our response, again largely unconscious, has been to go back in time to search for a revivifying and steadying formula around which we can build some kind of new social vision. I've called this impulse the "archaic revival" because I really think that history itself is empty of the kind of model we're looking for, and that in fact we have to go so far back in time that we actually leave the domain of history altogether. And I see this as much broader than what is called the "new age." It's been going on at least since Freud and Jung announced the discovery of the "unconscious." Surrealism, National Socialism, cubism and its glorification of the primitive, modern anthropology, the rise of syncopated dance and club music—many disparate phenomena in modern society point to the archaic revival.

ABE: I was thinking about Arnold Toynbee's assertion that when societies try to revive an archaic model they usually end up creating something like National Socialism which was an attempt to revive a pagan German folk soul. But you're transcending racism by going far enough backwards to some common human experience that is prehistoric?

TERENCE M: Yes. Prehistoric is a fairly neutral word, although not necessarily. But it is prehierarchical, pre- male dominance, pre- the styles of linear thinking created by the phonetic alphabet and print. It's a style that is much more fluid and emotion-based and I suppose you would have to say Dionysian as opposed to Apollonian. And the centerpiece of this is the shaman. This is the model personality that dominates any discussion of the archaic, and what I've done is carry out a detailed deconstructive analysis of what shamanism is, and reached the conclusion that it is essentially a reliance on the chemistry of certain plants to dissolve boundaries, to catalyze the imagination.

ABE: Now you speak of what is called in the native tradition "teacher plants." You speak of psilocybin, for instance, as being informative and educative, and you appear to see it as being involved in getting the "naked ape" to a higher level of consciousness. Can you talk about that?

TERENCE M: Yes. This is what *Food of the Gods* explores in great detail, the notion being that what orthodox anthropology and human evolutionary theory have overlooked (in trying to account for the emergence of human beings out of the animal substrate) is the impact of our switch from a fruitatarian and highly specialized diet to an omnivorous diet at the very moment that we were ceasing to be arboreal and were beginning to become binocular, bipedal animals of the African grassland. And psilocybin would have been present in those environments, because psilocybin mushrooms of many species have a preference for the dung of ungulate animals. Now those mushrooms would surely have been tested for their food value at the same time that many other potentially mutagenic compounds in foods were being exposed to the human genome.

The interesting thing about psilocybin is that at very low doses it increases visual acuity, and to my mind this would tip the evolutionary scales in a situation of natural selection towards selection of those individuals and their families that were admitting this exotic item into their diet. They would be better hunters and consequently better able to supply food to their children and raise them to reproductive maturity. At slightly higher dose levels, psilocybin, like many central nervous system stimulators, causes arousal and an energizing of the organism. Well, in highly sexed creatures like primates, this inevitably ends in sexual activity. So that's a second factor imparted by the psilocybin that would tend to force the outbreeding of the non-psilocybin portion of the population.

Finally, and most significantly, at the level of a truly boundary-dissolving intoxication, the psilocybin causes spontaneous outbursts of glossolalia (speaking in tongues). This may have to do with the elaboration of language. It creates a flood of hallucinagenic imagery, which may become the models for inspired members of the community to carve or paint or tattoo, or whatever. So, in other words, psilocybin looks to me like the chemical catalyst of the leap out of high primate organization and into human organization. And the way in which it achieves this effect is by dissolving dominance hierarchies; specifically it dissolves the construct in the personality that as moderns we call "the ego."

ABE: Let me just backtrack a little bit, because you've just covered a lot of territory. You suggest that psilocybin increases sexual arousal. At some point in the evolution of primates their sexuality became freed from the menstrual cycle. And animals, as you know, only breed at specific times, because they're only in heat at specific times. I'm wondering if something like psilocybin could have been the cause of creating what we would think of as "transcendental sexuality" in the sense that it transcends purely nature-based rhythms?

TERENCE M: Well, what it does is it tends to dissolve boundaries, and all primates, including very primitive primates right back into the squirrel monkeys, have what are called male-dominant hierarchies, in which females are strictly controlled by powerful males and assigned to them. I think what the exposure to psilocybin in the diet did was that it temporarily intervened in this tendency to form male-dominance hierarchies, and instead it was a catalyst for community, for group mindedness, for a more relativistic attitude towards ownership and possession of females, and it did this by promoting orgy, meaning group sexual activity. You know, the nearest relatives to the human line alive in the world today are the pygmy chimpanzees, and their sexual behaviors can barely be reported in a family publication. They are almost entirely bisexual, constantly sexually active in groups and apart, breaking and making pair bondings very readily, and I think that this must have happened over a long period of time. The protohominids, the psilocybin mushrooms, and the ungulate cattle were probably in association with each other for upwards of two to three million years, and it was a relationship of increasing closeness and attraction which ends finally about fifteen to twenty thousand years ago with the domestication of these ungulate animals and the establishment of the paleolithic religion of the Great Horned Goddess. I argue in my book, *Food of the Gods*, a kind of paradisiacal, quasi-symbiotic dynamic was involved there on the grasslands of the Sahara in the wake of the last glaciation. And what destroyed this was simply further climatological drying when the Sahara became a desert and we begin to get the institutions which we can recognize.

ABE: You talk about the relationship of psilocybin to the evolution of art. We know that totem societies go back an awful long way, and that totemism is, as Claude Lévi-Strauss pointed out, a sensibility, a culture form, and also an art form. Everywhere these kinds of substances were used we run across cave paintings, petroglyphs, that kind of thing. Do you think that psilocybin was responsible for that, too?

TERENCE M: Well, it has the quality of somehow empowering cognitive activity. It empowers poetics, dance, artistic productions in the form of carving and painting. It seems to somehow stimulate the organism to self-reflection in combination with self-expression. And so, yes, I would argue the evidence for the little scenario on the Saharan grasslands that I just laid out for you are these magnificent rock carvings in the Tassili Plateau region of southern Algeria, and they are not greatly different and certainly no less in quality than the rock work at Lascaux in France.

ABE: Something very significant happened to human consciousness in a very short period of evolutionary time.

TERENCE M: It's a great puzzle for evolutionary biology how it is that in a two-million-year period the human brain effectively doubled in size. There are evolutionary biologists—Lumsden being one example—who call this the most rapid transformation of a major animal organ in the entire fossil record, and it happened to us. Short of the intercession of God Almighty, theories have been thin indeed, and yet this goes to the existential core of what it is to be human. We stand apart from the general order of nature. I mean, you can talk about dolphin speech and honey bee dances, etc., but that's a long way from Milton. Science, in its rush to exorcise the paranormal, the occult, the inexplicable, has brushed over the major piece of evidence for something highly unusual going on, on this planet—ourselves.

ABE: You point out that the Americas are actually richer in consciousness-altering natural substances than anywhere on the rest of the planet. And yet, due to the experience in the sixties with LSD, we now see on television with the "Just say no" campaign that LSD and heroin and crack cocaine, speed, marijuana, psilocybin, and mescaline are all being lumped together as being the same thing, which makes this kind of investigation and exploration very difficult right now. Do you feel it likely that the distinctions among these different substances will again start to be recognized?

TERENCE M: Well, my book is essentially a plea for this. All the substances that you mention are lumped together under the category "bad," and then under the category "good" we get sugar, caffeine, alcohol, tobacco, and television. And what this is really telling us is that the style of the dominator culture is to suppress inquiry and to support various forms of sedation, addiction, and so forth.

ABE: Some of these mind-altering and addictive substances *are* bad.

TERENCE M: I certainly don't approve of the morphine-based drugs which are currently illegal. But I think the real anxiety about drugs has nothing to do with heroin use. It has to do with the feeling that was generated in the American establishment during the 1960s that they were actually losing control of the society, that such an infusion of psychedelic questioning threatened the very linchpin of society itself, and I would actually have to agree with them. I think the egocentric, dominator style that emerged in the West becomes very uncomfortable when the foundations of mental life are traced to a material root. This has to do with certain philosophical biases and the style in which modern science has arisen. Basically the epistemic bias of Western civilization makes it very restless in confrontation with the concept of transcendence or boundary dissolution achieved through drugs.

ABE: And yet we know that these substances, particularly sacred mushrooms, have been used by shamans of all kinds in all cultures for millenia.

TERENCE M: We know that, if by "we" you mean a vanishingly small percentage of an academically educated, intellectual elite. And this information did not even arrive in their understanding until the last century. Mescaline was discovered in the late 1880s; psilocybin was discovered in 1953 by Gordon Wasson; LSD did not have any currency until the early fifties. What we're actually talking about is an extraordinarily narrow window of opportunity to do research on these compounds before society got nervous and drove it all underground and made research illegal.

ABE: Still, I don't suppose either you or I would like to see a return to the excessive and trivialized use of psychoactive substances that went on in the sixties.

TERENCE M: That's right. What was absent in the sixties was any awareness of the ethnographic context in which these things had been used, very little mention of shamanism and so forth. And the other thing is that LSD is a unique compound in the following sense—that an inspired undergraduate biochemistry student, who is able to push together about $50,000 worth of financial backing, can, over a long weekend, produce ten, twenty, thirty million doses of this drug. With any other drug, psychoactive or otherwise, if you want to produce thirty million doses, you're talking about stainless steel vats the size of railroad boxcars and a true industrial scale of production. But LSD, because it is active in the millionths of a gram, so that theoretically you could get approximately ten thousand doses of this drug from a single gram, posed real problems for the establishment. And these are unique problems not having to do with its power as a psychedelic, which was considerable, but having to do with its unique characteristics as a commodity. See, that biochemistry student has automatically transformed himself into the head of a criminal empire. And there were many such individuals, which is, of course, unsettling to any agency charged with the maintainence of social order.

ABE: The responsible use of psychoactive substances has been going on for an awful long time. You seem to maintain that there is something unique about psilocybin.

TERENCE M: Well, I outlined for you my assumptions about its role in early human evolution. No other psychedelic could have had that role because it had to be a plant of the grasslands; it had to be a plant that required no preparation, no concentration or extraction, and psilocybin, it must be said, has this quality of activating a phenomenon for which, without blushing, we have to go back to the constructs of Hellenistic mysticism and just call it what it is—the *"Logos."* The Logos, an informing voice that has been silent in the mind of Western human beings for 2,500 years, suddenly comes back into communication with psilocybin. And the people who have had the most to do with it, Gordon Wasson and so forth, have always mentioned this in their writing. But I think it's such an extraordinary assertion that people don't even realize what is being said. In other words, it isn't that the mushroom allows you to understand things you never understood before, or that it gives you a new point of view, or anything so harmless sounding as that. It's actually that the mushroom speaks; it speaks to you in your native language, and it tells you things that you could never have figured out on your own, or at least I certainly never could have. And trying to come to terms with this as a rationalist without going off to cloud-cuckoo-land is quite daunting. Western science has no place in its pantheon for talking fungi. We may fund the search for extraterrestrial intelligence by radio telescope, but if you were to suggest to someone that extraterrestrial intelligence may actually be spread through the pastures and cowpies beneath our feet, they don't even hear that as a serious assertion. Yet shamanism, persistently, in all times and places, has insisted that it operated through helping spirits and ancestor spirits and contact with an animate intelligence resident in nature.

ABE: In Julian Jaynes' book, *The Origin of Consciousness in the Breakdown of the Bicameral Mind,* he basically defines the bicameral mind as the mind that is prerational and acts on the basis of hearing a voice. Are you talking about the same thing?

TERENCE M: To some degree. I mean, I found that book very interesting. It's over six hundred pages long and I think there's one paragraph on psychedelic drugs, a discussion of mescaline. He either was not aware, or decided to disarm himself of his most powerful argument. I think that the way to understand what happened back there before history is to think of the ego as a structure in the psyche analogous to a tumor, and the way to think of psilocybin is to think of it as a kind of psycholitic compound that was actually innoculating human beings for a window of several tens of thousands of years against the formation of ego, and that when the psilocybin religion died out and new religious forms took its place, ego was born. And with it came kingship, male dominance, concern for lines of male paternity, agriculture, accumulation of surplus, class structure, the whole panoply of institutions of which we are the unhappy inheritors.

ABE: How would psilocybin as a spiritually potent experience fit into the kind of urban, technologized society that we now have, or would you have to have one or the other kind of culture?

TERENCE M: No. I think that psychotherapy has been tremendously weakened and disarmed by allowing politicians to define what tools were legitimate and what were not. When LSD was first discovered by a Canadian they were getting 40% cure of chronic alcoholism with one exposure, and somehow the courage of the psychotherapeutic community failed at a moment when they should have hurled themselves against the "know nothing" politicians. They allowed an incredibly powerful set of tools for understanding the human mind to be placed out of their reach. I mean, it's as if the establishment of Renaissance science had accepted the Church's effort to ban the telescope, which means that we would never have evolved the edifice of modern astronomy and cosmology that we have. The psychotherapeutic community, perhaps because it always felt itself to be a poor sister to "real" science, just lay down and went along with that in the fifties and sixties, and now there is no psychedelically empowered psychotherapy. This is what shamanism is in the societies where it still is vital, and by studying those societies I think we could revitalize our own mental health care and mental health care maintenance systems dramatically.

ABE: You've witnessed some of those societies, haven't you, in the Amazon basin?

TERENCE M: Yes, and in eastern Indonesia and elsewhere.

ABE: Talk to me about the societies that function in this way in the Amazon.

TERENCE M: Over large areas of the upper Amazon basin of Columbia, Peru, and Ecuador, there is reliance on a psychedelic plant complex called ayahuasca. It's a prepared thing, made by combining two plants and boiling them together. But when analyzed chemically it is found to be a very close cousin to psilocybin. And early ethnographers, encountering these ayahuasca-using groups, were sufficiently impressed to claim that this was a telepathic drug of some sort. What they really meant by that was that incredibly intimate styles of decision-making had arisen around these plants, where these tribal societies were actually making decisions about migration, hunting, warfare, and pair-bonding based on information that was being group generated within the context of these shamanic trances. And this, to my mind, makes the point I was discussing earlier about the dissolution of ego. What it really means is that they were recreating this paleolithic style of group integration by using the psychedelic plants in the paleolithic style, which dissolves boundaries, and then, in a situation of dissolved boundaries, community concerns, group values are always given precedence over the wishes of individuals, even powerfully ranked individuals.

ABE: A lot of the spiritual traditions that have come into the West out of Asia, for instance, the Hindu, Buddhist, and Taoist traditions, seem to be saying that the use of psychoactive substances is really a bad idea, that you should avoid them and get where you're going through meditation techniques.

TERENCE M: Well, it's a stage in religions. When you study the history of religion, you find that if something is taboo, that's a clear signal that it was once very important. And in the case of Hinduism, out of which Buddhism developed—it was a reaction and a reformation of a portion of Hinduism— Hinduism rests firmly upon the Rig Vedas, and the Rig Vegas are nothing more than an enormous number of ecstatic poems dedicated to a mysterious intoxicant called Soma. And while we don't know what Soma was—this is a place where scholars labor endlessly—there is no question that it was physical, it was ecstatically intoxicating. In Western religion and spirituality an enormous number of our religious and spiritual strains of thought can be traced back to the Eleusinian mysteries of Greece. These were psychedelic celebrations of some sort. The evidence is pretty overwhelming. So these later religions, I think, are simply in the business of promoting priestcraft, and if that's your game, the first thing you have to do is to cast doubt on the notion that the individual can directly access "the Mystery."

ABE: What do you see as the future of psilocybin in Western culture?

TERENCE M: As we have circled ever more tightly around the mystery of the archaic we have seen the figure of the shaman come into view, and now hopefully the figure of the psychedelically inspired shaman. I think that this society is in a deep crisis and that first premises are now in question, and that, if we are allowed to carry out a reasonable inventory of our cultural tools, we will eventually have to accept the power of these things. The rise of our respect for the primitive, which has been going on for a hundred years, is an indication that we are slowly losing faith in our own methodologies. No one now believes in a leisure-haunted, electronic utopia. Most visions of the future are apocalyptic and bleak indeed, and the fact that the consequences of the Western style of being are to plunge the entire planetary ecosystem into crisis is going to force us to seriously rethink the premises of Western civilization. And I think the figure of the shaman is waiting in the wings. Certainly the youth culture, unconsciously, over the past thirty or forty years, keeps gravitating back toward that rhythmically boundary-dissolving, highly erotically charged dimension. And of course it's horrifying to the print mentality that is all probity and correctness, but all that is what got us into the mess we're in and it's pretty terminal now. I think eventually the depth of the crisis will force us to look outside the ordinary set of cultural answers for much more radical possibilities.

ABE: One of the fascinating things about this whole subject of psilocybin is, of course, that people can grow it very easily themselves.

TERENCE M: That's right. My brother and I are the authors of one of the best-selling books on the subject. We wrote *Psilocybin, The Magic Mushroom Grower's Guide* pseudonymously as O. T. Oss and O. N. Oeric, and it sold over a hundred thousand copies, and so did some of our competitors. So, yes, in the short space of a couple of decades, the psilocybin mushroom has gone from a denizen of the pastures of the tropical zone to a familiar sight in the attics, bowers, and basements of high-tech society.

ABE: Now, this shaman in the Amazon, he's using the substance that you describe, and there's a certain culture, a certain society that uses that in a respectful and sacred way. In your communication with these people, does it emerge that they deliberately use that substance for psychological healing and other forms of healing, or is it more of a mystical thing for them?

TERENCE M: No, the primary emphasis for them is healing. The distinction between physical and psychological is not so clear, but the incidents of serious mental illness in these societies is strikingly low. The hallucinations, the cosmic vistas and all that, are in a sense the frosting on the cake for these people. The shaman functions as an exemplar, a kind of superperson that everyone looks up to and trusts, believes in, and the shaman is able to be an exemplar because he actually has a living connection to the truly sacred, in contrast to, say, Jimmy Swaggart. In our society that cultural expectation of superhumanness and exemplary behavior is always disappointed because there is no genuine connection to real sacrality. Shamans who betray that are pathetic figures indeed and a society will turn on them with great vehemence.

ABE: You yourself have experimented extensively with psilocybin, and here we are having this highly intellectual dialogue about the thousand and one things. So obviously it's been possible for you to experiment with psilocybin and it hasn't turned your brain into mush. But isn't that one of the primary fears surrounding its use?

TERENCE M: Well, the brain-to-mush issue is one of the reasons that I am not an advocate of the vast cornucopia of synthetic drugs that keep coming onto the market. You see, with mushrooms or with ayahuasca or peyote or something like that, since we're not allowed to do scientific research on human subjects, we have to look at the ethnographic data and we know that people have been using mushrooms in central Mexico for at least two millenia. We can look at these populations, record the incidences of miscarriage, blindness, fetal deformation, retardation, and so forth. And we see that these are not factors. So, if you judiciously choose your shamanic plants with an eye towards the already recorded impact that they have on well-studied human populations, the debilitative possibility is easily avoided.

ABE: Now, would you group marijuana and hashish in that group of positive psychoactive substances?

TERENCE M: It's interesting. Cannabis is a category breaker. All these psychedelic substances that we've been talking about are chemically what are called alkaloids. Cannabis is technically what's called a polyhydric alcohol. Psilocybin occurs in many species of mushrooms; mescaline occurs in many species of cacti; other psychedelics usually occur in various places in nature. The tetrahydrocannabinol occurs only in cannabis. In terms of the social effect, yes, I would say that it functions socially as a minor psychedelic. In other words, it is boundary dissolving, it promotes introspection, reverie; it probably does not promote the kind of devotion to industrial social values that, say, caffeine does. But, nevertheless, caffeine is a serious addictive drug with demonstrable consequences on the liver, and yet it still is written into every contract signed between labor and management in any civilized country in the world as "the coffee break." Cannabis is unwelcome because it does not fit in with the model of the good worker/good citizen that has arisen in the wake of the industrial revolution. Nevertheless, its suppression and the amount of money and anxiety that is spread over that issue is one of the most bizarre and schizophrenic aspects of our whole approach to this thing.

ABE: Law enforcement agencies can more easily block marijuana and hashish because it's bulky, it has a distinctive odor, it's easy to track, whereas the white powder is highly transportable, and we have massive populations now addicted to cocaine and to crack cocaine. There are some social studies that point to the fact that people have only taken up those drugs at a point when they couldn't get marijuana and hashish.

TERENCE M: The only way you can take the profit out of the drugs is by making them legal, because the exhorbitant profits to be made from drugs are a consequence of their illegality. As an example—I haven't checked recently, but I imagine cocaine is still hovering around a hundred and twenty dollars a gram—airplane glue is a buck seventy-nine a tube, and can be purchased everywhere. Now, we do not have a large population of airplane-glue abusers in this society, and the reason is there is no glamor in it, and you cannot ride around in your neighborhood in a Mercedes after six weeks of dealing airplane glue. So it is absurd to expect these oppressed ghetto populations in the large cities of the industrialized West not to avail themselves of a product when there are enormous differentials between the purchase price and the sales price. If people have no other option and there's a commodity where they can double and triple and quadruple their initial investment, they're certainly going to avail themselves of it. Interestingly, most of the hard-drug epidemics that have harried the Western world over the past fifty years have been largely subsidized by government. Governments are the great culprits in this drug thing, and nobody wants to talk about this because it's just too horrible to suppose that our own elected, democratic institutions are somehow co-opted by the need for vast amounts of clandestine money, usually on the part of intelligence agencies and that sort of thing. The drug problem is a problem of the greed of mendacious governments, the failure of education, and a failure to provide people with other alternatives for how to better themselves.

3
chaos
and
creation

JOHN ANTHONY WEST

TOM HARPUR

JEAN HOUSTON

the riddle,
the sphinx, and
the "A" word

JOHN ANTHONY WEST

in conversation with

ALEXANDER BLAIR-EWART

An Egyptologist for more than twenty years, John Anthony West is the author of Serpent in the Sky *(1993),* The Traveller's Key to Ancient Egypt *(1985), and* The Case for Astrology *(1991) among others. At the time of this interview, John had just returned from an extensive period of research at the site of the Sphinx, where he and his colleagues had been probing the riddle of this mysterious and amazing wonder of the world.*

ALEXANDER BLAIR-EWART: Your book *Serpent in the Sky* is an introduction to ancient Egypt and to Schwaller de Lubicz. He's an exceptional character inside Egyptology, isn't he? He was a maverick to start with.

JOHN ANTHONY WEST: He's not an academic Egyptologist, which gives the academic Egyptologists license to ignore him, which they do. But he's an absolutely meticulous scholar. And he doesn't stick his neck out unless he can document it with particular interpretations. The thing to realize about Egyptology is that the only facts are the temples themselves, the inscriptions and reliefs, and so on. But the interpretation of those facts is by no means a scientific exercise. The proportions of the temple—those are the facts. What those proportions and measurements signify are a matter of interpretation. Other Egyptologists may say they don't signify anything. The Great Pyramid just happens to be one-eighth of a degree of longitude. In order to help people understand what makes Schwaller so different from all the rest, I use the analogy of Martians coming to Earth and watching a baseball game. And if they don't have any games on Mars, they can get very interested in this strange religious rite. They can measure the distance to the bases; they can even deduce some of the quite complex rules. But if you don't even recognize that it is a game, the information is total nonsense. Once you figure out that it's a game, then it all makes sense.

There were a number of other scholars even within the bounds of academic Egyptology in the nineteenth century who knew that there was something going on. They knew it was a game, but they didn't know what the game was. Schwaller figured out precisely what the game was and documented it in such a way that it really is irrefutable. And it's an important game, here and now in the last few years of the twentieth century, not that we're going to build pyramids and temples of Luxor again, but rather because Egypt provides us with a tremendous picture of how civilized people actually comport themselves.

ABE: Why does the study of ancient Egypt continue to be important today?

JOHN A.W.: It's because you can say there's really only one important philosophical question in the world, which is, is humanity on Earth for a purpose or not? The answer you give to that question determines the nature of an entire society. If the answer is yes, you produce Taj Mahals, Chartres cathedrals, temples of Luxor, and pyramids, etc. You produce Zen archery and Eastern martial arts and some primitive societies which aren't primitive at all, actually. You produce all kinds of dances and ceremonies, rituals and so on. If the answer to the question is no, you produce the twentieth century with its nuclear bombs and its poisoning of the earth, and the energy that would go into building cathedrals is building shopping malls. And you have a religion in its own right called the "Church of Progress." What we have now is a direct result of our having answered no, there is no purpose to our being here.

ABE: Very strange, this "Church of Progress." It demands a sacrifice of all of life. It's worse than the Aztecs.

JOHN A.W.: It demands the sacrifice of your heart. Only they don't cut it out of your body. They petrify it within. So what was it about Egypt that made it so important? Precisely because it's an example of how civilized people behave when they're answering that question with, "Yes, there is a purpose to our life." And one of the ways that is acted out is in the building of these glorious temples, tombs, and art work, genius and reverence spread across an entire society. In Egypt, the whole of society was engaged in extending its creative genius on every level.

ABE: Can we explore Schwaller's concept of "The Temple in Man"? He, along with his wife Isha and Lucie Lamy, were at the Temple of Luxor sometime in the forties and fifties?

JOHN A.W.: Yes, 1947–52.

ABE: He makes a remarkable discovery there because he's meticulous enough to measure everything and really look at it.

JOHN A.W.: He started out with a very simple aim. He was looking for the golden section pi. He had what psychics call a revelation, what poets call an inspiration, what scientists call a hypothesis (they always make it as boring as possible), that the Temple of Luxor was an exercise in harmony and proportion. Within a very short time he discovered not only was there the pi, but that the Egyptians were aesthetically, geometrically sophisticated in a way that he never envisioned. He had the background knowledge that allowed him to recognize what was going on. What started out as a relatively simple aim proliferated into this massive project in which the geometry and proportion, and so on, ran into a complete reinterpretation of the myths and hieroglyphs and symbolism. So he was finally able to offer this picture of a tremendously integrated civilization which hasn't been seen on Earth since that time. Art, philosophy, science, and religion fused into one inextricable motion.

ABE: When was the Temple of Luxor first built?

JOHN A.W.: Like everything else it was built upon earlier structures. The earliest parts found have been incorporated into the present structure and they date from the Middle Kingdom which is roughly 2000 B.C., but almost certainly, like every other structure in Egypt, it dates further back to the original.

ABE: So, approximately four thousand years ago, these human beings began to build this structure and into this structure they built a total harmonious imprint of individual man himself, the human being and his relationship to all of life.

JOHN A.W.: And it's curious that it is in Luxor and not in some other temple—Dendera or wherever. Luxor was the key to the whole business. It's a really amazing building.

ABE: What kind of people lived there?

JOHN A.W.: It's like this great genius operating on every possible level simultaneously. The proportions of the geometry, the way the reliefs fit into the spaces, and the way it all fits together is absolutely mysterious. As though they thought in geometry and then could apply the reliefs, the sculptures, the sanctuaries, the symbolism, and mythology to the geometry simultaneously. The deeper you go into it, the more incredible it seems.

ABE: These men were not like us?

JOHN A.W.: Presumably they were like us. They were individuals. There are enough documents around to show this. They had criminals and they had lawsuits and they had wills.

ABE: What is it that we have lost or forgotten?

JOHN A.W.: We seem to have lost touch with the universal principles, the living experience of the organic creation. Everybody knows the movement of birth, fertilization, growth, death, and renewal, ultimately finding spiritual resurrection and salvation. But our science of the Church of Progress finds these to be accidental corollaries.

ABE: There was this incredible integrated awareness and then it was lost just like that. What does that point to for us?

JOHN A.W.: It wasn't completely lost. It was carried on through the ages into Chartres and Europe. Mayan temples manifest a somewhat similar understanding in a different context. It's written into China and Japan. It has never really been lost. What has been lost is the ability of an entire civilization to live it.

ABE: I'm incredibly interested in what it was that you discovered when you were in Egypt not very long ago researching the riddle of the Sphinx.

JOHN A.W.: I've been working on this theory for going on twenty years now, based on Schwaller de Lubicz's very simple observation that the Sphinx was weathered by water, not by wind and sand. His theory, in my opinion, was demonstrable, and that all you needed was a geologist with the right kind of expertise to look into that question, see if it was weathered by water, and if it was, the question would then be: Where did the water come from, and when? I knew that the Sahara is a relatively recent desert, but that it's been desert at least since dynastic Egypt and before. The current dating suggests that it has been desert since about 10,000 B.C. In between 10,000 and 15,000 B.C., there were long periods of terrific rains, high floods, and all sorts of things, a very confused period. Before that it was fertile savannah.

ABE: Would that flood period have connected to an ice age farther north?

JOHN A.W.: Well, the current thinking is that it was concurrent with the melting of the ice from the last ice age. But at the moment I think you can say without any hesitation whatsoever that the theory is correct. The Sphinx was weathered by water and is a hell of a lot older than anybody thinks it is. This is sure. How much older? This is where the geology starts getting fuzzy because, when you go into geology, as in any other science, the stuff that's put out there for the layman all looks as though they have all the answers. As soon as you start going into it, however, you see that everybody's arguing about it, and it's by no means hard. What seems to be hard, as it were, is the sequential chronology. In other words, though nobody can really put a date on it, it's certain that the desert comes last. Before that there was this long period of very heavy rains, and I mean "the deluge" jumps to mind. It's very hard not to think of that in terms of Old Testament deluge. And before that it was savannah. Now that's certain. But the dating is up for grabs. I mean, from my point of view, whether it's 8000 B.C. or 14,000 B.C. or 40,000 B.C. is beside the point. The main point is that it was built by a civilization of which we have no record. And when you really look at the Sphinx and the temples around it, you see that it's an even more staggering piece of work than even the Pyramids or the temples of Egypt. So effectively it upsets the whole applecart of history. Needless to say, the people who make a living selling apples are not happy about this.

ABE: And now you are able to prove your theory?

JOHN A.W.: I've got my geologist, Robert M. Shoch, backing me up on this a hundred percent. Now he's a very conservative guy, and he starts getting a bit edgy when you start bandying about dates, because we can't yet geologically put a strict date to it. But he certainly agrees with that chronological sequence. So it's fairly obvious that whenever those rains were there, the Sphinx was there before that. Oh yes, by the way, I should say that it's not just water weathering, but it's quite distinctly rain. In other words, lots of precipitation over long periods of time. This you see not so clearly on the Sphinx itself, because it has been repaired and rerepaired so many times over the past five thousand years that it's tough to get a really clear picture of the Sphinx itself. But where you get an absolutely pristine clear picture is on the stone walls of the ditch surrounding the Sphinx ...

ABE: In the oldest layers of stone?

JOHN A.W.: Where it's been cut away in order to free the body of the Sphinx. And there you see that the walls have been weathered back ten, twelve feet from the original cut. You see, this doesn't happen overnight.

ABE: What is the Sphinx made of?

JOHN A.W.: Limestone. The technical word is "competent," a fairly competent limestone.

ABE: It would take a fair while to wear limestone back to that extent. Chartres and most of the cathedrals in Europe are made of limestone and some of them go back to the eleventh or twelfth century. And they're showing very mild wear at this point.

JOHN A.W.: That's right. Again it depends a lot upon the kind of limestone. If it's a harder limestone, it's going to wear a lot less. On the other hand, Europe is Europe, and it's raining all the time. In Egypt, of course, it hardly ever rains. There is lots of hard scientific work still to be done here, but I think you can say without any possibility of doubt that all of history and the whole notion of the so-called evolution of human civilization has to be rethought right from the beginning on the basis of this simple fact.

ABE: Who do you think those people were who built the Sphinx?

JOHN A.W.: I do not know.

ABE: Have you got a theory?

JOHN A.W.: Some of my colleagues and I got to laughing about it; it's become known as the "A" word, because as soon as you say the "A" word everybody gets all excited. *[laughter]* The opposition freaks out and starts getting hot under the collar. The "A" word is, of course, Atlantis and Plato's myth.

ABE: Through my own cosmological, cyclical investigations I was driven to the conclusion that Atlantis existed where the Mediterranean Sea is now.

JOHN A.W.: Well, that's a very plausible scenario, because it's quite well known that the Mediterranean wasn't full not so very long ago, and that it could well be that that civilization was existing on the bottom, and that the Sphinx was sort of the outpost. Maybe the Sphinx was to that civilization what Abu Simbel was to the dynastic Egyptians. That's one scenario.

ABE: The thing is, how do you explain away the vast proliferation of different cultures in the Mediterranean basin, even within recorded history? Where did all those different cultures come from?

JOHN A.W.: Again, that's a good question, and very difficult to answer. I mean, human beings are human beings; they could have all thought it up independently, more or less at the same time, the way you see it happen with scientific discoveries nowadays, where people working absolutely independently and with no knowledge of each other come up with very similar discoveries around the same time, as though it's in the air. So you just don't know; you can't answer those questions, really. But since I spoke to you last there's a new card been thrown on the table. Have you heard about the people who are working on the face on Mars, the monuments on Mars?

ABE: Yes.

JOHN A.W.: Well, they've been in touch with me, and I'd heard about that discovery, but never looked deeply into it. I've always been a bit hesitant about it because the Sphinx theories were outrageous enough to begin with. But when I peruse their material really carefully, unless the photographs or the computer enhancements are a total fudge, it sure does look interesting.

ABE: Yeah, that huge pyramid...

JOHN A.W.: To me, the proof is when the geometry starts giving you those figures, because the geometry's no accident.

ABE: Would you describe what those Viking computer-enhanced pictures show on Mars?

JOHN A.W.: Well yes, they show something that looks very suspiciously like a gigantic face which looks up into the air. All you'd see from the ground was a profile. A huge head with a kind of headdress around it, and then, not connected directly with it, but connected to it geometrically—in other words, at quite precise distances and angles from it—are a number of structures that do not look natural, including a five-sided pyramid. That pyramid just doesn't look like something that could be formed naturally. The researchers, for reasons too complicated to go into, date that construction at about 200,000 B.C., and they think that the Sphinx and the Giza pyramid are connected in some way or another to that original scheme. Interestingly enough, once when we were sitting near the Sphinx, Shoch was looking at this weathering on the ditch and suddenly said, "Gee, this is scary, this stuff looks like it's hundreds of thousands of years old."

The first viewing of the Sphinx is often revelatory. I mean, it really packs a wallop like nothing else on this Earth—what struck me was that this dated from some kind of unimaginable antiquity, and that it was built by people so advanced beyond us that it was very hard even to conceive of what they were like, what they thought or how they felt, that it was built by superhuman beings who nevertheless ostensibly were us. And of course that was a gut feeling, that's not science. But when we talk about dates it looks so outrageous that if you have any scientific background, or you believe anything you were taught in school, you would just want to dismiss it out of hand. Yet when you go into it, even that kind of outrageous figure has to be borne in mind. I mean I'm not saying that it *is* that, but once you realize that the Sphinx was built before the rains, and the rains were somewhere between, say, 10,000 and 15,000 B.C., well then, it's at least older than

15,000 B.C., and it could be a hell of a lot older than that. We don't know.

ABE: All of the Neoplatonic cosmologies place it firmly in what we call the Atlantean epoch.

JOHN A.W.: Yes, there are legends and myths all over the world that suggest that high civilizations were around tens of thousands of years prior to modern history. And, of course, why not listen to the ancients? I mean, it was their job to keep intact the old knowledge. If I want to know something about the Egyptians, I listen to the Egyptians rather than the Egyptologists.

ABE: Yes, indeed.

JOHN A.W.: Quite frankly my view of modern scholarship and modern science is that it's mostly a catastrophe. There's not much of it that's right and an awful lot of it that's presumption, assumption, and opinion, and just plain hubris. So it seems, on the basis of this Sphinx theory alone, that it's time to go back and look into the old legends and myths and see what checks out, what corroborates, what cross-matches, and so on. There's been a fair amount of work along these lines, which proves again, beyond any possibility of doubt, that there's an astronomical, astrological content. And then there are many of these myths and legends found all around the world that date from time immemorial. So, really, we're effectively establishing the context of an entirely new science on the basis of this very simple fact that the Sphinx was weathered by water in the distant past.

ABE: Incidentally, John, in the revised cosmology that I've been working on through astrology for many years, the planet that rules Egypt, or the force point in the cycle, is Mars.

JOHN A.W.: Interesting that you say that, Alexander, because the ancient word for Giza or Cairo, apparently, to the ancient Egyptians—I didn't know this myself—was the name for Mars.

ABE: Ahh... that's beautiful.

JOHN A.W.: So there are a lot of connections, and I'm just now starting to explore this Mars connection material.

ABE: Now, you may not be able to offer scientific proof, or whatever, but I want to get back to the "A" word, and back to the Sphinx. What impression do you have of the kind of people who would have built the Sphinx?

JOHN A.W.: Well, it's hard to say. But you get a sense of a kind of superhuman quality, particularly when you look just at the scale and perfection of the Sphinx. When you look at the temples around it, built of blocks that each weigh upwards of two hundred and fifty tons, that are jigsawed into place as though they were children's toys, you get the sense of a people in command of a kind of prodigious technology that is at the same time philosophical and spiritual. And you can't look at the Sphinx without getting this tremendous feeling in your gut that you get from a tremendous work of art. A great work of art puts you in touch with the gods. That's what art is for, to put you in touch with divine or cosmic principles. We've lost track of that, of course, in our barbarous civilization which we like to call progressive. But that's what ancient art, ancient sacred art, was for. And that's what you get when you look at the Sphinx and its temples. Indeed you get it from all of Egypt, but especially from the Sphinx and the temples around it. And if you go into it deeply enough—which is difficult to do with the Sphinx temples because they're so badly beaten up and weathered that it's hard to get the measurements—but when you measure these things carefully you get the constituent harmonies, geometries, and proportions, and they in turn can give you clues as to the original function, which, in fact, is not known in the case of the Sphinx and its temples. Not only do we not know when the Sphinx was built, or who built it, we don't know why it was built, although the Mars guys and I have some pretty interesting speculative ideas about that.

ABE: Can you talk about them?

JOHN A.W.: Well, one of my ideas is that in some sense or another the whole complex of Giza and other similar places was intended to act as a kind of tuning fork that's meant to respiritualize the earth, or to spiritualize it, as the case may be; that it's kind of a gigantic, scientific-religious instrument that's designed to, let's say, put people in touch with the gods, which are of course within. That's my gut feeling, but attempting to prove that is something else again. In the geometry, and in fact to a certain extent in the geology and the geomorphology, as we get into it, we're starting to find real clues. The people who are working on the Mars material came up with a somewhat similar explanation from a purely mathematical standpoint. So we've got something interesting going on, and it's going to take some years to develop. I think we've got a variety of people with expertise—not just your usual Aquarian dreamers—but people with real expertise in very specific areas, and we seem to be converging on a kind of new science or new paradigm.

ABE: Does this research lend credibility to the idea that the earth at one time was populated from another planet, or that there was a time when there was a transplanetary civilization?

JOHN A.W.: Why not? I mean, it could just as well be the other way around, that they could have been populated from us. And, of course, also coming into this whole paradigm now are these amazing crop circles that are showing up everywhere which are demonstrating the same kind of geometry as the formations on Mars, and which is in turn connected to the geometry on the Giza plateau. *[laughter]* It's a bit mind-boggling, but I don't mind speculation as long as you know you're being speculative, and you don't say that something *is* until you have some kind of real proof that it is, at least from the point of view of science. If you want to go and talk channeling and revelations, well then you don't have to talk science, and I have nothing against that. But for my purposes, in this kind of an inquiry, I do need science.

ABE: Where are you going to next take this investigation?

JOHN A.W.: When we first went there we were looking for underground chambers to see if there was anything to Edgar Cayce's "hall of records" and that sort of thing. And we did, in fact, discover some rather suspicious-looking or -sounding cavities and/or chambers in the area of the Sphinx. Because we were kind of casting our net wide, we didn't do detailed enough work so that we could absolutely spot them, and we can't really say on the basis of the seismograph whether they are man-made or natural structures. But they are suspiciously unnatural looking in terms of the way they are placed and the fact that soundings taken elsewhere on the plateau don't give you those cavities or chambers. So one of the next stages would be to get back there with the seismographs and do much more detailed work so that we can pinpoint these things. If we can pinpoint them more precisely, then the Department of Antiquities would drill and drop down one of those little minicameras to see if something is there.

ABE: How deep are those cavities, John?

JOHN A.W.: It was hard to tell. The impression that we got from the seismograph work was that they might have been chambers or cavities that had collapsed. So we just don't know. But a Japanese team who was there a couple of years ago, using a totally different method of underground sounding, came up with rather similar results. So there's *something* there.

ABE: Would you say that the result of your recent investigation there in Egypt on the site of the Sphinx and the surrounding temples definitely proves that the Sphinx is infinitely older than we previously thought it was?

JOHN A.W.: Yes. Well, I wouldn't say infinitely, but it's many, many thousands of years older than anyone thought, and on that basis alone the whole of history and the notion of the so-called evolution of human civilization has to be totally rethought. Yes, I can categorically say that.

because we are not a race of angels

TOM HARPUR

in conversation with

ALEXANDER BLAIR-EWART

Tom Harpur has had a rich background that includes both the academic—Rhodes Scholar, Professor of New Testament and Greek—and the practical—parish priest, global journalist, newspaper editor, TV broadcaster and author. He is a host on Vision TV and a regular columnist on ethical and religious affairs with the Sunday Star *in Toronto. Among the many books he has authored are:* Harpur's Heaven and Hell *(1983),* For Christ's Sake *(1986),* Life After Death *(1991),* God Help Us *(1992), and* The Uncommon Touch *(1994).*

ALEXANDER BLAIR-EWART: Just to help our discussion, let's say that the "Logos" is this Presence that our presence stands in, our humanness, our awareness when we are most wholly ourselves, present, real, and alive. This Presence spontaneously arises when I want to connect with *[gestures towards Tom]* here, and I want to be met by who is here, with the acknowledgment that there is a spiritual being, a human being here. And this Presence, the Logos, opens me constantly to this quality of "we" awareness.

So there is this all pervasive Presence, which is Eternity itself. It has taken different forms, various shapes, and has been given many names and images by different cultures. And in contemporary culture, people are looking around in this huge supermarket of spiritual possibilities to try to find this Logos. From a Christian point of view, do you see the new age movement as being a valuable opening into a reawakening of this awareness of the Logos, or the Christ, as it is called in the West, or is it that if they simply concentrated on Christianity as we know it, they would get there anyway?

TOM HARPUR: I view the new age movement for the most part positively, which makes me rather a pariah among many theologians, particularly those in the conservative mode who see it as demonic. If you read right-wing, fundamentalist, Catholic publications right now—and that's a growth industry, too—the new age movement in all its manifestations is one of the signs of the Antichrist. And, of course, so is the new environmental movement, the feminist movement, almost anything you can look at that's happening around us. Global thinking, in terms of any kind of world federalism—that also is Antichrist. But I think you're right, that the new age movement is certainly a symptom of our hunger for the Logos, for meaning or spirit, a profound witness to the vacuum that exists because of the dry dust of traditional orthodox Christianity. I just don't think it's cutting it. It is with some people, but if you look at the world picture, I don't think traditional orthodox Christianity is cutting it. It has played itself out and I think, personally, that it was a distortion to begin with.

ABE: In actuality, then, how do these two things, the new age movement and traditional Chrisitianity, connect?

TOM H: One of the things I try to stress whenever I can is that we need to, at the very minimum, learn from the new age movement: one, that the spiritual hunger is there and the search is there; and two, that many of the things which are speaking meaningfully to people in the new age movement are in fact within the tradition from which we come, whether it's meditation or mystical experience. It is all there, but we haven't drawn on it, with some exceptions, as you say, with Creation Spirituality and Matthew Fox, where you have a creative thing that's alive with possibilities. But by and large there is this hunkering down on the part of mainstream Christianity in the face of this new manifestation, this threat as it's perceived. And so I don't know yet whether or not to be optimistic that this lesson or this message is going to be learned or heard by "traditional Christianity."

ABE: There's this human and divine Presence that embraces all that is, and what it calls for is unity amongst human beings and a conscious relationship with everything that is. This awareness doesn't say we can't use the tree, it just says, "See that it is a tree, that it's something that lives, and your relationship with it should be based on that."

TOM H: Well it *participates* in the Logos or is an expression of the Logos. For me it's an enfleshment, and I think for Matthew Fox, also, it's an incarnation, if you like, of the Logos. So is every living creature, and so is every human being. And I agree with you that this is what constitutes our fundamental humanity. When I said earlier that orthodoxy was a distortion, I was thinking about my little book *For Christ's Sake* and other books like it that are trying to get to the biblical basis and see what it was that Jesus discovered, and who was he anyway? Because I think the instinct of the Johannine author of the Fourth Gospel or whatever later editor put the prologue on there about the Logos, was right, that the historical Jesus to begin with discovered this Presence, that it was within Him, that God, the Kingdom of Heaven, or the Logos was within Him. And so fully possessed was He by it or so open to it—there are other ways of describing it, too—but the whole Lucan idea of the way in which Jesus was totally filled with the Holy Spirit of God for the first time as a human being, totally possessed by It, that to me is where His divinity lies.

People talk about the divinity in Jesus. But I wouldn't want to talk about His divinity without talking about ours, too. Not in a Shirley MacLaine sense, but it's just that while we haven't participated as fully or opened ourselves as much to the Logos as Jesus did, we can be Christs in that way, or we can be another Jesus, if you like.

ABE: What is the metaphysic of the Antichrist?

TOM H: Metaphysic of the Antichrist?

ABE: Yes. What is the metaphysic of the Antichrist? Is there some way to arrive at some clear apprehension of the metaphysics of the Antichrist? There ought to be some way, instead of merely being able to fling this epithet at people, to get at some kind of clarity about what the Antichrist is, so that we'll know whether or not someone deserves the title.

TOM H: I am, according to my critics. *[laughter]* But I think it is the attempt to come up with a metaphysical explanation that ends up with something like a personal devil. So I don't think that's a helpful direction in which to go. I'm not sure I'm interested in speculation about that.

ABE: Let me see if I can encourage you to do it, because I think it's important. Okay, so we have this whole new age movement in all its many forms. All of these people in one way or another are concerned about the human quality of their existence and how they are relating to other people, where they are and whether or not they should be where they are, and so on. I mean, there's conscience operating there. So, would Antichrist be something like the conscience*less* activities that we see in the degradation of the planet, in the proliferation of nuclear weapons or chemical warfare?

TOM H: I think it's anything that denies the fundamentally human, the fully human. Then, of course, you can ask, What is the fully human? and we're back at the Logos again. Wherever there is substance, as Jung would say, there is shadow. So, if there is such a thing as the Logos, then there would have to be the not-Logos, or even stronger than that, the anti-Logos. So, if I were pressed, I would say it would be anything that denies the face of the human in us.

ABE: Now, here's the question. Does such a fragmented entity actually have any power, ultimately? Is it something to be feared?

TOM H: I think it's to be taken very seriously. I wouldn't say feared, because I think the perfect love is supposed to cast out fear, and the knowledge that you can really love, which is the knowledge that the Logos brings, properly understood it seems to me, is where the ultimate control lies, that it is meant to cast out fear. So fear is too strong a word, but to be shunned, to be avoided, to be fought at times, yes.

ABE: In traditional Christian thinking, which you've already defined as a kind of distortion, there is this fear of the new age movement, all of these millenarianists declaring, "These are the end times." So, the appearance of the new age movement? "It's the Antichrist. It's proof positive that Jesus is coming and we should be happy about that." Would there be some way to dialogue our way to the point where new age people realize that actually they're involved in the search for the same thing that Christians are, and have some of the Christians a little less worried about it?

TOM H: Yes, that's what I'm saying. If we could be a lot more open, instead of putting up the barriers and calling names, and share more with each other as part of our interfaith dialogue, then I think it would be productive for both sides. Parts of my book on healing, for example, in some sense could be written off as new age. But it is really grounded in something which belongs to the Old Testament, as we wrongly call it, and the New Testament, and which is deep in the Christian tradition. So, in the dialogue we might be made more aware of what it is we really have. We might also help some of the seekers out there be a little more encouraged to look again, those who have either written Christianity off, stereotyped it, or seen it as the enemy. Have you read *The Celestine Prophecy?*

ABE: Yes, I guess everyone has.

TOM H: It sees the church as the enemy. It's the church that wants to suppress "the manuscript" because of the insights therein. And then you read a lot of books on reincarnation and they will tell you the church deliberately repressed or suppressed any teachings about reincarnation, even to the point of butchering the New Testament to get rid of them. A lot of very poor scholarship at work there and some paranoia. They on their side tend to look at the church with a certain amount of hostility. So dialogue, yes, and an openness on both sides.

ABE: I actually wonder, what is the difference between sin, redemption, and grace and karma, reincarnation, and enlightenment? I guess in the one case you can be forgiven and in the other case you have to take your lumps, no matter what.

TOM H: I think in both cases you take your lumps. You can be forgiven, but if you've been an alcoholic parent, the consequences of that go on and on.

ABE: I deeply suspect that very few people in the West are able to actually think the thought karma, reincarnation, enlightenment, and so what they do is replace these three words with sin, redemption, and grace.

TOM H: That could well be. I think the average holy man from India is totally shocked at what passes for the doctrines which are supposed to come from Eastern mysticism. In other words, it's like Chinese food; it's been changed to meet the market here. So I agree. They're talking about similar realities, but in a different way, and at a fundamentally different level, it seems.

ABE: Is Christianity going to survive the encounter with the late twentieth century, with the new age movement on one side—which is definitely here to stay—and technology on the other? You see, we hear so much on one hand about the church going through a revolution. On the other hand, there are all these establishment right-wingers who are going to hang on until the bitter end. So, is Christianity, in that form, finished and is that possibly good? I mean, if we say it's a distortion in the first place, maybe that way of being Christian has to die away in order for a re-enlivening of the whole thing to take place.

TOM H: That's a very important point, and I think it's moot. I mean, one would have to be a prophet to see it clearly, but I think it's moribund in many ways. I talked to a very brilliant Nicaraguan liberation theologian the other day, and he was saying that the Curia in Rome and the establishment as such is really unknowingly setting about the total dismantling of Catholicism as we know it. And it may well be that in the plan of God the churches have to die so that something fresh might be reborn. There will always be vestigial groups hanging on, and as I sometimes say in my column, they will come under the Ministry of Culture, get grants for quaint activities and things like that. So that's not beyond the bounds of possibility. If that happens, so be it. I mean, then something new and better can be born. I guess the reason I keep writing and speaking about these issues is that while I see the death of the churches as a possibility, and maybe even as a good thing, I still try to fan the embers and flames of renewal and of rebirth, wherever I see them, because there is so much there that is good. And the potential to absorb and to change is there if it's allowed to happen. It depends very much on the leadership. But I'm not inspired by the leadership I see in Canada at the moment in any of the churches.

ABE: So here we are, we have this historically Christian culture with its overlay of technology and new ageism, and it's like Beckett's play *Waiting for Godot*. There's no announcing voice anywhere that any of us would actually harken to. There's no prophet in this wilderness. What is it that people need to see happen for us to cut through all of the theological nonsense, old and new, and actually be *present?* What are we waiting for?

TOM H: We're waiting for the reality to break through, and unfortunately the vases in which it is meant to be contained or the conduits through which it is meant to pour are blocking it. There's a certain human craving for someone to tell us that "this is the way," I suppose. I would be fearful, personally, if somebody arose who was a totally luminous kind of figure and everybody went, "That's what we were waiting for." That might be the Antichrist. *[laughter]*

ABE: Obviously the only way the Antichrist (if there is such a creature) can "get us" is if we're not doing it ourselves, and we're not sure—is that messiah real or not? Obviously the only way for us to have any kind of ground of certainty—and I don't mean intellectual ground—is to actually stop waiting and decide that the messianic age can begin now, here, this afternoon, in this beautiful room.

TOM H: Well, perhaps it *is* beginning here.

ABE: And what are we looking for? Miracles? Are we still shouting out, "Give us a sign!"? Some people are saying, "Well, the new age movement is a sign," and others are saying, "Oh no, it's the wrong sign. No, over there, Rabbi Schneerson or one of his disciples in New York or Israel is maybe the messiah. There's a sign over there. Let's look at that." I mean, are we actually unbelievers? Are we the children of Israel saying, "Show us a sign. Show us a sign," when we don't really need one?

TOM H: But the sign is within you already.

ABE: Right.

TOM H: It's within everyone. And so I think it's a mistake to go running hither and thither after Matthew Fox or the Vineyard Church, or whatever.

ABE: Does it actually, then, turn out that all of us, for whatever reason— fear of the Antichrist?—have a heavy investment in this *not* being a numinous time, and that that's why it isn't?

TOM H: Yes, I think you could put it that way. But I think it's an unconscious heavy investment. And the hierarchies of the church are very obvious examples. But it doesn't stop there, obviously, because the laity in the main are totally apathetic, as well. There are small groups like the Coalition of

Concerned Catholics, but in spite of what happened in Newfoundland with the scandals and everything,* maybe you get a few hundred concerned Catholics. The rest of them simply want to continue going to Mass and don't want anybody rocking the boat. They don't care whether the priest is living a double life or whatever. If it's drawn to their attention, they won't like it, but they're not going to start something. They don't care if the Pope is unreasonable or stupid. They have a vested interest at an unconscious level in keeping the status quo, as we do politically in other ways.

ABE: So, what is it then, that stops all of us from crossing this line which is always now? What stops us from crossing this line from waiting to Being? What is this actually? Is it lack of faith?

TOM H: Yes, if by faith you mean trust, as opposed to an assent to X number of propositions. Part of the discovery of Jesus of this Presence of which we speak, it seems to me, was the discovery that It was within. I think that His consciousness changed, and part of the change of consciousness was this awareness that entering into the Kingdom, or accepting one's being and incarnation of the Logos, having God within you, could not be earned. It was simply a matter of trust. And that's why He uses the analogy of the little child. It's a trust in the universe, if you like, a trust in yourself understood in terms of the Logos being the higher self, or however you want to name it. It's an act of trust, and it's almost too simple. I think that St. Paul maybe in a twisted way was saying, too, that that's what he really found, after being a Pharisee of Pharisees and trying so hard, and suddenly realizing, "God, I can relax." This is the point of Rome, it seems to me, however else you interpret it, that he just suddenly realized he could let go and relax and he was in Christ or Christ was in him. He likes both metaphors. We're too sophisticated, or we think we are, and it's too easy, too obvious. And so all of those things go into the reason why we don't grasp it.

ABE: What I see all over the new age movement is the "seeker," and the "seeker" is the Christian, and the Christian is the "seeker." The new age movement is largely an unconsciously Christian movement. The seeker or the pilgrim, this person who is looking for God, the Presence or the Logos, is filled with a certain kind of attitude, a cultural need, something that has developed throughout the history of the West. The seeker wants to arrive somewhere. As you said with Paul, there's something in us that wants to say, "Ah, now I'm here." But if you look over the whole geography of the new

*The sexual abuse of boys in Catholic orphanages. The award-winning docudrama The Boys of St. Vincent was based on it.

age, Christian, native, Buddhist landscape, the seekers can't land anywhere. And then the restless seeker has to move on to the next thing, restlessly looking all over the place. Could it be that the very seeker is our problem? I mean, is that what Paul realized, that he didn't have to carry this brilliant Talmudic initiation all his life?

TOM H: He didn't abandon it. It was there and it was like Jung's mud in the alchem. It's the mud that eventually the gold comes out of. I think that for Paul it shed light backwards and forwards for him in the experience, so that all that he had done wasn't wasted. This is why he is so thoroughly Jewish. The scholarship of the last forty or fifty years has discovered again the Jewishness of Jesus, the Jewishness of Paul. What happened, though, what transformed his way of looking at all of that, was that he no longer had to strive to *make it* with God. All of that before was seen as a means to an end, the end being somehow to get right with God, to be forgiven, to feel at peace, reconciled, whatever. And he glimpsed that it was a gift of Grace, that he was never ever going to make it that way, no matter what he did, that it was already given to him. The prodigal son discovers his father is waiting. It's nothing the prodigal son has done. He's done all the wrong things, but the Grace is there, the father is on the road to meet him. When Paul realized that it was God actually out there running to meet him, if only he could see it, his goal suddenly shifted. He was no longer a seeker in the sense of the ultimate, but more in terms of: how does this live itself out, how can I be more nearly the man God wants me to be? It's a struggle.

ABE: Now, what is he actually fighting with?

TOM H: He's fighting with his shadow, using Jungian terms. He's fighting with his self, his id, with his lower nature, because he says, "Oh wretched man that I am, the body of this death." He wasn't antibody at that point, I don't think. He simply decided "'I'm conscious of an unlived part of my life, which is the shadow." And there is a constant struggle and warfare over that. He said we have this "treasure in earthen vessels," which is a rather nice metaphor.

ABE: Two thousand years later, here we are, here's Paul sitting in the armchair. What are we fighting with here? What would we have to fight to be here as the living Logos? And we've already touched on it in the conversation. If you, using the word as a verb, *presenced* in that way, you are going to take terrible risks. I might persecute you for that, for instance. I might say, "What do you think you're doing. It's very inappropriate of you. Don't be present in that way. That's not expected behavior." All of these reactions. We go to the therapist and fight the id, the shadow, the complex, the neurosis. But it's not actually what we're dealing with in the Logos space between us.

TOM H: Well it's there, whether we like it or not.

ABE: It's there, yes. Is it possible for us to objectify what it is here that is keeping the Logos separated? Because that's what it comes to for society, for the church, for everything. What is this barrier?

TOM H: It is the shadow side of our humanity. It is a fact that we don't want to be totally open with one another. I mean, we do and we don't. We want it as long as it doesn't involve this, that, and the other. You know what I mean? So it's a guarded openness. We have to, it seems to me, accept our humanity. For me, it is very important to get the humanity of Jesus, whereas the churches have gone off the deep end, making Him a god up there somewhere. Part of our acceptance of our humanity is obvious stuff but it's very important. We cannot be pure spiritual beings, not yet, not now.

ABE: Why not yet? Why not now?

TOM H: Because we are incarnate. The Logos has become incarnate. It's enfleshed, and part of this enfleshment means, it seems to me, that pure spirituality, total, utter, is not only impossible, it's a dangerous illusion right now. I think there's a real danger of people becoming hyperspiritual, disconnected from their bodies, from their shadow, from all that is this composite thing called a human being.

ABE: I agree with you about hyperspirituality. But on the other hand, what I'm trying to look at is the entry into the "living here," of being more present as a physical being, more present as a psychological, mental, emotional being, and so on. If as a conscious being, I experience myself as the Logos and as a man enfleshed, then why am I fearing to manifest my love for the Logos in the way in which I am present in the world?

TOM H: First of all, who's to say it isn't happening? I think it is happening.

ABE: Of course it's always potentially happening.

TOM H: And part of what we need to do is just to recognize that and not get too fine tuned about it. But we're afraid of being misunderstood. Everybody has their image, their persona in place. People get fed up or whatever, but they don't go very far with the expression of their feelings. You can get hurt very quickly.

ABE: We have an infinite capacity to hurt each other.

TOM H: Yes. And we're not all at the same stage.

ABE: I suspect that somewhere a small group or community of people will actually decide to cross that line with each other in absolute trust of the Logos, probably very hard-headed, capable people, too, who will respark the community of living spiritual beings. We call this the Body of Christ in the West. And it can actually ignite at any moment. But it seems that we spend so much time contemplating, as you say, these lofty metaphysical nuances that we forget that what we're talking about is simply a quality of Presence.

TOM H: I don't have any problem with that. I say *amen* to that. That would be a step forward in consciousness, and I think it's actually happening. I do believe that. I get letters all the time from people and I am very struck by the number of people who don't sound to me to be kooks, who are having or have had in recent times an experience of what I would call "cosmic consciousness," or of awareness of the Logos, if you like, and of feeling this sense of the unity with all. In particular, over the last five or six years—and I've been twenty-five years in mass media in this field. There are things happening out there, in spite of the church's rigidities, and in spite of the idiocies of some aspects of the new age.

ABE: Every moment, this living, breathing Presence, it's always new, and my trouble is that I can easily become too old, too knowledgable about it to meet it. That in every moment I have to erase everything I think I know about all of this in order to become living Presence. So that the minute we have a formalized Christianity, or new ageism, which is becoming formalized, too...

TOM H: The rituals creep in right away.

ABE : Yes. So, there is this moment of new age something in the air, and then it, too, is gone. And the problem is transmission. We don't have a culture now that transmits this living Presence. That's the question for the church, for society. How can we engender a culture, a community of men and women, where the "Logos" is what makes itself present as opposed to all the other things that we drag around?

TOM H : Before you get the culture you have to have a massive transformation of consciousness. It has to be more than just a little cell here and a little cell there because we're talking now about something massive, something global. People throw out the term "quantum leap of consciousness." I think I see signs of it happening. Who knows what kind of culture would give you that spontaneity, that immediacy, that ability to shed the crap and the commercialism and all the messages from the information highway? God, what a highway! And to be really present with one another, Martin Buber's I-Thou, that kind of immediacy. I think that's only going to come in small cells.

ABE : I don't so much mean culture in that formalistic sense. But, look, here I am, I'm late twentieth-century man or woman, I'm dying of alienation, I'm ill inside, I'm living in pain, and all I want to do, actually, is fall asleep into the TV or into being a celebrity or something like that. My life is totally empty because there is nothing real in it and my soul is dying. So my need is urgent. And if we are the people who are presumably seriously involved in these issues, I mean, are we just existing on faith, or does the moment of action come?

TOM H : I think each one of us begins where we are, first with ourselves. And then, if you're a communicator, you do it, obviously, in that way. You see, I really believe that if that person with no soul who you were describing, with a dead soul or an alienated soul, *really* has the hunger to the degree to which you put it, then something will happen. What alarms me is when there's the absence of that longing. And I'm heartened by the new age movement because it shows that there are many people who have this longing. Now, whether it's sufficient for them or not, or whether they'll be palmed off with something that's less than bread, with pseudo, ersatz spirituality...

ABE : So, what do you see happening with all of this? What has to happen before there's a sufficient transformation between people for a new culture to begin? You pointed out earlier that you think in a way it's already happening.

TOM H: Yes, I do. There is a horrible word which I don't like—networking—but it is going on. I mean, that's one good thing about the Internet and the other forms of it which are not electronic. Again, I mentioned people talking about mystical experiences or cosmic consciousness. The people one hears from nowadays who are really tuned in, say, to the environmental movement at a deep spiritual level, well, they've never heard of Matthew Fox, and so on. I'm very encouraged by that. And I don't believe in the idea of the critical mass, that you get a hundred meditators together and then something clicks. But there is some truth in the idea that once a sufficient number of people begin to have this hunger met or partly met, entering into the new experience of the Logos, or however you want to express it, that connections will be made and are being made. I think that has to happen, obviously, on a much greater scale than it is now before the direction in which we're moving is going to significantly change. But around all these issues, whether it's nuclear arsenals, poverty, or whatever, there's a rising awareness, it seems to me, that it's not just a logistical problem, but a spiritual problem, a problem of consciousness, and a heightening of that consciousness.

It seems to me that either that's going to happen or we will have total disaster. It sounds gloomy, but on my off days I really do believe that those who go around blithely thinking that technology is going to solve all our problems are really crazy, or that the nuclear peril is now behind us and we can forget about that because the Cold War's over. Nevertheless, there is this rising and it is global. Whether it's sufficiently massive is up for grabs. But I am optimistic at the moment in that something...well, it's obviously the activity of God. I believe that everything is in the hands of God.

ABE: The way in which we're speaking of this god, Him/It, He/She in its name of "Logos," carries the implication that Logos is something unchanging, that everything changes within or around the Logos, but the Logos itself doesn't change. Is it possible that something has happened within the Logos in the last few centuries, which is actually responsible for this changed world that we're now living in? And that our difficulty is that we have to learn something completely new, which is how to relate to the Logos in this new relationship mood in the way that it is here now? We keep looking for the Logos of the Bible, for instance. But what if it isn't there anymore? Nobody in the Bible could have imagined the world we are now in, not even begun. And yet here we are, we're in it. So, is it somehow that our deepest assumptions about the issues of Christianity and the Logos and culture need to be completely reexamined?

TOM H: Well, we certainly need to do that. I don't think, however, it follows necessarily that the Logos has changed. But I think there needs to be a fundamental re-envisioning. And yet, if God is the kind of god who communicates, which is partly what the Logos is about, a communicating god, then God communicates today or He didn't communicate then. So, what is God saying to me now in this moment, in this instance? It's very hard for anyone to say, "Okay, let's start from scratch." And I don't think you can, entirely. But I think that attitude is what we have to have. Personally, when I go back to the New Testament, I want to try to get beyond the words and the whole thing to what is the reality that is being talked about here? If you boil it right down, what is going on here? And how would that speak afresh today? How can I encounter that today in my life, know it as a reality? The people in church who sit with such dead faces, is that what they really want? Maybe they don't want to hear about Moses and the historical Jesus so much as they want to encounter God right now, here. And they're not getting it. They want the bread that we were talking about.

ABE: So you feel the Logos doesn't change.

TOM H: No, I don't think so. I am quite aware of process theology, and there are some attractive things about it.

ABE: No, I'm not talking on that level. I'm not trying to discuss new theological theories. But just in the sense of, look, this thing, this indescribable, ineffable, it's living, it's conditionless, it's moving. It's actually the source of all life. It's alive.

TOM H: That's right.

ABE: You fall out of it into your ordinary consciousness and then you wake up again. And each moment is completely new. As it says in the scripture, "Behold, I make all things new." But why does it make all things new? Because It itself is constantly new. It's living, moving, changing.

TOM H: Just like the light streaming in the window here is not the light that was streaming in when we started the conversation. So the Logos is always new and yet unchanged. It's unchanging, but the manifestation, the perception or consciousness, is constantly shifting.

ABE: You can never doubt that it is the Logos. So, in that sense it is unchanging. Yet it's living, and it's the font and source of everything that lives and changes. So it is present as me or you or him. It is a principle, an uncontainable, ineffable, eternal Presence. It is also an individual being. Let's say, it's you. Let's say that here you are, you're Jesus. Now, it seems to me the big problem in religion is that we have difficulty squaring how this absolute principle, if you like, is an absolute principle on one hand, but it's also a man. It can be any man. So we keep getting fixated on the anthropomorphic, the individual.

TOM H: I wouldn't make the sort of one-to-one equation that you're making, that is to say, "You are the Logos sitting there, and I am the Logos sitting here." I prefer the idea that we all share in humanity. So you are humanity sitting there, you embody humanity, and you and I embody the Logos. We are an expression of the Logos. But I would never make the statement, "I am the Logos," or, "The Logos is me." The Logos is expressing itself through me and my being is an expression of that. And no, it's not just a principle, as the Stoics sometimes suggest, but it is actually a living presence; it is personal.

ABE: So you hold that traditional view, then, of original sin and the fallenness of man.

TOM H: How do you leap from that to original sin?

ABE: Well, you suggest that you, Tom Harpur, wearing blue jeans, that you're not the Logos, that you're only some sort of container for It. You're a vehicle and It is embodied in you as humanity. But It isn't you. Why isn't It you? What is it about all the rest of you that puts it outside the Logos?

TOM H: If It were I and I were It/Him/Her, then we wouldn't have any problem because we would be five billion angels, not human beings, living on the earth, and we wouldn't have this problem of how to know the Logos. It's Plato's idea that the ideal form expresses itself in the particular, and the particular is not the pure idea. So we share in the Logos. The Logos is that in us which is of God. And ultimately, I suppose, since all things come from God, all of us is from God. I'm saying that we are enfleshed, and that is not the opposite of the Logos, but it's not to be identified with It either. So, you end up with pantheism, don't you, if you pursue your tack? Ultimately everything *is* the Logos. Everything is divine, everything is God. And I take a step back from pantheism. Panentheism, yes, but not pantheism.

ABE: If you experience and then postulate the essential unity of all that is, ultimately how can anything be outside it?

TOM H: I don't think it is outside. And that's the subtle difference between saying pantheism and panentheism. All things are ultimately held together by the Logos. But I wouldn't be conscious, neither would St. Paul have been, of this interior moral struggle, if he or I could make this bald statement that Tom Harpur *is* the Logos.

ABE: In the manifestation we definitely have a "this/that." You know, there's this and then there's that. And we're very happy about this because there couldn't be any individuals if there wasn't the this/that. Now, you can take the next step and say there is a this/that because this is a fallen world and we're sinful creatures, and that the only way to get back to the Presence, the Logos, is to beg for forgiveness. But the minute you have the acknowledgement of the this/that as fallenness, you can build original sin on it. In the West we've taken the this/that as proof of error. The fact that we're here in the flesh, it's error. So we have developed a theology that does not allow us to realize that this *is* the Logos sitting right here.

TOM H: The whole business of original sin and the doctrine of the Fall is highly problematic and not a very good attempt to get at the problems and questions of evil—why we aren't a race of angels, and so on. I think they did the best they could at the time. I don't think it's a very happy, very adequate theory, but I'm not sure that I have one that's superior to put in its place. Better minds than mine have struggled with it and been unsuccessful. But the idea that the taint of sin has been passed down to us through procreation from an archetypal Adam, from some golden age, and that we've fallen from that, I think, is simply a religious myth which has limited value and has led to a great deal of confusion.

ABE: So are we perhaps more closely identified with the Logos than one would traditionally think?

TOM H: I'm now saying the opposite of what I was saying before, but I mean, while I wouldn't want to say that I am the Logos sitting here, I don't really go too far with the totally depraved, wretched, impossible-to-do-any-good view which has come out of the doctrine of the Fall. You know, in Calvinism and in Fundamentalism you are a totally depraved sinner and unless you're washed in the blood of the Lamb you can do no good thing. Well, I've met atheists working in the house of the dying in Calcutta who were doing good things.

I don't personally believe that the this/thatness of the world is a direct result of, or necessarily implies, a cosmic fall. I believe very much in the whole evolutionary theory of modern science, and that there was a golden age, if you like, in the sense of the mind of God. I think we're being pulled from *in front* towards what God has in mind for us. And that there hasn't been some catastrophic event prior to which we were pure beings of spirit and now are pure creatures of clay.

So there is that *of* God in us. There is also that which denies God, or which would put itself in opposition to God, and that is a result, I suppose, of the gift of human freedom.

jesters in the court of chaos

DR. JEAN HOUSTON
in conversation with
ALEXANDER BLAIR-EWART

For more than twenty-five years Dr. Jean Houston has lectured and conducted seminars and courses at universities throughout the U.S., Canada, and Europe. She has served on the faculties of psychology, philosophy, and religion at Columbia University, New York University, and the University of California. She is past-president of the Association for Humanistic Psychology. In 1985 she received the National Teacher-Education Association's award as Distinguished Educator of the year (USA).

Dr. Houston is director of the Foundation for Mind Research and author of Life Force *(1980),* The Possible Human *(1982),* The Search for the Beloved *(1987),* Godseed *(1987), and* The Hero and the Goddess *(1992). She is also coauthor with her husband, Robert Masters, of* Mind Games: The Guide to Inner Space *(1990) and* Listening to the Body *(1979). She has written numerous articles and created hundreds of instructional audiotapes in the field of human capacities.*

ALEXANDER BLAIR-EWART: They don't seem to have the concept of the shadow in Hindu India or in other Eastern cultures. The shadow is a very Western idea. And I think it has a lot to do with the fact that Christ comes,

He goes down into Hell, faces the darkness of Satan, and overcomes all of that. Where would you begin in looking at the shadow in its broadest sense?

JEAN HOUSTON: I start with the notion of homo duplex, man the doubled being. And of course this notion of homo duplex is a conundrum that has haunted the human race since its inception, especially the Western human race. *[laughter]* St. Paul speaks to this when he says, "The things that I would do, I do not. The things that I would not, I do." And at least in the Western consciousness the shadow is built into the substance of reality. We feel ourselves divided beings in a reality divided within itself.

ABE: Yes. The contrast of light and dark.

JEAN H: Now, what I then do is I look at whether this has always been true. Because when we were primordial organisms, floating in an early ocean, our fundamental existential problem revolved around the issue—and we weren't very bright—"This is me, but this is not me. I can eat that." Gradually this immune response, which is the ability to recognize that which is other, and to react effectively against it by creating antigens, became a vital part of all biochemical development. And it forced the creation of the early forms of memory. It wove the membrane between selves, the boundaries between the organs, and provoked the early nerve sense to specialize in ways that produced our central nervous system. Then there's the immune response's effect on the phylogenetic development of our unconnected brain. Three brains from three different evolutionary parts of biological history which don't talk to each other, fear each other, and, I suspect, confuse each other no end. So our thought processes have their origin in this early immune response and the ability to say, "This is me, and this is not me."

You see, the structure of our mind, the orders between conscious and unconscious realms, the gates that keep us from too close a connection with archetypal existence, and ultimately from spiritual realities, may be maintained by a psychophysical equivalent of the immune response. But the problem is, I think, that in protecting ourselves and insuring our survival, we have come to treat almost everything as a virus—offerings of love, incursions of grace, presentiments of union. The political debacle of the last ninety years of the divided world is the statement of the immune response writ large and running riot. We are being pushed, as it were, to a conscious control of our own systems of divisions and boundaries, so that we do not atavistically respond between peoples and nations as we did when we were much simpler organisms protecting ourselves in primeval oceans. And I wonder if there isn't, perhaps, some metaphor in the fact that evolutionary governance is upon us at the same time that we have so much breakdown and rising disease in the functioning of the immune system.

Now, certainly in the grand scale, things split off, break apart, break down, are cast out. The creation of planets comes from the shredding of stars. The child is torn out of the mother. Schism and division are built into the very condition of being. Whenever we deny a part of ourselves, in my experience, it always rises up to haunt us, for schism, in its very nature, demands reunion. The Greek myths, it seems to me, tell us that the gods demand that all your faces be seen. The thickness of reality requires that you recognize all parts, even if you may show more devotion to one or another.

ABE: Where does the development of ego fit into all of this?

JEAN H: In the Western world at least, ego, which I consider to be just one image among the multiple images of the psyche, rose to its present inflation by repression of the other contents of the psyche, thinking it could control them and control the world that it was objectifying and conquering. Instead, the insular arrogance of ego created mayhem and space became reduced, our objective reality of space became reduced to an inventory of materials to be manipulated and shaped into forms able to be consumed by the voracious mouth of ego. I think the point is that the repressed always rises. And it carries in its wake the possibility of evil.

I think that evil can be seen as the corruption that ensues from the repression of a fullness of perspective. Evil can also be seen as the jester in the court of chaos. Its sleight of hand, its cruel jokes, ironic twists, keep us diverted from seeing the creative purpose in chaos. And that's why there's so much interest in chaos and chaos theory. Chaos, which means the great shadow and the great dispersion in its original sense, lives in a dialectical marriage with cosmos. And cosmos, which means creation and order, always comes out of chaos. The "big bang," if there was such a thing, or a continuous banging, as I suspect, [laughter] is the ultimate chaos of the dispersion that has in it the seeding of the coming cosmos. So that throughout history, whenever you have periods of chaos, you find beneath this surface the seedings of a new cosmos, a new culture. The cosmogenic time, more often than not, does not emerge out of stable, steady state growth, but rather out of the chaotic shift when everything is shaken up. It is then that you decide whether you will grow or you will die.

If I were evil incarnate, I would not fight against chaos. I would undermine its energies, so that it could neither bang, shake, shift, or seed the order, the cosmos that's trying to emerge. The power of evil is to divert and dissipate energy, intention, commitment, to lure people into self-indulgence and narcissism, to promise absolution while sanctifying sloth. And so we have in the Old Testament a God that blew upon the waters of the deep and created cosmos, and in Hebrew the word deep is tehom, which is etymologically linked to the Tiamat, the ancient Middle Eastern dragon goddess of chaos.

ABE: Yes.

JEAN H: In a wonderful book called *Sophia*, Caitlin Matthews studies in the first chapters the Black Goddess, who is Kali, who is chaos, who is Tiamat, and it is in this great, creative chaos that all the energies of creation are stored. In order for your spirit to blow strong enough to create cosmos, you need a certain water level of chaos to blow upon. And so, present civilization, as well as planetary necessity, is the extraordinary vehicle to engender the required density of chaos, the density of what we are coming to call the shadow, to provoke in us the desire for cosmogenesis as we enter upon what I could perhaps refer to as the beginning of type one high-level civilization, when we become responsible for biological governance, in which we deepen and complexify our psyche, in which we become the mythic beings that we once objectified and in which we lived daily life as spiritual exercise.

I think that chaos and the shadow is a movement towards consciousness, which is also a movement into conscious creation and conscious genesis, where we become copartners of the evolutionary process. And having now the responsibility, as we do, for the first time in history, at least on such a broad and democratic a scale for evolutionary and biological governance of the planet, having the powers once thought to belong to gods, we stand in dread before the inner shadows of our being, feeling that the evil that we do can now have the consequences of a Götterdämmerung, and not just another foolish mistake in history. I think that's one of the reasons why we are examining shadows. My fear is that we will look at them psychologically and we will tend to pathologize instead of mythologize.

ABE: Yes, and lose the creative potency.

JEAN H: Because we are living in mythic times.

ABE: You know, Jean, what you have just given birth to in me, as I am listening to you, is a transpersonal ecology.

JEAN H: Yes.

ABE: We are being driven for the first time in millenia to experience ecology, or nature as consciousness, as a part of us. Now we are faced with that accumulated shadow, the accumulated rejection of our relationship with the All, with everything that is there in Gaia or the Great Mother. And so the shadow rises, like the Beast rises out of the sea in Revelation.

JEAN H: Well, if you want to use that image of Revelation, that's an interesting one, because the Beast has many heads.

ABE: Yes. Multiple consciousness.

JEAN H: And I think that what is rising in us are many heads. I've often said that if schizophrenia is the disease of the human condition, polyphrenia, the orchestration of our many heads, our many selves, may be the extended help we need. We are finding levels and layers within ourselves that we are frightened of, and which we then objectify through psychological or industrial language as the shadow. But the shadow may be—and of course that occurs in the Book of Revelation—the rising of the deeps and of the multiple levels of our persona, our personality, of the structures of our psyche which had been limited, repressed, and isolated in the long, long ice age of the industrial revolution.

This whole question of the shadow rose tremendously, as you probably know, in the second and third century, in the Gnostic movement, when, due to the Pax Romanum, the Roman peace, and the ecumenism of the empire, people lost their localness, they lost their relationship to earth, star, sea, and spirit. And everybody was on a kind of jet-set donkey *[laughter]* all over the world. With these hundreds of thousands of people spilling out all over the empire, their local religion tended to be repressed, and there was this tremendous rise of a sense of not belonging anymore, for the first time, maybe, in history. Ecumenism always gives a sense of not belonging. There are many facets to Gnosticism which are glorious, but there was this level of saying, "I am a project. I do not belong to this world, my psyche and my soul really belong to the world beyond this world."

ABE: So there were the seeds of nihilism.

JEAN H: Yes. And the Roman Empire's religion of salvation could take over. You know, "All right, you don't belong, but you *do* belong in Christ." I think there is something of this going on now. It's interesting, Alexander, that you write about these new psychological saviors, *[laughter]* whoever they might be. And people flock to them because they are presenting almost a Christlike perspective of giving and salvation. We're going to see much more of that. We're going to see a lot of salvation figures. It's an interesting historical phenomenon that at the same time that so many people feel that they do not belong, there is the rising cry from the Earth that says, "By God, *you do* belong." Psyche and soma are part of the same substance. The mind and soul's apertures, extensions, *are* our body. And what we have is the denial of the parts and the looking for salvation, either in the salvational figure or the big bang, the god beyond the god, or the archetype to channel, etc.

ABE: In all of that psychologizing I sense an incredible missing of the mark, where, at the very moment that you expect to hear the bell ring, there is a dull thud, as if something essential has been missed.

JEAN H: Yes, well, that was also true of Gnosticism, wasn't it? That it never had its sense of "thereness." Ironically, in the Gnostic texts, in the Gospel of Thomas, Jesus says, "You're looking for the Kingdom? If you look up in Heaven, then the birds will get there before you. *[laughter]* If you look in the sea, the fish are going to get there first. Look right in you. This is where it is. Wake up! Wake up! Wake up!" The *gnosis*, the knowledge, is at hand, it's in your body, it's in your mind, all parts of you. And those parts always rise up. But in such a time of radical urgency, many people of real spirit and depth are in a state of radical deconstruction, not destruction, but deconstruction. And they are being stripped away. It's like the *kenosis* before the pleurosis, you know, the stripping before the filling. And that's also the place of the dark goddess, isn't it, the shadow, the depth of self that allows you to be stripped, to be humbled, before you can be filled again. I see this as a very positive, very creative construct. But I think that coming out of the structure of the West the shadow has been objectified as evil, has become something that we fear, whereas other, primal societies tend to welcome it.

ABE: Whenever I look at this whole shadow issue there is a person who comes and sits beside me and won't go away. Every time I think about the shadow, up pops Friedrich Nietzsche, and he turns around to me and he says, "You see, I told you. You're living in the time of the last man." And the last man says, "Alas, alas, the time is coming when the arrow of man's longing will no longer shoot itself at a star. Alas, the time is coming of the most despicable man, the man who can no longer despise himself. As ineradicable as sand fleas, the last man lives longest." He says, "We have invented happiness," and he winks. On one hand there appears to be an ardent and courageous sense of "now is the time to face what the last millenia have made of us, and whatever it is we want to know." On the other side of that, which is a much larger movement, is this sense of wanting to blunt the edge, to say, "Oh, you've just become aware that there's a shadow? Don't worry, we can fix it for you. We'll make you happy. You won't have to really face what this means to you. I mean, it's not *that* disturbing. Don't be afraid. We'll take care of it." And the people who are saying, "We'll take care of it," to me, are an extension of the church. I mean, they're priests, people who will absolve you of the sin of having a shadow in the first place. But like all priests, they seduce you away from the actuality of your experience.

JEAN H: I think that the ardor and courage you speak of is the true life of shamanism. Shamanism is prepolitical and depoliticized. It never got politicized. There's no priest, no bureaucracy, no hierarchy. It's the soul that is willing to do the hard work of consciousness, descend into its own depths as a necessary journey, and not with any pride. The journey is required. In the twenty-fifth chapter of Nietzsche's *Gay Science*, when the madman comes to the town saying, "God is dead. God is dead," the people laugh and say, "What happened? Did He go on a voyage, is He gone, does He have a cold?" And the madman says, "Well, you don't see Him. The churches are singing dirges for Him. You don't see it. I've come too early." Now it was about 1886 when he wrote that, and the world has turned around 106 times since then. But now it's true. The archetypes are crumbling. We're at the point of the bowling alley time for the gods. *[laughter]* The ancient archetypes are crumbling in the psyche, so that they can begin to reconstitute, and can enter into time and be regrown again. Our responsibility is so enormous. We are in cocreative time with psychic space, with archetypal space, and this last man is the last man of a certain order. And we feel both chilling despair and utter exhilaration over it. An utter regenesis re-creation.

ABE: We were talking about the qualities of the new archetype that is emerging. I have this sense that something that we can barely recognize yet is being born within us.

JEAN H: Yes, I think so. I think we're involved in, *whew*, a total revision of the earth's story, the human story, and most certainly the Western story. I don't believe that we've ever, in known history, been at this point. I suspect that the present shifts in culture and consciousness are announcements of this historic happening. I feel that you were right on the button when you talked about Nietzsche, only he said it a 110 years too soon. I think its high pattern is one of regenesis, an archetype of cosmogenesis or world building. But, for this regenesis, this archetype of regenesis to emerge fully, we have to revision our own depths, then shift focus from our shadow to our possibility. We're still so absorbed in our shadow, we don't yet see our possibility.

ABE: In a way, the accumulation of our shadow by now would also include all of the "positive" images that come to us from the older cultures.

JEAN H: Yes, that's right. The problem is that if we look at the older cultures, we'll see the positive images, but in questing for meaning and self-understanding, we unfortunately seek too often to pathologize instead of do what the older cultures do which is mythologize. We reach for and embrace, almost with relief it seems, words that label our sickness, words that maintain us as helpless victims. We come home to illness. *[laughter]*

ABE: You know, in that morphogenic field sense, sometimes I find Buddha ranting and raving inside me, or Jesus Christ, Moses, Zoroaster, Plato, and there are times when I'm sincerely and deeply saturated in these intelligences, these beings. Yet at the same time there's an underlying sense that they're saying goodbye in me. And there's sadness in it because it's like all of these ancient gods are receding, leaving us alone in a new space, a new clearing. So we have to find a new vision and a new meaning. And we barely know where to begin.

JEAN H: True. These archetypal structures, both past and present, are always available. We're made out of them. But if they're perceived through the lens of alienated culture and consciousness, they appear as warped, even demonic versions of what they truly are. And that's why I think the great clearing has to take place. I mean, has the warped archetypal energy played itself out in the horrors of the twentieth century, in Hitler's utilizing archaic strata of Teutonic and Scandinavian myth and archetype, refashioned in Wagnerian mythic operas? *[laughter]* What are archetypal patterns about? I think they're about primarily relational patterns that serve to bridge spirit with nature, and mind with nature, self and universe. They're the essential elements within the structure of our psyche, and without them we would live in a gray, flat world.

ABE: We need those bridges because we have become separated.

JEAN H: Yes.

ABE: And now we feel less and less separated as ecological or transpersonal ecological reality presses in on us.

JEAN H: That's right. But, you see, the archetypal dimensions, in order to have any continuity and comprehension, will have to be encoded into myth, because they are so much larger than our local story. And myths may be the most fundamental patterns in human existence. They're source patterns, I think, originating from beneath us, behind us, in this transpersonal realm that you're talking about, yet are the key to our personal and historical existence. That's why I often say they're the DNA of the human psyche. But as our lives are becoming more mythic, compared to the lives of our ancestors of two hundred years ago, what has happened is that these patterns are unfolding or uncoding faster and faster in culture, through art and religion, architecture, drama, ritual, ethics, social custom, and mental disorders. And this is where I think James Hillman is quite right, that because we have no rites of passage, because we have no dramatizations, they play themselves out as psychosis. "Why mental disorders?" I keep asking. I think it's because the dominant pathology of the culture is often the shadow side of its innate genius, and the psychopathology of one generation is probably the expanded reality pattern of the next.

ABE: I have this sense of the next few centuries as being a distillation and a dying away of everything that we have been throughout our whole history.

JEAN H: I suspect that time is a nested resonance of waves. For example, let's take North America, especially America, and if we follow through your thought, it may be a time compression of, let's say for the fun of it, the

Roman Empire. *[laughter]* So that in this time-compression scenario we're living in about the time of the fifth century with the breakdown of the Roman Empire. And the next ten years is almost a compression of that two thousand years from the Dark Ages, through the Middle Ages with its new kinds of federation and guilds, a federated Europe, a federated Asia, to a renaissance of all kinds of cultures, and then an age of exploration of outer space and inner space, and then to some kind of tremendous diaphanous event.

ABE: I have this feeling that at the end of this three-hundred-year Armageddon that I sense ahead of us we will have outgrown social mores and religions and ideology, all of these things that we use to contain, protect, and impose order, and that we'll reach a state of natural order in which every being will naturally be in its right place in the universe. And yet I'm also aware that that world of the future will be a very dynamic one because, in a sense, there will be no barrier between beings, and that what you are is what you will be, and the other will be that as well, and the interplay of the totality of what each human being is will form that culture. So in many ways it will be a fiercer and more terrifying place to be than where we are now, and yet in another way it will be a much more fulfilling and whole place for us because it will be reality.

JEAN H: I know many people who feel they're living that way now. Are they prefigural events?

ABE: Yes, time seeds of the future.

JEAN H: You know, becoming a mythic being is a phenomenon that I'm finding worldwide, perhaps because the people who come to my seminars, regardless of where in the world I'm teaching, generally come because they either hear the call of the mythic path, or they're caught somewhere along it, probably in the belly of the whale. *[laughter]*

ABE: Are you referring to people who feel that the future is being played out in them already and that if they survive, just simply survive it, or pass through it, by that very tiny act of survival, something will have established itself?

JEAN H: Yes, they are creating a morphic field.

ABE: A living seed of the future.

JEAN H: But also that history itself is a kind of a shadow cast back by eschatology, that there's something like a hyperdimensional transcendent object beyond space/time that is casting what we might consider the shadow back in time, and that we capture it and we play it out to a kind of fullness. And that we are, in the words of T. S. Eliot, redeeming the time, redeeming the unread vision of the higher dream. Something like that.

ABE: André Malraux talks about that, too. He talks about how we are the first civilization that has ever had access to all of the past.

JEAN H: And that is why so many have experienced the entire life of the soul, and by extension the soul of the world, mythically. It's almost like the neoplatonic notion of the *anima mundi*, the soul of the world, and in this time of what, I think, is whole system transition, we are becoming able to hear Psyche speaking through all the things and events of the world, not just in myths.

ABE: Do you have those experiences where on a particular day you wake up, you feel peculiarly energized, something seems to be grinding inside you, something is moving...

JEAN H: Oh yes, yes.

ABE: ...and you turn on the television and a volcano just erupted?

JEAN H: It's like catching an evolutionary vibration and being a distillation chamber, an alchemical alembic for the world soul.

ABE: So, it's the breakdown of anthropocentric humanity.

JEAN H: Oh yes, and cosmocentric humanity. I mean, we are historically in the next two or three hundred years becoming responsible for evolutionary governance; we're going to start going out and redesigning planets. *[laughter]* And then probably in a thousand years we'll join a galactic milieu. So the psyche is accelerating. To keep up with this outreach, we have this accelerated inreach. But I think that you're quite right, that we become microcosms of the whole. We are part of the great order of things, and it is this tremendous vision in our lives which is what is giving the archetypal quality to our lives. That's why people study myths nowadays. It's the first opening to this disclosure, that when we begin to study the personal particulars of our lives in relation to the universal, it's the mythic events that inform us of the unfolding and the uncoding of the soul in the world. This allows our consciousness to become part of a soul-directed living, and I think that's why there's so much tension now between soul and world in our public and private spheres. Because the tension and the shadow is required in order to disappear, and we discover ourselves to be characters in the drama of the anima mundi.

4
turtle
island
songs

OH SHINNAH

STARHAWK

LYNN ANDREWS

warrior
wise woman

OH SHINNAH
in conversation with
ALEXANDER BLAIR-EWART

Oh Shinnah is an internationally known native American teacher, writer, singer, composer, and ceremonialist with Tineh (Apache) and Mohawk lineage. She has served on United Nations committees, initiated a plenary session with Mother Teresa for the United Nations Conference of Spirituality, and originated the Suicide Hotline in Chicago.

ALEXANDER BLAIR EWART: When you look at what has happened on this continent for the last few centuries, standing where I imagine you might be standing, what does all of that look like to you?

OH SHINNAH: Well, it's a horror story. I mean, two hundred years ago what we call Turtle Island was paradise. It was. And with industrialization and the white wave that came over, paradise has been turned into a cesspool, to the point where we are endangered as a species. In our prophecies, at least the Chirikahua Apache's prophecies that I know of, and the Iroquois Six Nations' prophecies, the reason why the white people were received the way they were was because they were supposed to bring a technology that would free the people from hunger, from want. So they were received with an open hand. And they turned that opened hand into a fist by not recognizing Native rights, our desire to caretake this land. According to the original instructions, our purpose was to act as caretakers for Mother Earth, and we're in a position right now where it's almost impossible to do that.

I view it as a horror story. If these white brothers and sisters would have come with an open hand, it would have been a different story. But they didn't; they came with a closed fist. And they believed that they could own the land, instead of caretaking the land. They lived for the greed of the now. Most of these people in big business don't even think about future generations, don't even think about their own grandchildren. It's what they can get right now for themselves. And I believe that there's a very amazing and wonderful thing happening, because in our prophecies we talk about how there are a lot of people that incarnated into the dominant society having been Indians in other lives, because this society is the one that is in control. They've chosen to incarnate in the dominant society so they can help make the kinds of changes that are necessary for the survival of our species. I mean, we are an endangered species. People don't realize that.

ABE: The whole human species or the Native American species?

OH SHINNAH: I think that the two-leggeds are an endangered species everywhere. I mean, look at global warming and the ozone, and corporate management, big business not caring, what's going on with the rain forests. One of the reasons why they're tearing down rain forests over in Indonesia is because the Japanese have decided that it's a status symbol to build houses out of hard woods. They own two-thirds of the standing timber in the northwest of Turtle Island here in the United States. And they stockpile it in Tokyo Bay for toothpicks and chopsticks and what have you. I would love to talk to those people. It's not that they're noncaring; it's that they're not informed. And education is the answer, but people have also got to take risks and be willing to die for what they believe in. And that's where I'm coming from.

ABE: There is this process of education, the process of changing consciousness, there's ecological consciousness on TV, but where else is it, really? It's all moving very, very slowly, too slowly.

OH SHINNAH: It is taking too long, but I can also tell you this, that there is progress. I've been talking about recycling for thirty years. My family were always recyclers. You know, in the Second World War everybody did. And it's like the stone that goes into the pond that creates the ripple. Well I feel like that stone that's gone into the pond, because I can turn on television and I do see ads about recycling and so on, and it is a developing consciousness. What we have to do is kick it into high gear. If you're not a part of the solution, you're part of the problem. There's no more middle road; there really isn't. In this country, especially, we have to take control of politics. I think what we have to do is dissolve all the borders and speak for each other. I was deeply involved in the issue of Native American religious freedom, and when I was in one of the plenary sessions at the One in the Spirit Conference held at the United Nations, they asked me, "How do we do it?" I said, "Go back to your countries, go back to your religions, and tell these people to write to this government, tell them that we don't need missionaries, that we have a living and viable religion." And they did, and because it became a world issue, America was forced to create a law that is called the Native American Religious Freedom Act, which also gives us a right to save land. You know, the temple of my church is the dome of the everlasting sky. It's not a building. When they were going to do the offshore drilling in Mendocino I invoked the Native American Religious Freedom Act to stop it. I said, "Under this act you can't do this, because this is my church."

So I really feel that progress is being made, darling. I mean, it's the sense of hopelessness that confines us. We have to hold to the light. We have to hold to a future that is going to be free of malice, and we have to hold to hope. If we don't have hope and we don't have faith, then we'll blow it off. And people like you and people like me, we've got to go to those big businesses and say, "Screw you, buddy." Sanctions work. I know that the Japanese quit doing the drift-netting of tuna because of sanctions. Both Canada and the United States quit buying tuna that was being produced by Japan. So, if we do the same thing with wood and cars and everything else, it will make a difference, because these people don't understand anything but money.

ABE: Do you see the way in which Native spirituality is permeating more and more of "white culture" as an authentic process?

OH SHINNAH: Oh yes, I do. And it's in our prophecies. In the original instructions that were given to the Native peoples, their work was to be caretakers for Mother Earth. One of the reasons why people are more interested in what Native Americans think is because it's the Earth itself that's speaking to them. And the only way that they can learn about how to be caretakers is through Native people, because everybody else has pretty much lost it.

ABE: There seem to be some Native teachers who are very unhappy with that. Why do you think that is?

OH SHINNAH: Well, I think it has to do with jealousy. I think that it has to do with believing that you can own spirituality. When you really look at it, anything that's going to make life better is right. And I don't care where it's coming from. Whether it's Native or Russian or Chinese or whatever, if it's going to make it better, it's right. And I think that the problem is that the Native people have lost so much that they feel like their spirituality is being taken away from them as well.

ABE: I was talking to Florinda Donner recently. She's one of the Castaneda group. I'm wondering what you think of what Castaneda has done from that point of view?

OH SHINNAH: Well, his first book I thought was fabulous. Actually, I think that most of his books are pretty good. You know, in the beginning he was doing a Ph.D. dissertation and he really didn't understand the Indian humor. He took it all too seriously. But basically, except for the one that he did about women, which was totally off the wall...

ABE: *The Second Ring of Power?*

OH SHINNAH: Yeah.

ABE: What was off the wall about that?

OH SHINNAH: The way he presented the women. I know some of those people down there, and they're not like that at all. They don't deliberately set out to destroy somebody's life, and that's the way he presented the women in that book.

ABE: He portrayed that as being part of their sorcery task, to help him to wake up.

OH SHINNAH: But if he'd have awakened, behind it, he wouldn't have presented it the way he did. I also believe that his heart was in the right place, and they're not lies. I mean, these are real experiences that he had, but they're very subjective.

ABE: You, I imagine, come from, or are working within a way of being, a spirituality. Is it a particularly Native spirituality? I know you describe yourself as an eclectic.

OH SHINNAH: Well, yes, I'm a fourth-generation Theosophist. I was raised in Catholic school. I call myself an Apache/Catho/Buddha/Jew. *[laughter]* But basically my understanding and comprehension of the world is from a Native perspective. My father is full-blood Apache and I learned wonderful things from him. I've worked with a lot of Native peoples in South America, Mexico, and here in the States. But I feel it's a weaving, that the tapestry is beautiful because of all the threads that come from different directions. And so I really am eclectic, though the core of my being is Native. I was an invoked spirit, I was born into a crystal spectrum. All the events of my life have been primarily Native American. But I'm also a sister of the Violet Flame, which is an ancient Egyptian order of women who were keepers of knowledge and tradition and esoteric understandings that had to be committed to memory. So I really don't know what I am. *[laughter]* But basically my truth is Native.

Native peoples who follow a traditional spiritual path are not prejudiced. If you meet an Indian that's prejudiced, they're not truly Native American, because we don't hold any kind of prejudice. The white house, the white knight, and Mr. Clean is an attitude. It doesn't have anything to do with race; it's an attitude. And if people choose that attitude, then they're wrong thinkers.

ABE: What would it take, do you think, to bridge the gap between the white person in the street and the Native community?

OH SHINNAH: I think that spirit and ceremony is the only way. When we share ceremonial practices like sweat lodge, smudging, going to Mass, there is a union that happens that transcends skin color. I think that the Earth is the healer. If we really get ourselves concerned and involved in solving the problems of ecology, all those other things will go away, because we're all working for the same purpose, and that purpose is the survival of our species and all other species, and the Earth itself. I think that transcends any color, any race, any religion, and that's the way out.

ABE: You've been involved in helping people with suicide. What do you think is the cause of that suicidal impulse in people? Can one generalize about that, or is it always specific?

OH SHINNAH: Well, I think it is very individual, but there are also many people who are so sensitive that they can't handle the aggression that's going on in the world today. In Japan, the highest suicide rate is among Japanese children. When they get to eighth grade, if they don't have the right grades, they can't go on, and it dishonors the family. So they commit suicide.

ABE: You're saying sensitive people pick up on the collective malaise, and then become overwhelmed by it?

OH SHINNAH: And don't know what to do, so they just want a way out. Whatever it is, with the kids in Japan, the education with Indian kids here, the alcoholism, it's an overlap, it's a general kind of energy that exists everywhere in the world. And the people who are really really sensitive can't handle it. I was suicidal. I was very, very suicidal, and I don't know where I got the strength to continue my life. But something touched me in a way that gave me the strength to continue. If I'd have been younger, maybe I would have killed myself. And I think that it's general. There is an energy that exists that overwhelms the sensitive.

ABE: Do they have a name for that as a being in the Native tradition, the "Death Stalker" or something? Or am I way off base there?

OH SHINNAH: There is a word like that. In our tradition it's *chehistu*, an encompassing energy, an overwhelming force.

ABE: And that's what comes to people when they're depressed and amplifies it?

OH SHINNAH: Yes, and they choose to go out through chehistu, to "walk away" from what hurts you.

ABE: What do you think the spiritual results of suicide would be? I know that different traditions say different things about that.

OH SHINNAH: I think it's only acceptable if it's done as an act of conscious will. If it's an act done to punish somebody else because you're

121

angry with them or because you're disappointed or depressed, that's not right. If it's a conscious act... for example, I had cancer. I had Hodgkin's disease and I survived it. They told me I was going to be dead in two years. But if that ever came back on me, rather than let my children watch me waste away to nothing, I would electively use suicide as a means to get out of it, and that would be chehistu, a conscious act. I already told my kids, "If this cancer ever comes back on me, I'm not going to waste my life, I'm not going to waste your money. I'll bring all of you together and I will kill myself."

ABE: How did they react to that emotionally?

OH SHINNAH: They absolutely approved of it. They understood what I was going through when I did have that cancer, and they understood what they were going through. And I wouldn't do that again. I would just say, "Over and out."

ABE: Is there some orientation that a person can have towards chehistu where, as in the case of young people, it's inappropriate for them to be doing that?

OH SHINNAH: Well, children don't know what they're doing, anyway. I think that they would have to give themselves time to find out whether they could work things out in their lives. I don't think it's correct for children. If a child has leukemia, that's another story, you know. That's already a death sentence. But for people who are older, they have a right of choice. Young people don't know what their life is going to be like, anyway, and I think that they have to give themselves the opportunity to experience life.

ABE: There is Doctor Kavorkian in Michigan who has been taken to court and charged with murder for assisting people to commit suicide. What do you think of that?

OH SHINNAH: He gave them a chance to make a choice for themselves. It's not something that he forced on them. So I think he's a very brave man. I think he said, "You know, you've got two ways to go, here. You can die horribly or you can die peacefully." And he didn't kill them. They injected themselves. People should have the right of choice. I feel the same way about abortion. But I also feel that you've got to look at all the issues before you make that kind of decision, and seek the clarity and guidance of people who really understand the spiritual ethic involved. And I don't see that happening a lot. Some women use abortion as a way to get away from the problem, without really looking at it as an ethical and spiritual experience. My people have a way where you make an agreement with the child within, and you talk to it and you say this is the wrong time for me. We even have a ceremony where you can pass that child's spirit onto another sister who has had trouble getting pregnant. But it's a very conscious act. I think that has to be the issue, and I think that that's what this man Kavorkian is doing. He's giving people choices.

ABE: I've heard you described as a warrior, or that you describe yourself as a warrior.

OH SHINNAH: I am a warrior for Mother Earth. I have been initiated by my people as a warrior. I had to go through all of the conditionings, spiritually, physically, everything.

ABE: What kind of training is involved in becoming a warrior in the sense that you're using that word?

OH SHINNAH: Well, it's developing an impeccable nature. There were tests that I had to go through, like, I was stood one time between two plants that were exactly the same, but because the soil was different on either side, one would kill and one would heal, and I had to know the language of the plant people so the plant itself could tell me which one would not hurt me. I had to sit two nights in the snow naked so that the inner fire within me was ignited, so I wasn't damaged by the cold. It's not easy. I can hit a moving object from a moving horse with a bow and arrow, always accurate. I used to ride rodeo, and did these demonstrations. To be able to hit a moving object from a moving horse is not an easy thing to do. And to always be true to yourself and to the world; when you make a mistake to be able to admit that you made a mistake. To be a warrior is to always act for the good of the whole instead of the self. That's basically the most important thing that I learned in my life, that I don't act for me as a person, I act for the good of the whole. Action is the key word; you don't just sit back and do nothing. For example, I go into a restaurant where I know the owner and I stand up and I scream, "Why are you still using Styrofoam? Hey, Charles, come out here and tell me why you're still using Styrofoam!" He gets really upset about it, you know, but I do it anyway. I bring my own little containers when I'm going to take food out of the place. And I love the food there, but I don't love Styrofoam, so I told him plain out, "I'm going to tell everybody, and if I have to stand right here in your restaurant and say it, I'm going to do that because you're wrong."

ABE: How does he react to that?

OH SHINNAH: Well, he's trying to find another way to do it. I mean, it's even been written up in the newspapers here. It's really funny. I went into a bar restaurant in Boston, and they had a drink on the menu called a Mayan Whore, and I screamed at this dude, "Well, you got two of us, didn't you? You got two minorities. You got Indians and you got women!" I created a little street theater in this bar. My daughter Heather, who's built like Mae West and was born on the same day as Mae West, went in there dressed as Mae West and said, "Well, I'm looking for my competition." *[laughter]* Or two guys who come in with briefcases, order drinks, and they see this Mayan Whore, upon which they open their briefcases and there are pies in there which they shove in each other's face. And then there are people running through there screaming and hollering. I walk up to the owner and say, "Well, I see this Mayan Whore but I certainly don't see any Bald Jocks or anything like that here. *[laughter]* And it worked. The owner finally capitulated. *[laughter]* It was plain street theater. Well, that's what the warrior is. You don't capitulate to systems that you don't believe in. If you do, you're not a warrior. Regardless of what it is, you have to confront it if it doesn't hold true for you, and that's the act of a warrior.

ABE: As you know, most people are afraid of doing that. They will very rarely do it themselves.

OH SHINNAH: They want somebody else to do it for them. And that's the act of the warrior. You do it for them. And then sometimes they get pissed at you, and you have to stand up to them, too, and say, "Hey, I'm out here doing it. What are you doing?"

ABE: So more people should find their way to a place of courage, because it's really passivity, isn't it, that makes people suicidal?

OH SHINNAH: Exactly. If you're not a part of the solution, you're a part of the problem. And the problem can become oppressive to the point where you don't act, so you want to die. Action takes us out of that. It isn't enough to think about how you feel. You've got to act on how you feel.

ABE: How can we survive this next phase of planetary confusion?

OH SHINNAH: Spiritual survival is the point. You have to develop a spirituality that is concise and strong. How to live in an ordinary world as a spiritual person. We call this the age of purification, and that purification is not only of the Earth but of ourselves. So I teach people how to do that, how to keep yourself clear, how to purify yourself, how to let go of things that don't hold true in your life, how to take care of your body in a right way, because that's a big part of it. You can't talk about just physical survival without the spiritual aspects, and you can't talk about spiritual aspects without taking care of the body. People need to understand that this is the age of purification for ourselves, for the Earth, and that we have to be active in the process, not passive.

ABE: When you say "age of purification," how deep is that purification of the Earth going to go, do you think?

OH SHINNAH: That's something we don't know. We could blow it. All you have to do is look at the prophecies of the Hopi people. They talk about our present period as a time of decision—either we get it straight or it's over, and there's no middle road. I'm sure you're familiar with the prophecies of Nostradamus. Well, they're very much like the Apache and Hopi and Iroquois Nations' prophecies about this time.

ABE: And they're saying, essentially, that this purification has to take place. Do we already know what the nature of that purification is, and we're just not doing it, or...?

OH SHINNAH: We're not doing it. It has to do with cleaning up our act. If you don't recycle your garbage, you're part of the problem. We have to be conscious about how we use everything, and that includes the purification within ourselves. If we carry around inner garbage, we're part of the problem. This is the time of true purification, and either we get it straight now or it's over.

ABE: I know there a lot of people who would like to do something, but they don't know how to start.

OH SHINNAH: I sort of kick their buns *[laughter]* to help them get started. And it starts simple. Just recycle your garbage. When you start recycling your garbage you see the garbage that you make, you see the abuses that you condone, and it's not just physical. All of a sudden that reflects into your spiritual life as well. We really need to be in touch with that infinite nature within us. We are mind, body, soul, and spirit, and spirit is infinite nature, that god/goddess aspect of our being. Our soul is our finite nature, and what we need to do is bring mind, body, soul, and spirit into harmony, so that there isn't conflict, so that we can always act in impeccable ways, and strongly so. Most people aren't willing to put their life on the line, but now we've got to be willing to die for what we believe in, or we're lying. I'll put my life on the line—I've been shot at; I've been in jail. And I'll do it again, because I am not going to sell my life short, and I'm concerned about the future and the children. If it takes my life to make that possible, then it can have my life. There is no middle road. All the governments of the world are trying to buy a middle road. But that's not the way it's going to change.

# of witches
and wisdom

STARHAWK
in conversation with
ALEXANDER BLAIR-EWART

*Psychotherapist, writer, teacher, political activist, and witch,
Starhawk is a founding member of Reclaiming: A Center for
Feminist Spirituality and Counseling in San Francisco,
California. She is the author of* Truth or Dare *(1987),*
Dreaming the Dark *(1988),* The Spiral Dance: A Rebirth of the
Ancient Religion of the Great Goddess *(1989), and* The Fifth
Sacred Thing *(1993). She was featured in the National Film
Board Studio D productions* Goddess Remembered *and* The
Burning Times.

ALEXANDER BLAIR-EWART: What kind of witch are you?

STARIIAWK: Well, perhaps I had better define witch as I use the word. A witch is somebody who has made a commitment to the spiritual tradition of the Goddess, the old pre-Christian religions of Western Europe. So I am a witch in the sense that that is my religion, my spiritual tradition. I am an initiated priestess of the Goddess.

ABE: Do you have a sense of past lives?

STARHAWK: Yes, I do. I think most witches believe in some version of reincarnation.

ABE: Do you feel you've been a witch before?

STARHAWK: I feel I have, yes, quite a number of times. You could say that the work that I attached myself to somewhere way back had to do with the Goddess and the Craft and keeping the tradition alive.

ABE: I've oftened wondered to what extent the kind of witch that you are now is the same as a pre–Judeo-Christian-Islamic witch. There's obviously been some kind of evolution there. Can you talk about that?

STARHAWK: Certainly in the Craft, the rituals that we do today are not the rituals that they did in 25,000 B.C.; there's no way they possibly could be, because we're not the same people and we're not living in the same culture. We like to believe that we have roots that go back that far. Some people believe they are a sort of direct transmission; other people believe they have more a spiritual sense of connection. And we have ongoing debates within the Craft about that. But to me, what's important about witchcraft and about the pagan movement is, essentially, that it's not so much a way of seeing reality, as it's a different way of valuing the reality around us. We say that what is sacred, in the sense of what we are most committed to, what determines all our other values, is this living Earth, this world, the life systems of the earth, the cycles of birth and growth and death and regeneration; the air, the fire, the water, the land. In that sense, we're very much aligned with the same kinds of understandings as in the Native traditions from this continent, and from Africa and other tribal cultures.

ABE: We have a technological society which sees all of nature including people as resource. So we have resource ecology, and we have deep ecology, which is the awareness of the sacredness of nature. I wonder if you can talk about how much of an uphill climb it's going to be to get technological world humanity—and I think it does embrace the whole world now—to stop seeing nature as resource, and start seeing it as Being.

STARHAWK: There's no denying it's an uphill climb, that it does require on the one hand a real radical transformation of our values, our way of life, our economics, our material culture. I happen to believe it would be a very healthy transformation. People often portray it as, "We have to sacrifice this, give up that," and in one sense we do. We certainly can't go on driving our huge cars everywhere. But in another sense, I think that the benefits that we would find, spiritually, emotionally, psychologically, physically, from those changes would far outweigh any losses. We would look back on what we had and say, "Why were we afraid to make that change?"

ABE: Our culture is afraid of that change.

STARHAWK: It's tremendously afraid of that change, and it's full of very strong vested interests that do not want to make that change and will oppose it in every possible way. At the same time, my basic belief is that the Earth is a living being. She is an organism and She's intelligent. She's smart and She's not suicidal. *[laughter]*

ABE: I wonder what the role of theology is in that worldview. For instance, a lot of people in Canada, and certainly mainstream society, first became aware of you through the Matthew Fox/Creation Spirituality controversy. Can you talk about that involvement with Matthew Fox and Creation Spirituality?

STARHAWK: Yes. Matthew Fox is someone who is really trying to make some of those transformations from within the Catholic Church. He believes very deeply in ecumenism, that the church needs to learn from other traditions. So he brought me in, as well as other Native teachers, African and American teachers, to share something of our traditions as resources for people to draw on, not in the sense of trying to turn nuns into witches, although there's often not that great a difference. And it's been a wonderful experience for me. I've met wonderful people there. But a couple of years ago the church hierarchy decided that they were going to crack down on Matt and silenced him for a year. He's now out of his year of silence, teaching again and speaking.

ABE: There is the other part of this question, which is the relationship between "paganism" in the widest sense and Creation Spirituality. Can that marriage actually work?

STARHAWK: I think it does work. There is a difference between my theology and Matt's theology. And it's really a difference of about a word.

ABE: You mean "He" for God, as opposed to "She" for God?

STARHAWK: No, because I think Matthew would use both, and actually so would I at different times. But the difference is that Matthew Fox talks about God being alive *in* Nature, whereas for pagans God *is* Nature. There are pantheists and there are panentheists. This is what keeps him from being a heretic. *[laughter]* But I don't have to worry about that, not ever having been in the Catholic Church to begin with.

ABE: So basically you're talking about the immanence versus transcendence metaphysical debate?

STARHAWK: In some ways it's not really an either/or thing. If you look into the mystical part of any of the traditions, you find that there's a place where whatever that is that we like to call God, Goddess, or whatever is both immanent and transcendent. But pagans come down more on the immanent side, and tend to stress that as focus, and say, "Look, it's not that there is some external spirit out there living in the tree. It's that the tree itself is sacred." And I think theology does make a difference. I think if we define God, if we define the sacred as being outside the world, then the world itself gets profoundly devalued, because what we call sacred really is what determines our values, what we as a society, as a culture, are willing to risk ourselves for. What we say has a value that goes beyond expediency and beyond human ends. So you can imagine if we were to say, "Okay, water is sacred," as it was to many of the ancient Goddess traditions, to the Keltic tradition, to the Native Canadian and American traditions of this land, then the idea of polluting the water would be a heresy, would be unthinkable. And that definition of the sacred really makes a whole lot of sense because if you look at what people called sacred—the water, the air, the fire, and the earth—those were the things that we needed to live, to support life. It only makes sense that you would protect them, that they would be the primary value of a culture, of a society that wanted to survive.

ABE: What is it going to take for people to feel that, because, obviously, if they don't feel it, they won't do it?

STARHAWK: I think there are many possible ways to come to feel that. For me, one of the reasons I do rituals and teach rituals is because it's one of the most important and most accessible ways that people can begin to feel that sense of sacredness in the cycles around us, in our own lives, in nature. I would hope that people could come to feel that sense of sacredness through reflection, through education, through exposure to these ideas. My fear is that people will only come to feel that through great ecological catastrophe, which we seem to be heading into more and more. We're in a state of tremendous cultural denial about what we've done to the Earth, and it's always hard to break through that denial.

ABE: Do you feel it's something that we should be teaching our children in school?

STARHAWK: Absolutely. In fact, I think we'd do better teaching our children, if instead of having them sit at desks all day, locked up indoors in school, which you and I wouldn't stand for, we took them out... In a novel I've written, one of the characters starts a school where she takes kids out and says, "You need to learn about something from beginning to end. We're going to learn about water by going up to the Sierras, the mountain range in California, and find the source of the stream, and follow it all the way down. And we're going to learn about mathematics by learning how to read a compass, and about physics by learning how to steer a raft down the rapids."

ABE: The Anglicans have female bishops, and so on. The Catholic Church and the Protestant churches, I guess, are still pretty adamantly antifeminist in that sense. What do you see the future role of women in the Catholic Church and in Judaism as being? Is there going to be real change there? Is real change even possible?

STARHAWK: I think there will be real changes, or women will simply leave those traditions and gravitate to other traditions where they can have the kind of power and responsibility that they are entitled to. I see the Catholic Church from outside, but it appears to me that women have always really supported the Church in the sense that it couldn't have survived without the work of the women of the religious orders. And those women are pretty angry about their position. I think they're in a dilemma. There was an article in the paper about how the Church is feeling such a loss in terms of priests and nuns and people coming into the clergy, especially priests, that they don't have enough chaplains to provide for the troops in areas of conflict. The average age of a priest is sixty something, and the other religious warriors are getting on beyond that.

ABE: There's a real change coming there, regardless of what Rome decides about it. Does the same thing hold true in Judaism, in the synagogues?

STARHAWK: Well, Judaism actually has made some changes. In Judaism you have the reform, the conservative, the reconstructionist, and the orthodox. And the orthodox is the slowest to change, though there is a big feminist movement within it.

ABE: That's within Hasidism?

STARHAWK: Not only within Hasidism. Hasidism is just one branch of orthodoxy. But the conservative and the reconstructionist and reform now all do ordain women rabbis. For example, there's a prescription in Judaism where you need ten men to make what is called a *minyan*. My grandmother was never in her life counted in a minyan. You could have forty women and eight men and you still couldn't say certain prayers. But after she died, when we went back to Minneapolis where she was buried to have a headstone setting, we were discussing with my uncle how the service was going to go, and could we say certain prayers, and he said, "Well, we'll have so and so, and so and so, your cousin Stevie and Ruthie and you, and that's ten. And I said, "Since when did you start counting women in the minyan?" And he said, "Oh, we do that all the time in our synagogue," which is conservative leaning to orthodox. Now they're very orthodox, they keep kosher, very strict. And I thought it was a very hopeful sign that even though my grandmother was never counted in her lifetime, her children and grandchildren around her grave had become full human beings.

ABE: Theologically speaking, Judaism and paganism are diametrically opposed worldviews. How do you reconcile those two things?

STARHAWK: Well, yes and no. Superficially it might seem like that. But to me there are a lot of elements in Judaism that go back to an ancient earth-centered tradition. All of the holidays, all of the festivals are celebrations of the seasons and the cycles and the different forms of renewal that nature takes. And paganism is pretty eclectic. Paganism is polytheistic. It says you can have many gods and goddesses. It says you can have many different ways of naming the truth and seeing the truth.

ABE: I see what you're saying from that side. But from the point of view of what we'll call the "people of the book," the Jews, the Christians, and the

Moslems, they all have a monotheistic he-god. So how would a bridge be possible from that side?

STARHAWK: Well, fortunately, it's not my task to make that bridge from that side. It's my task simply to live with my own contradictions, and I guess as I get older I feel more and more comfortable being a Jewish pagan, or a pagan Jew.

ABE: Which raises the subject for me of rituals. Can you envision future rituals that would be in the true sense syncretistic and really work? Are you involved in the creation of new rituals?

STARHAWK: Oh yes, I've done them. One of the things we've been doing over the last couple of years is, from time to time, creating rituals that are multicultural, multiracial. We did one for Samhain, which is Hallowe'en. One particular year we had three Samhain rituals, three public rituals, because over the years we had this continual problem of getting bigger and bigger. One year we did a ritual for over a thousand people, which was very exciting, but enormously exhausting to organize and costly in terms of space. So we decided we could do three smaller ones more easily than one big one. The first ritual focused on the idea of Samhain as a time to remember our own beloved dead and mourn those who had gone, and kind of visit with our relatives. The second one honored the ancestors of many cultures. And the third was Samhain as the new year, creating a vision of the future.

The ritual for the ancestors of many cultures was planned by a group including myself, Louisah Teish, who is a priestess of the Uribe traditions, Raphael Gonzales, who is a Mexican American very much involved with some of the old Aztec traditions and Native American traditions, and many people from a lot of different groups. We gathered together a lot of people and asked them to make an altar to their ancestors. So when you walked into the space, there was a Hispanic altar with the skeletons and the skulls and the candles and the paper cutouts and the marigolds, and there was a Keltic altar with all kinds of things from Samhain. And there was an African altar that had African cloth, foods, birds and grains, and things. And there was a Middle Eastern altar, a Jewish altar with a challah and Yorzeit candles, and there was a Japanese altar with sushi and those kinds of offerings. It was just gorgeous, and people had time to circulate and to look at all the different items and to bring their own offerings and place them on the altars that they felt drawn to. When we invoked the directions, we used a drum rhythm that came from a different culture to call each direction, and dancers who moved differently for each direction. We took people on a trance journey to go back to the cave of the ancestors, and to see what gifts their ancestors had left them and to see which ones were actually useful to them at this time, and which ones should have been discarded a while back. *[laughter]* And we did a spiral dance. It was a very, very wonderful ritual, because it just had an incredible life and color and richness to it.

ABE: You're pointing at something that is very much the essential ground of the new age movement, which is one-worldism and the embracing of every religious and spiritual tradition. But there is this sifting going on of what in the traditions are useful and valuable, where the live seeds are and where the dead husks are.

STARHAWK: Right. And also the idea of being able to bring together all of those differences, without turning them into a bland kind of mud. But really having respect for the differences and to bring them together in such a way as to retain their individuality. There was some criticism of that ritual afterwards by some people, which was that there needed to be in it more acknowledgment of the reality of racism, the reality that we are living in a world that doesn't value these differences, that the vision was so far beyond what the day-to-day reality of people's lives are, that it was hard to make that leap for some people. So one of the things I would like to do in the long run is work with that idea, work with how we could do that kind of education within the context of a ritual.

ABE: I'm wondering what your perception of the new age movement is at this stage?

STARHAWK: Well, you know, it's hard to say. It seems that the movement is so vast and encompasses so many differences, that it's almost hard to talk about it generically. I think I have seen over the last few years a greater level of political awareness and involvement, that people are saying less that this is a way to escape from the world, and instead are saying, "We have to figure out a way to make this relevant to the real problems that we're facing." That's where I would hope the new age movement will go.

ABE: One of the things that has been emerging over a number of years, but now seems to be mainstream inside the new age movement, is the Brotherhood movement. How do you see the Brotherhood and Sisterhood movements? Is there a new male/female reality working there? How do you perceive the emergence of what could turn out to be a new patriarchy?

STARHAWK: Well, that is really something that happened for women back in the early seventies with the feminist movement. I guess I feel cautiously optimistic about it in terms of what's happening for men. I think that men have been tremendously harmed by this system, which I prefer to call wararchy, instead of patriarchy, because I think war is so much at the center of it, at the heart of it. And a young man pointed out to me that calling it patriarchy, which literally means the rule of the fathers, was hard on men who were really trying to reclaim the role of father, trying to function as a real nurturing father. So I'm kind of playing with that change of language. But I do think that men, as a whole, men as a class, still retain so many more privileges than women do, that there's always a danger that this just becomes one more way for men to get something new without looking at some of those other changes that need to go on.

Robert Bly talks about the difference between being a wildman and being a savage. I'm not sure if those are exactly the terms I'd use, but I think there is a difference between free, untamed energies and violence. And I would really like to see the men's movement take on the question of violence, both interpersonal and domestic violence, and organized violence and war, and ask, "What does it mean to us as men that we have been conditioned for five thousand years to see ourselves as weapons, as expendable, as machinery of war? What is it really going to take to change that?" I think men pay a tremendous price for the privileges that they have. And as we're seeing now, that price is the body bag. The price is, especially for a young man, that your life is expendable, your life is considered something your society can decide to throw away.

ABE: You've always been associated with radical politics. Can you express a general overview, or what the most important part of your radical political approach, the cutting edge of your process, is at this stage?

STARHAWK: In terms of my thinking, I guess, I don't feel like it falls into the old lines of left and right, you know, socialist, communist, anarchist, whatever. I think all those things are breaking down anyway. For me, I think the conflicts that we're seeing played out politically right now are conflicts about what is sacred to us, what are the overarching values that our society is going to hold. And for me, what is sacred is the interconnected systems that sustain and support life, both the natural systems and the cultural systems. So that puts me, I guess, politically on the side of Native peoples and their struggles for land rights and self-determination. It puts me on the side of nonviolence as opposed to violence, on the side of the environment and fairly strict and far-ranging changes to protect the environment.

ABE: When you were in Toronto several years ago, it was for some National Film Board of Canada films that you had been involved with.

STARHAWK: Yes, *Goddess Remembered* and *The Burning Times*, which are about the history of the Goddess tradition, and the suppression and burning of the witches. There is a third film now called *Full Circle*, which talks about the emerging Goddess movement currently. They're beautifully filmed and they're important parts of history that people should know about. Often a response we get from people who have seen them is, "How come nobody ever taught me this before? I've been to school, studied history, I've got a degree, and nobody ever told me this information."

ABE: What kind of people come to your events and lectures? I guess they're predominantly women, are they?

STARHAWK: With the lectures it's a pretty mixed crowd. The workshops tend to be predominantly women. Often I do things that are just for women. But I also do events that are mixed. Some of the people who attend these come out of the new age community; some come out of the politically active community, the peace community; some of them out of the feminist community; some of them out of the mainstream churches, people who are looking for something that they haven't been finding there.

arousal of
the inner fire

LYNN ANDREWS
in conversation with
ALEXANDER BLAIR-EWART

Lynn Andrews has been a bright light on the new age scene for many years now. Often accused of being a female version of Carlos Castaneda, Lynn has authored many bestsellers including Medicine Woman *(1981),* Flight of the Seventh Moon *(1984),* Jaguar Woman *(1985),* Star Woman *(1986),* Crystal Woman *(1987),* Windhorse Woman *(1989),* Teachings Around the Sacred Wheel *(1990),* The Woman of Wyrrd *(1990),* The Mask of Power *(1992),* Shakkai: Woman of the Sacred Garden *(1992),* Woman at the Edge of Two Worlds *(1993), and* Walk in Balance *(1994).*

ALEXANDER BLAIR-EWART: Are you working in what is called pan-Indianism?

LYNN ANDREWS: What do you mean by that exactly?

ABE: Well, there is a pan-Keltic movement encompassing different Keltic traditions from the Isle of Mann, Normandy and Basque, Irish and Scottish, Ionian, etc. And there is pan-Indianism, where the distinctions between the different tribes, the different approaches to spirituality, are being smoothed out. What are the implications of pan-Indianism in the long run, both for Native spirituality and for non-Natives getting involved in it?

LYNN A : I'm glad you asked the question, because there has been so much confusion around my work, and it's probably my own fault, because I didn't make it very clear in the beginning. The women that I work with are my benefactors, my real teachers, Agnes Whistling Elk and Ruby Plenty Shoes. They are certainly Native American women, but they are not tribally affiliated as medicine women. They are really shaman women, and there is a big difference. Medicine woman denotes that you have grown up in a tradition, and then been raised into a position of being a sacred person, a holder of the sacred pipe, a medicine person. That is not what Agnes and Ruby are. They are part of the Sisterhood of the Shield, which is a very different kind of thing. The Sisterhood of the Shield is an ancient gathering of women that has been in existence for a very, very long time, and they are from different indigenous cultures from all over the world. They're Native women but they are not Native Americans. So I think there's been a confusion about that and it breaks my heart in a way, because there's been a misunderstanding, and a lot of people have not read my books, yet they think that I have something to do with teachings about Native traditional ceremonies, and that's just not at all what I do. I talk about an ancient power and way of woman, and I'm sure there are similarities in lots of ways, but it's certainly not traditional.

ABE : In regards to feminine magic, by all accounts feminine magic was very powerful in Atlantis, and I wonder if you have any thoughts or any awarenesses about what role feminine magic played, for instance, in the downfall of Atlantis, or if it was a counterforce.

LYNN A : I don't know for sure. I know that it was very powerful in Atlantis. I have not worked on that area personally for a very long time, so it would be incorrect and inappropriate of me to comment on that. But I know about that personally from the Sisterhood. The Sisterhood is an extraordinary group of women who have taken me through a process of evolution, beginning with Agnes about fifteen years ago, and moving me from one member of the Sisterhood to another. So I went from Agnes to Ruby whom I worked with very closely, and then I started working with Zoila who helped me with my book *Jaguar Woman*. Then I went to Australia and worked with Ginevee, and then to Nepal where I worked with a Nepalese hill woman, and so forth. And so I haven't gotten to that round yet, but I am sure that we will before I am through.

ABE: The reason I raise that is because there is a lot of tradition in the Keltic and in the Saxon magic about it being a carryover from Atlantis.

LYNN A: I think that all of this truth seems to be the same. It has different ceremonies, it has different works, but I think the essence of what I am learning is exactly what the Kelts learned, and I think the source of that truth is probably the same. I think because we are on a feminine planet, the source of power is always female. If we were on a male planet, it would be reversed.

ABE: What would you have to say to contemporary new age men about the direction they should be moving in, in terms of getting to a place where they would be good company for you?

LYNN A: *[laughter]* Well, I think that men come onto this planet to heal the female side of themselves. And I think they've chosen that as what they came here to do. Of course, as we're all born into this physical dimension we forget why we're here, and half of this life is a process of getting back to remembering who we are. Men are in a very difficult position, I think, because they are born into a patriarchal society, and everybody in their family says, "Hey, buddy, it's a man's world out there." This little kid looks out there and he's frightened. Now this is something that may be very unconscious, but they don't really understand the energy here.

I think what happens is that men look for that goddess/woman, that incredible warrioress, that can teach them how to really live. And men have tremendous things to teach women, too. But in terms of how to live in common with the female element of nature, for instance, the energy of female consciousness is something that men need to learn about. Just like women need to learn certain ways of projecting that femaleness out into the world. We tend to hold within us more, I think. A man needs to learn how to live with the woman. He has to give the woman the chance to do that, he has to listen to her somehow, has to be able to see her and her reason for being in his life. Men have an incredible amount to learn in terms of being able to balance their own nature and to make that part of the world. And I think that women can help them do that. Men are so afraid, and they have to build this huge ego to defend the fact that they really don't know what they're doing in terms of the energy of this planet. And this ego presents a huge problem in relationship with a woman.

The other problem is that woman is taught that it's a man's world out there and that she's not going to be loved if she takes her power. So then there is a real problem, because then the warrioress never exhibits herself; she never becomes that warrior; she's afraid, she holds herself back and becomes what other people want her to be. A woman's self-esteem is in a very difficult position today, just the way society is structured. And a lot of what I address in my books has to do with feminine consciousness, because that's what's missing. It's hard for women also to take their power and be the goddess for the man in their life, and I think men test that goddess unconsciously.

ABE: Yes, definitely.

LYNN A: And women have to understand what that is. So often a very powerful woman will fall in love with a man and she'll just collapse. She will become a doormat. She will *fall* in love and lose her power and then the man wipes his feet on her.

ABE: What role does sexuality play in all of this? There is an emergence now of Tantric knowledge. Various people are working with that. Do you see this as a positive development?

LYNN A: I think it's one path. I looked at Tantric practice a long time ago, and felt then that it was certainly a path. I have worked with the kundalini, although we use a little different terminology.

ABE: What do you call it?

LYNN A: We call it the arousal of the inner fire. My book *The Woman of Wyrrd* is about the arousal of the inner fire, not in a sexual way, but in a way which leads you back into past lives, because, as I have been taught, the blood is what carries your lifetimes and your actual history. You have to be able to tune into the fire within, literally. And the arousal of that inner fire is not unlike the arousal of the kundalini; it's a process that is similar to that but with a different end in mind.

ABE: You are saying that your past lives are imprinted in your blood, and your blood, of course, is the basic vehicle of your astral body.

LYNN A: Yes.

ABE: So how would you tune into the forces that are living in your blood?

LYNN A: Well, the way I did it is the way I described it in *The Woman of Wyrrd.* My teachers built a dream lodge for me, and again I don't mean a traditional Indian dream lodge. I'm talking about a dream lodge where I literally learned how to do something called double dreaming, or dreaming within the dream. It's a kind of astral projection, but not really. You know, so many things that are part of the unknowable are absolutely impossible to explain. The only thing I can describe is how I got there. If I wanted to teach you how to do this process, I could get you strong enough to teach you what you needed to do to get there, but it is difficult to explain.

I got myself physically very strong before I even attempted the process. But essentially I went into the dream lodge and I did a ceremony. Before that I had worked a great deal with astral projection, moving in and out of my body, etc., and then moving into the arousal of the inner fire. So I could finally do this ceremony and successfully move back to sixteenth-century England, into a lifetime when I had had a teacher who wanted to work with me again in that lifetime so that I could learn something that I needed for this lifetime. It became very clear to me that we do carry a spirit shield from one lifetime to another, and that spirit shield is imprinted with symbols and learning in each lifetime as you go along.

It was very interesting. I had never really delved into past lives too much—I felt that you could get lost in your imagination so easily. But Agnes explained the need for doing this by saying, "When you are moving into the third and fourth rings of power, the last rings of your learning and teaching on this physical plane, it's like being this stick." And she held up a stick with her hand and balanced it using her finger as the fulcrum. She then tilted one end of the stick and said, "This is like your learning with the Woman of Wyrrd, the woman of the mists. You've learned many things in this past lifetime." Then she poked the stick and it fell from her fingers. And then she picked it up again, balanced it, and then made the other end tilt, and said, "That is your future lifetime. Both the knowledge of the past and the future is all contained within your blood. To access that knowledge you must understand it through the process of double dreaming, which is brought to you through the arousal of the inner fire."

ABE: So are we talking in a way about time travel from a spiritual point of view?

LYNN A: From a very spiritual point of view. It's hard to explain because it doesn't seem like time. You know, once you move into that world there is no time. We need time only for the relative world, the physical world, so that we have an agreement that you and I are separate, you in Canada, me in Los Angeles. We have an agreement that we are a certain age and so forth. But actually you move out of that time frame to go into double dreaming. That's why it was so difficult to come back into my body. Have you ever done that?

ABE: Yes.

LYNN A: It's like coming back into a carcass. Whew! It's so uncomfortable.

ABE: In terms of that phenomenon where the body becomes paralyzed when you're in that state, if your body didn't become paralyzed you'd turn into a channeler.

LYNN A: Yes.

ABE: In a natural, healthy trance, you're supposed to be as one dead. The body is supposed to be paralyzed so that nothing else can enter it. And the channeling path is a whole other path where you're stuck with being a communication station for other beings.

LYNN A: [laughter] Yes, that's right.

ABE: The first time you go into that trance state is deeply disturbing because, of course, when you try to come back into your body, as you say, you're coming back into a carcass. But after a while you learn that all you have to do is imagine your finger moving, for instance, and your body will then move and you'll get back in.

LYNN A: Well then you know intimately what I'm speaking about. It was interesting, because when I moved into that lifetime as Catherine I was a young girl and I had an extraordinary teacher whom I called the lady of the mist. She was actually two women and she presented herself to me at first like Danu really, and then became an old grandmother. It was only towards the end that I realized who she really was. She was just so magnificent, and in that dreaming I would dream within that dream. That was the extraordinary thing. I actually dreamed within that dream. That was a first for me. It was incredibly lucid. I remembered all of it and wrote it out exactly as it happened.

ABE: The remarkable thing about this, Lynn, is that each one of us contains a past that is as ancient as the Earth itself. The whole of time is in each one of us.

LYNN A: Yes. And isn't that a beautiful thing to say?

ABE: And it's only through the rediscovery of that that we can protect our humanness in the face of technology and in the face of what is happening in the world. We need that deeper spiritual and cultural and reincarnational richness to balance the world that we are now in. In this sense I agree absolutely with you that the feminine has to be nourished, it has to grow, it has to get out there, to awaken. If it doesn't, all culture will die.

LYNN A: I think we are lost without it, but I think it's happening.

ABE: You're obviously very active in all of this. You write each one of these books as part of your ongoing experience. What is the essential message of *The Woman of Wyrrd?*

LYNN A: The essential message is that we can take our power in life, and when I say power I am talking about finding that place of passion and true destiny that lives within each of us. Being able to express that truth in the world. It is about finding that place of passion, about how to strip away the unessential in your life so that you can move into that place of healing and truth that is within each of us, that place that we are all trying to find. I look around me in my life, and I find that so many of us, because of the stress of twentieth-century life, have sold out in so many ways. We've sold out in our relationships; we may have sold out in terms of the job that we are doing—we probably had dreams as a kid of wanting to make an extraordinary mark in life, something really special, and instead we settle for a job to just pay the bills. Not that that is a bad thing, but what happens when you sell out over and over again in little ways in your life is that you also sell out that dream that you had, and *The Woman of Wyrrd* is about understanding your own dream, being able to find your dream, and then living that dream.

The Woman of Wyrrd was really such a departure for me, first of all to even delve into past lives the way I did in that book. And it was so fascinating to me to realize that there really is a reason for all of the pain and all the suffering, all of the tremendous struggles that we face, besides all of the joy that we have in our lives.

ABE: It's a very interesting cutting-edge process where many of us, given that our auras are as evolved as they are at this stage, are now beginning to rerun all of our past-life content in these bodies, bringing all of that into the present and getting ready for that epochal shift into Aquarius. How have you handled that, knowing that there are literally hundreds of thousands of people reading your books and thinking about you? Do you feel that energy? Do you work with that energy?

LYNN A: Oh yes, very much. It's been a tremendous onslaught of energy, and it runs through my body day and night. Fortunately I know how to focus myself and how to discipline myself. And Agnes helped to prepare me for this.

ABE: There's always that cyclical patterned process in one's life, and the reason I'm bringing this up is to see if I can get you to talk a little bit about people accepting the totality of themselves and accepting that they don't have to be perfect at every stage of their process, that sometimes you have to have acne as an ugly teenager to grow up into a beautiful woman or man. I'm wondering what experiences you have with that in working with people, where they have to deal with, say, the dark side of themselves, or the dark side of the world?

LYNN A: I think that's what this stage is really pushing us into. As Agnes so clearly told me in Tibet several years ago, "We're giving birth to a new eon of time," which they call a magical child. A magical child is truly an androgynous being that is totally balanced between the male and female energy, and represents a whole new birth of consciousness. And when there is a giving birth, which is what we are doing, there's tremendous energy coursing through each and every one of us. The reason that I give seminars all over the country is to help people clear out the psychic debris that they are carrying so that that energy can move through them freely, without hurting them. It is so important to realize that this energy that is coming in is being experienced by everyone. That is another one of the reasons I wrote *The Woman of Wyrrd*, so that people could begin to see that there's a pattern, there's a whole process that goes beyond just this lifetime, and that our imperfections are actually gifts. Those gifts are signposts along our journey towards enlightenment. If we can move through each of those weaknesses, if you want to call them that, and make them strong, then it's just passing another test of power towards that place of truth that we are searching for. We're going home, really. We're finding our way home. I think that's why the

Brotherhoods and the Sisterhoods are becoming more available.

ABE: We are all very conditioned about what enlightenment or liberation or spiritual evolution should look like, and it looks as if, since the sixties, there has been a steady shattering of all of those thoughtforms, and we're beginning to realize, when you talk about the magical child, that it is play, it is something completely new, in a way, even though it draws on all of these ancient roots. And when you talk about moving the debris out of the way, probably part of that debris is our own conditioned ideas of what spirituality is supposed to look like.

LYNN A: We all have ideas of what spirituality is supposed to look like. That's how the religions of the world come to be. Unfortunately I don't think that most religions teach you about enlightenment. They teach you about organization. Enlightenment is quite another story, and it's a process of going within, finding that sacred witness inside of you. That sacred witness is part of what I'm trying to show people with all of my writing. There are so many areas that you have to deal with, your emotional integrity, etc. You have to go around the sacred wheel, which is physicality in the South; emotionality in the West, strength and wisdom, the adult part of your being; spirit in the North; and in the East, illumination.

ABE: What kind of woman are you predominantly?

LYNN A: In the sacred dream, death and rebirth, transformation, the West. I live a lot in the West. And of course I live a lot in the North because I am teaching so much. I try very hard to live all the way around the wheel all of the time. I think that's very important. It's part of what I'm teaching in *The Woman of Wyrrd*, which is how to live balanced so that you can have a magnificent relationship, a really powerful, passionate relationship, a love relationship.

ABE: Say more about that.

LYNN A: *[laughter]* Well, I talk a lot about Windhorse, who is my spirit husband, and what that means. In the shamanistic sense, in the ancient sense, it has to do with marrying that counterpart spiritually within yourself. That is, when you meet your spirit husband, it isn't just part of your imagination. It's a true being that lives on the other side, who is married to you in spirit. And when you marry that being in spirit, then you are ready to get married in the physical, because you're complete. You aren't then moving towards someone out of need. You're moving towards someone out of just really wanting to share, of wanting that opportunity to love. And that can be many different things. I explore a different kind of relationship in *The Woman of Wyrrd.* I meet someone in that lifetime who is the reincarnation of a spirit man that I know in another sense, and it is very clear that in that relationship we both have to retain our power, and how we do that is very interesting.

ABE: There's such tremendous fear, particularly in North America, of powerful emotions between men and women. And the only way that gets represented in the movies, for instance, is in films like *Fatal Attraction* or *9 1/2 Weeks, Bittermoon,* or whatever.

LYNN A: It's sad that we cannot show the good side, how wonderful that can be.

ABE: You're in touch with a lot of people all over this continent and other continents as well. When you talked earlier about finding your dream and then living it, there's also obviously a larger collective dream involved in all of this.

LYNN A: I'm intimately involved with and have dedicated my entire life to healing this planet. I looked out at the world and flailed around for a while trying to figure out how do I do this, and as I was working with Agnes and Ruby I realized, of course, healing always begins at home. One has to heal the individual. How do you do that? What better way than to just tell my story? I have had an extraordinary opportunity to work with these powerful and magnificent women and the experience that I have had has healed me. It has had such an extraordinary and profound effect on my life. So when I was early on working with Agnes, she said, "I want you to write about our life together. I want you to write in detail about how this work has affected you, how you have come along in your process of apprenticeship so that perhaps other men and women will gain courage from what you have been able to do and are still in the process of doing, and will be able to manifest their dreams in the world and find their true path." In healing the individual, which has to do of course with each person taking their power...

ABE: What does "taking their power" actually mean?

LYNN A: Taking their power means manifesting their truth in the world, rather than other people's truth—once they are balanced and healthy and strong, then the world around them becomes healthy and strong. So that is the way I have approached the healing of Mother Earth, through the healing of the individual.

ABE: What role does love in the deeper sense play in your life and in what you do?

LYNN A: Love is everything. As far as I'm concerned, love is what we're working with basically. It is the path of heart, and the path of heart has to do with finally stripping away, like layers of an onion, to the center, to that stillness, that magnificent, central, powerful, sacred witness that dwells at the beginning, at the still point of the storm that is you. Once you are in that place, then you can truly love.

ABE: Where you do you see your work going?

LYNN A: I guess hopefully I am working towards enlightenment, whatever that means. And enlightenment is, going back to what I was just saying, moving into the stillness. As my teachers have so often said, you have to know about the physical world, to deal with it on every level. You have to deal with the foundations of your sacred lodge, meaning how you live in the physical world, how you deal with your body, how you support your family, how you deal with the world with integrity, with care, with beauty. And when you have moved through the physical world and understand the lessons that you have come here to learn, then you can at last give it up. Because you cannot give up something that you haven't had. I think a lot of spiritual people don't understand that. They want to give it all up before they've experienced and learned the lessons that they came here to learn.

ABE: Yes. The thing that I find very interesting about the Keltic mysteries and the Native mysteries is that they are life embracing, whereas so much of what has come from Asia, for instance, is very life denying.

LYNN A: Well, they are different devices. I look at all of that as just a device. I think there are a lot of different ways to move towards enlightenment, and it depends on who you are. Each person is vastly different and unique in their process. I do think that we have probably been here many times, and that you may have been here a thousand times. Maybe the person that you are seeing at the moment has been here only ten times. Who knows? So your lessons are very different. Perhaps some people need to learn that lesson of being an ascetic in India or whatever. It's not my path. I think that what I am doing is what I need to be doing, certainly the path of heart, the path of love. Embracing all of life and understanding Nature in the most intimate and deepest sense holds great lessons for us. Nature is definitely our teacher and not the other way around.

ABE: How does what you're doing connect to the Gaia consciousness?

LYNN A: Well, very definitely Mother Earth is a being, and a true being, and I have felt for a long time that all of my work with the Sisterhood has to do with healing the Mother, the Mama as we call her. She's our Mama. We are given life from Mother Earth, and she's definitely alive. Things are alive in different ways, and beings of the planet are all part of us, all part of that oneness. So very definitely I am deeply involved with that concept.

ABE: That's the awakened feminine. In your view, what would the ideal awakened man be like?

LYNN A: For me, the ideal man is someone who lives with a foot in the physical and a foot equally balanced in the spirit, and of course equally balanced male and female shields. He's able to move with great facility between those two shields, being able to carry the female, when it's appropriate, and the male, too.

ABE: Do you think you're likely to meet such a man in this lifetime?

LYNN A: Oh, I think so. The ideal person to me, man or woman, is a balanced being, and that balance means of course that you have gone through all your stuff, taken your environmental cloaks, gathered lifetime after lifetime, and peeled them away one by one to get down to the essential truth of being. That truth is very simple, really. You learn all of this knowledge and wisdom and all of these tricks, and finally in the last analysis you say, "Hey, I've done it, and I've done it well. Now what I need to do is get very still, and be." But to get to that still point is a tremendous journey.

5
Jung
and beyond

MARION WOODMAN

ROBERT BLY

JEAN SHINODA BOLEN

being a
true self

MARION WOODMAN
in conversation with
VALERIE ELIA

Marion Woodman is a Jungian analyst with a private practice in Toronto. She is a prominent lecturer and workshop leader and the author of numerous books on the quest for personal transformation, including: The Owl Was a Baker's Daughter *(1980),* Addiction to Perfection *(1982),* The Pregnant Virgin *(1985),* The Ravaged Bridegroom *(1990), and* Leaving My Father's House: The Journey to Conscious Femininity *(1992).*

VALERIE ELIA: There is a saying: "May you live in interesting times." Well these certainly are. There is so much unrest and upheaval in the world, and it seems to me that we can't escape anymore from the world culture that pervades our lives. It must be very challenging for an analyst working today.

MARION WOOODMAN: Yes, we have to face what we're in, and to not face it is to go into an addictive behavior, which many people do. We are in a unique time because we have made one world now through technology. You know, the Persian Gulf is in our living room, Oka is in our living room, Jerusalem is in our living room. So we really are in one world, being called upon to be citizens of the global village. And yet we have no idea what that is. We are so confounded with our own prejudices, we have no idea how to be a citizen of the global village. But at the same time as we are being called upon to be whole people in a whole world, we have the technology also to destroy ourselves. With acid rain, the ozone layer, the rain forests, overpopulation, all these things, ecologists who know what they are saying are telling us that if this situation doesn't reverse in eight and a half years, there is going to be an irreversible process towards our own self-destruction. So our situation is unique and what's happening at the collective level shows up in the dreams that come into my office. In terms of the depth of despair, I've never seen anything like it before in my practice.

VALERIE E: People are dealing with unwanted forces and structures within themselves to an unprecedented degree. Where are we, then? What stage are we at?

MARION W: Well, I think that we are going through the death of the whole power structure on which the planet has existed for fifteen hundred years. The concept of conquering nature, of conquering each other, paying no attention to the planet's soul, much less to our own individual soul, is now being called into question. It's not going to work. We've got to learn what love is, and I think we have no idea yet what that is. Most people think of love as something that you are neurotically bound to, dependent on, or need in order to survive. That's not love. So I think that the death of the patriarchy is one thing. But coming out of that is the birth of a totally new consciousness.

VALERIE E: And the sense that where there is power there is not love?

MARION W: Well Jung says, "Where there is love there is no room for power."

VALERIE E: But you know, as I look around, power is everywhere and it's always been thus. To be successful is to be powerful. You make the statement: "Men and women unconsciously trapped in power drives have no individual freedom." Is the operative word "unconsciously"? If you consciously use power, is that okay? Is there any place for power?

MARION W: Yes, of course there's a place for power, but I would keep using the word "empowered." I think that if people don't find their own individual empowerment, there is no hope for the planet whatsoever. If we operate out of a mob psychology, and if there aren't enough individuals with the power and the strength and the courage to go against the mob, we are going to end up in total despair, and I can't see any hope but being ruled by tyrants, because in that psychology where you have victims you have tyrants.

VALERIE E: And yet even if we start to see changes in government, a new leader who says let's put an end to the old patriarchy, let's give more women a chance to make changes, if the tree is rotten, if we keep the same old structures, what's the difference?

MARION W: It won't work. And I also believe that many women are worse patriarchs than men. They are into power and they parody men's power attitudes and the desire to control.

VALERIE E: Are they at that point acting as patriarchs rather than matriarchs? Is patriarchy inherently negative?

MARION W: No. I wouldn't say so. I would say that in the old matriarchies which are now coming to light, we can see that to act from a matriarchal principle is very different than to act from a patriarchal one. They are a much more cooperative society; they tend to be more peaceful. India, for example, in our modern world, would be quite matriarchal. Granted they are in great difficulty with overpopulation, but it tends to be a much slower culture, much more in harmony with the rhythms of nature, not given to fighting and trying to dominate. So to come from a matriarchal structure would produce a very different world. But women who are identified with patriarchy accept patriarchal values, consciously or unconsciously, and they will try to carry out the aggressive, impersonal, assertive kind of value system that leaves no room for personal relationship, for the taking of time to be present and living from the inner reality. What I'm talking about is living the authentic life.

VALERIE E: In this country we have a constitution that is unique in the world, that gives women great protection, and right now the provisions of the Charter of Rights and Freedoms are constantly being tested, and from that are coming laws that will protect women from discrimination. Do you think this is the way to go, to use the law, which is a continuation of the old power system, to bring about changes? Is that how change comes about, or must it be organic?

MARION W: It's got to be organic, but I think of the people I know who are going through divorces, and without the courts, they would be in terrible trouble, they would have nothing, no possibility of living their authentic life, because they would have no money. And I think the same is true with the educational system. While that organic change is going on, people still have to learn to read and write, and granted it is based on competition and goals and patriarchal values, but it has to go on. I feel the same way even about the Church, because again the hierarchy there is overwhelming. Certainly nuns are trying to do something about their situation in the Catholic Church, and they are working to find their own empowerment within that structure. It seems to me that if that organic process is going on in enough people, and if they begin to care about their own creativity, living their own inner life, those systems will change from the inside and the old system will come clattering down at some point.

VALERIE E: Can I ask you a question about how you deal with power in your own life? Being a teacher and an analyst and maybe to some people a guru, you're in a situation where you're attracting more attention, larger crowds. Do you find it difficult not to come from power?

MARION W: Well, I do. Just like old Cyrano de Bergerac who loved his white plume and his power, and who then saw his shadow on the wall, that great huge nose, I keep very close to the earth by seeing my shadow on the wall. So that through my own analytic work, having to daily face my own shadow, I stay human, I think. Mind you, at night and in the morning I do a great deal of journaling. If I know that something is coming up where the power issue is going to come in, I look at that very carefully. And so I watch my dreams to see if there are power figures. I watch my journal, and I watch my own body, because it will react to power, power coming from other people, or from myself. When I see this dynamic in my life, I immediately go off by myself and do some deep breathing and try to come back into the receptive mode, which would be, for me, the feminine. So, yes, there is a huge danger of becoming inflated.

VALERIE E: Which is what I think happened to a lot of people in the new age movement.

MARION W: Yes, but you know, "What does it profit a man to gain the whole world and lose his own soul?"

VALERIE E: And sometimes you don't even notice that you're losing it.

MARION W: Oh, I doubt it, because if you're paying attention, it will be in the dreams. You will see the little girl go into the mud, or you will see the young woman that has been maturing raped in the dream images. You will see the animals becoming sick, and coming and biting the hand, and saying, "Look, I'm here, pay attention to me." And I think that the breakdown of the immune system in so many people is the soul saying, "If there's no room for me, if I cannot be paid attention to, I'm not interested in living." There's a profound death wish in an immune system that turns against itself.

VALERIE E: You say pay attention, yet what I see are alienated people who don't know why they're working at the job they're doing, who don't know why they're living the lives they're living. They don't know how they became this person that they seem to be. Where does it begin, this long road away from what you call the "authentic self"?

MARION W: Well it begins in infancy, if not in utero. And it goes back to power. If the parents don't want the child, if they don't want a child of that gender, I'm sure the child knows that in utero. You can see it in dreams. Often there's a trauma at the birth where the child either doesn't want to come into the world, or doesn't want to come in, in that body. And then, so often, even tiny children, if they are living who they are, realize they are not acceptable to the parents. So they learn to please the parents, not to live by their own musculature and their own body, not to act out of their real anger or their real joy. They are trying to please somebody else. And gradually they please the teacher, they please the boss, the husband, the kids, the grandchildren, and they're not living their own life at all. They're living a mask, and they have masks on their belt, and they just choose whatever one is right for the particular situation.

VALERIE E: Society rewards this false self a great deal. Many of our famous people are coming from this inauthentic self, and maybe that's what fuels it.

MARION W: No question about it.

VALERIE E: Is it possible to live to your death out of this inauthentic self?

MARION W: Of course it is.

VALERIE E: Does the true self make rumblings, try to come out and be seen?

MARION W: Yes, and that's why most people, I think, go into analysis. The rumblings have become so loud that they have nightmares. Their body is breaking down. They don't know what to do. They cannot make relationships that last. They find themselves replaying the old tape in every relationship, or they can't hold a job. For whatever reason, nothing is working. Now, you can escape from that with alcohol or drugs or food or TV or sleep. You can get into the addictions, and that's what our society is. Our whole society is addicted. And the alcohol or the abusive object will bury the soul, so that it will shut up.

VALERIE E: But if you're lucky, it will make rumblings and be heard and you'll have a breakdown.

MARION W: You'll have a breakdown in your body, either physically or psychically, and you will start to listen to the soul. I know that a lot of people say that analysis, particularly Jungian analysis, is elitist. But many people do not make the choice between the authentic life and the inauthentic life. They just muddle on until they are too sick to do anything.

VALERIE E: Well, if you are a famous actress, and you have been operating out of this inauthentic self, you get tremendous rewards. If you become conscious and go into therapy, would you be in danger of losing this gift, if we can call it that, this skill of performing?

MARION W: No, I don't think so. In fact, I think you'd be much better, because if you have worked in the depths of your own soul, it will show in every sentence you speak, it will have a resonance that goes into the soul of your audience. People know that you're coming from a true place. But it seems to me that here's where the differentiation would come in, where I would say the "masculine sword" has to come in. If you're an actress, you know that you are going to put on a mask, because you are going to be acting somebody else, right? But you try to identify with the person you're playing. You identify so that your body changes its movement, your whole gestures, everything changes, but it's resonating at a profound level in your gut. So it sounds authentic. Now when you step off the set, hopefully you know enough to take the mask off, and then you go back to what may be a very introverted world. You come on the set again and you put on the mask.

VALERIE E: If you don't take off the mask, if you continue to identify with this famous person...

MARION W: You are in big trouble, because you will be identified with an archetype.

VALERIE E: Take someone like Marilyn Monroe. We don't remember her as a great actress, but she...

MARION W: She had the fire, the light.

VALERIE E: She represented something to us. Would we remember Marilyn Monroe if she was a healthy, conscious person?

MARION W: I don't think it has anything to do with consciousness, Valerie. Marilyn Monroe was a very abused child, and where there is very little ego, the person very often can open to the archetypal energy that comes through, so that they just become that archetypal energy. And if there is no ego that says, "This is the god that is coming through me, or the goddess that is coming through me and it is not me," sooner or later you die in your own fire, because that's not who you are.

VALERIE E: What does it say about us, about the symbiotic relationship that we have with these icons? If we want these icons around us, then we are really a part of the whole process.

MARION W: These icons are necessary.

VALERIE E: Why?

MARION W: Because we are human beings. We are part animal, part divine, and we have to be in touch with our own divinity, and these icons keep us in touch with the divine. For most people the Church no longer keeps them in touch with the divine in themselves, and so therefore they set up false gods. But by identifying with them they do experience their own inner light.

VALERIE E: So, they serve a positive purpose as well.

MARION W: Yes, because they take us out of the two-dimensional world. I mean, life is three or four or five dimensions, and we have got to be in touch with that, otherwise again we go back into the addictive behavior, to try to find—I guess the only words to use are God and Goddess. Life is just boring, you see, without that archetypal dimension.

VALERIE E: Archetypes are interesting, and in Jungian psychology there are many puzzling but interesting concepts, some of which are not easily understood. Is Jungian psychology destined to attract a middle-class, well-educated constituency, or does it have something to say to larger, disadvantaged groups?

MARION W: Well, I don't think it has anything to do with education. Often professors are the hardest people in the world to work with, if we're talking about education, because if you reduce analysis to an intellectual experience, it's very dangerous. It's more dangerous than not having been in analysis at all, because you think you know something. If analysis doesn't touch the soul, doesn't touch the feelings, doesn't touch the body, I think it is dangerous, because one can become very inflated.

VALERIE E: But it does have an intellectual appeal.

MARION W: When you're on the outside looking in. But once you're in analysis and you are working with the dreams, and watching the instinctual images that are coming out of the body, you begin to understand that there is a totally different process going on at this level. And if you're not in analysis, you're working with the logic of the so-called rational world that we live in. There is a particular logic that goes with ego consciousness in the world out there. But in analysis you realize there is another logic that is operative in the unconscious world, and there is a process going on with very different values, emotions, and responses. And the dream is like a photograph from the unconscious of what went on yesterday. So that you may have thought you had a wonderful interview, for example, and you look at your dream, and it says, "Watch it, that person is a snake in the grass." Consciously you didn't catch that, but the unconscious does. So more and more you start to realize that the wisdom in the unconscious is beyond anything the ego could imagine.

VALERIE E: That intelligence that lives in the unconscious, can we leave it there? How do we know that it isn't doing more important work by being left unanalyzed, being left alone?

MARION W: Well, Jung says that what is not brought to consciousness comes to us as fate. So that if you don't bring it to consciousness, you live it out in your relationships, in your body that's breaking down.

VALERIE E: Have you ever questioned that? I think, well, if we were meant to remember our dreams, why isn't it part of our waking day?

MARION W: Most people are putting all their energy into consciousness. They wake up with an alarm clock and bang! their feet are on the floor and they're moving right into consciousness. But when you're away on holidays and you lie in bed and think about your dreams, they're there. We have lost the art of dialoguing with our dreams. I mean, children will tell you their dreams and they have an uncanny sense of the meaning of an image.

VALERIE E: It's an art that we're not in touch with as much as we could be.

MARION W: Yet primitive peoples have it. Native Americans have it, and children certainly are very much in touch with that other side. But if we take no time for listening to the unconscious, listening to our dreams, looking at our symptoms, looking at the messes we are making in our relationships because we're unconscious, then we blame somebody else for our troubles, and that of course is what Jung calls "projecting the shadow." Women blame men, men blame women, one nation blames another, the shadow is projected onto somebody else, and until we can take responsibility for our own power structures and our own envy and jealousy, hatred and greed, the situation is not going to change.

VALERIE E: A criticism that is often aimed at Jungian psychology is that it's kind of a magical world of dreams, of synchronicity, where everything has great significance, and that this child's world is one we should leave behind as adults, otherwise we live in a regressive, pre-egoic state. How do you feel about that?

MARION W: Well, first of all, anybody who says that it's a magical world has never been in analysis.

VALERIE E: I don't mean that the world is magical, but rather that the concepts are imbued with some kind of magic.

MARION W: I still say, Valerie, that someone who says that hasn't been in analysis, because anybody who has been in analysis has gone through the agony of recognizing their own evil. They have recognized the body reacting to pain. The agony of the body is as great as the agony of the soul in analysis. Our culture pays no attention to the soul, in fact it doesn't honor it in any way, so that if you begin a soul journey, you're an outcast so far as this society is concerned. And anybody who calls that magical, I think, is setting up a resistance; they are afraid of it, and therefore it's magic.

VALERIE E: Why would they be afraid of it?

MARION W: Because the culture, since Socrates at least, has tended to kill people who try to live an authentic life. I mean, just look at the number of people who tried to live an authentic life and who got massacred. And it's not much different in our society today, although I think many people are now feeling so empty that they are trying to find something that is authentic. But it is frightening to find yourself in a position where you have to live out values that are ridiculed and rejected by the society. Society calls it "navel gazing," calls it selfish to spend an hour on your dreams every day. But if you don't spend an hour a day working with these inner images, there's no way that you can integrate the power.

You see, when you're trying to change your life, or allow your life to be changed, you have no idea who you are or where you're going, because your parents did not supply any model, or you wouldn't have to change so radically. You have no models, because you are trying to find your life. So all you have are the images that are coming from your own interior world, and often these look very bizarre. But if you work with them and try to walk like the gypsies that appear, for example, in your dreams, or you try to move with the image, it's like your Olympic high jumper who is going to break the record, who is going to go where nobody has gone before. He has to stand until he can imagine himself going over that high bar. When he can imagine that, his physical body can catch up to the imaginal body. Until he can imagine it, he cannot jump it, and it's the same with dreams. If you don't work with the images, and dance them, paint them, compose music from them, work with them in the way the soul always works with imagery, through art forms, they won't become part of you.

VALERIE E: Are these images archetypes?

MARION W: They are archetypal images, and they carry the energy of the archetype. I can see why people call that magic, because it's like a child, the divine child. Every moment is a creative moment, because you are bringing consciousness to every moment. So that you're painting the flower of your dream and all of the energy comes up and you're trying to get it, and all of a sudden it becomes something totally different, and if anybody's watching that, I guess they'd think it was a bit magical.

VALERIE E: Can we talk a little bit about relationships and the role of archetypes in relationships? If you have a relationship with a man and you see him as a certain, perhaps archetypal, image, and you don't see him as a human being, and if he does the same with you, what have you got?

MARION W: You've got a pathological neurosis! *[laughter]* Because people say that's being in love, when in fact what you're in love with is your own image that you are projecting.

VALERIE E: Don't you think lots of relationships at least start out that way?

MARION W: Of course they do.

VALERIE E: When you see somebody across a crowded room, what are you seeing? You don't know this person. There must be some kind of image telegraphed to you.

MARION W: It's telegraphed from inside you, coming from the unconscious. Here again we're talking about archetypes and that energy that is so huge that it's bigger than the ego, and the ego becomes identified with that energy. That person out there is somehow stirring up the archetype in you. He either looks like somebody you love or looks like your father or your brother or somebody that is in the depths of your unconscious that you want to connect to in order to be whole. So gradually we realize the projection we put on somebody else is a part of ourselves that we've put out. When we come to that realization, we then have to ask, "Well, do I love this man?" It's pretty sobering to realize that you are in love with your own projection. And then you have to look at the person behind the projection, and it's the same thing for men and women. So, it's at that moment, when you realize that this is a totally other human being you're relating to, that human love, which very few of us know very much about, is released as a genuine energy between the two people.

VALERIE E: That moment of seeing the other person as a human being is a scary moment.

MARION W: You don't even know who it is! The projection has fallen off. The person on whom you had put the projection will feel the loss of energy; it's like taking the crutch out from under a crippled person, because that projection sustains the person who is carrying it. And you think, Oh, I am very special. In his eyes I am a princess. But it's boring, also, because you know he's not in love with you. He doesn't even see you.

VALERIE E: He must feed you at the very place you need to be fed, otherwise you wouldn't be there.

MARION W: That's right. But it's flattering and it's inflating and it's very dangerous, because it is not you. And that's where performance comes in. You are terrified of losing the person's love, so you keep performing what the person wants you to be for fear you'll lose him, for fear you'll be abandoned, for fear you'll be rejected. And there is an awful lot of rejection and abandonment in our culture right now. But the fact is that we abandon ourselves, our own soul, and the poor soul in its abandoned condition sends up its despair and grief to consciousness, and then people again project and say somebody else is abandoning them. We have to look at what we're doing to our own inner world, and not blame others for abandoning us.

VALERIE E: One of the types or archetypes that you talk about, the "demon lover" is both fascinating and frightening. A charming, yet ultimately cold man who bewitches women, like Don Juan and the Phantom of the Opera. Why are women so attracted to that man if he doesn't feel?

MARION W: He seems to feel. He's not macho; he's the kind of man who has been close to his mother and therefore understands the feminine unconscious. He knows how to ritualize courtship, how to bring her flowers, how to quote the poetry, how to write the letters, how to give the gifts, and he can do this through ritual. Now it doesn't look like that, of course, to a woman who is receiving it. So he gains his strokes by winning the woman, but once he's won her, he may start to look for the next one to win.

VALERIE E: And he can win each successive one over, even though they differ, one from the other.

MARION W: Yes, very much so. A woman who has lived her life through her father or her brother cannot live without that relationship with a man, whoever that man is who is carrying her projection of the demon lover. And it only becomes a demon lover because eventually it starts to take over her life. You know, there's the image of the demon lover sucking the blood out of the neck. It is sucking the life force because she is trying to live her own life; she's trying to get her job going again; she's trying to get on her own feet, but she feels that she's not really there. She's not, because her soul has been given over to this man who has gone away and left her.

VALERIE E: So while women feel terribly angry towards this demon lover, they are part of the equation.

MARION W: They will not even feel anger towards him. I would say the basic emotion is yearning. They are yearning for him; if he would phone, if he would come, if only, if only she could connect with him, then they could live again, and that yearning can take them to the streetcar tracks or into unconscious suicide, or the body can become very ill.

VALERIE E: Anna Karenina.

MARION W: Anna Karenina. And of course many, many women, many great creative women, have been caught in this. But you see it's the feminine as victim—in Shakespeare of course you have Othello and Desdemona—who never blames the man. That's part of it; they think it must be their fault; they're not good enough.

VALERIE E: Why can't they blame the man?

MARION W: Because their concept of the feminine is that it will serve the masculine. Therefore they must have done something wrong. They are pretty well identified with the masculine principle. I think to try to heal that kind of yearning without dreams is almost impossible because it doesn't make any sense at all to love the person who is destroying you. Now men can get into this, too, with the femme fatale. They will be so in love with a woman that it's like an umbilical cord; the life force goes through the connection between that woman and them, and if she cuts it, their lifeline is cut off. But they are the mothers' sons who believe that masculine law is to serve the feminine.

VALERIE E: So you have a relationship between the mother's son and the father's daughter.

MARION W: The one serving the masculine and the other serving the feminine. It's where you get the liebestot, the love/death marriage. Very romantic and full of fire and energy. I mean there's no other relationship quite like it.

VALERIE E: It sounds like a relationship that one can become very addicted to. On one level you feel very alive.

MARION W: Yes, because you are identified with archetypes, and that energy is flowing, and any normal kind of relationship is going to be pretty dull in comparison. But a relationship between two human beings demands a different kind of courage, a different kind of patience and strength. You're not just swept off your feet by the glories or the lightning. But if you've had the lightning, it's pretty boring without it.

VALERIE E: You have said that if you leave a relationship at a certain point, you will have to pick it up at that point in the next relationship. What is difficult to know is when you are leaving at a healthy stage, when you are okay to leave, and that you are not running away from something.

MARION W: It's very hard to know, because often the partners are not at the same level of working through their inner problems. The woman may be far ahead at one point and the man far ahead at another point. So, if they are not in sync—and it's very rare that we are—it's very hard, and I think that one has to be extremely patient. But if one partner refuses to do the inner work, I don't think there is any possibility of growth. The unconscious moves very slowly, and if you have a big investment in a relationship, it's worth waiting, providing your partner is doing everything possible to bring their material to consciousness.

VALERIE E: So even if you feel you are being hurt by that other partner, if you feel that he is willing to work on it and you are willing to work on it, then it's not necessarily destructive.

MARION W: No, and you have to look at your own dreams, because very often you will find that destructive partner in your own dreams, and if you go to work on your own inner material, as you change, your partner is going to change. The unconscious changes the atmosphere, and by the time you've worked out your own inner mess, your partner may have worked it through, too, so that you both come through to a different level.

VALERIE E: What can each one of us do to build a better relationship?

MARION W: I think that it's our responsibility to develop our own masculinity and our own femininity, men and women each developing those two energies, so that they are in harmony within, and if that harmony is operating within each partner, it will be operating within the relationship. I think it's crucial that we separate our archetypal projections from our human partners, so that we have the divine marriage inside and the human marriage outside, and we're not asking our partner to be a god; we aren't asking ourselves to be a goddess. We know that at the creative level, that is, when we are writing or dancing or whatever it is that is our creative work, the inner marriage is going on. The soul is open to spirit, and it's out of that marriage that you are creating. That leaves the human relationship free to be human with all the ecstasy that can go into a human relationship.

VALERIE E: When we follow any teacher or teachers, there arises the question of power. Could you talk about that?

MARION W: Jung said that there is nothing more dangerous than a Jungian. He'd say, "God preserve me from Jungians!" Because if you are a Jungian, well, it's like what Blake said about Christ. He said that as soon as Christ died, the Church buried him in ecclesiastical alcohol. In other words, the spirit that wanted to be renewed every moment is suddenly buried in ecclesiastical dogma. He was interested in releasing the Christ energy, you see, out of the alcohol, because he believed that the new day was Christened, and so on. And it's the same people who put Jung in a coffin and embalm him and say, "This is classical Jung," or "This is purest Jung." The minute you do that, it's dead. Jung said that he had gone as far as he could in his lifetime and it was up to people to go where they could in their lifetime. I never hesitate to think my own thoughts or have my own ideas about what's going on. More than anything I encourage creativity in my analysands. I would never say, "This is what the dream means." But I would say, "What are your associations with that image? Let's keep going until we get to the depths of that image." So I would say the same thing: "God preserve me from Jungians," because that's death to the psyche.

pulling
out the pin

ROBERT BLY
in conversation with
ALEXANDER BLAIR-EWART

One of the patriarchs of the modern men's movement, poet/wildman Robert Bly is both revered and reviled because of his commitment to honest communication and a life passionately lived. He has authored, edited, and translated numerous books, including the best-seller Iron John: a Book about Men *(1992),* The Rag and Bone Shop of the Heart *(edited with James Hillman and Micheal Meade, 1992), and* Night and Sleep *(poems of Jelaluddin Rumi, translated with Coleman Barks, 1981).*

ALEXANDER BLAIR-EWART: Men and women don't seem able to enjoy each other, which is a real shame. And there's a big negotiation going on before the party, like "How are we going to define how we're going to have fun here?" But nobody is really having any fun.

ROBERT BLY: These are all very deep problems. I think that women and men are ill suited to each other. That's a fact of human life, because men have been specialized in one direction and women have been specialized in another. And if the men were not specialized to kill animals and people, no one would be around at all. So therefore men did a great deal with other men, specialized as they were, and women did a great deal with other women, specialized as they were. And the suffering, or as they would say in the ancient world, the goddess Necessity made them overlook how ill suited they were to each other. I know, on the farm, when I was a boy, my grandmother worked a tremendous amount and the men worked a tremendous amount, and they hardly noticed they were ill suited to each other.

ABE: They didn't have the time.

ROBERT B: No, they didn't have the time. Now you have a completely different situation in which people don't do that physical work as much, and men and women are noticing how ill suited they are. Well, unacceptable. Somebody must be wrong. Some feminists suggest that it's the fault of the patriarchy. The patriarchy is why men and women are ill suited to each other. But the more you hear that, the more it's like ex-president George Bush complaining about Congress. The more he complained, the less real it seemed to be. What I'm saying is that the pin has gone in and *both* men and women are asleep. And that's a very different explanation. You're talking about waking people up, then. I mean, compulsory education, among other things, has put the pin in, and that's not arranged only by men. In the United States the overwhelming number of grade school teachers are female. So the women are very much involved in the putting in of the pin, both for girls and boys.

The adult men in the United States, not as much in Scotland or England, have withdrawn or been pushed out of the whole process of childhood development. For example, I think the greatest mistake in consciousness in this century is the belief that fathers are not important. And both men and women have accepted that. The men have accepted it more grudgingly, but nevertheless they've basically accepted it, so that when a man gets divorced, he may simply say, "Well, I'll let her raise the children." As a matter of fact, in my father's generation, it was thought that the woman would raise the children and the father would earn the living. But the very fact of earning the living in the presence of the sons helped pull out the pin.

ABE: What is the result of this negation of the father?

ROBERT B: The disasters that have come about from this simple belief that fathers are not significant in the raising of the sons or the daughters are multiplying all over the planet. When you're looking at gangs in the United

States, you know, you're looking at young men who have no older men at all as models or mentors. Women are terrified of those young men, and justly so. But I have been attacked over and over again, for example, in *Ms.* magazine, where they as much as accused me of starting the Gulf War! *[laughter]* Schwartzkopf and Bush and I started the Gulf War. And then there's the idea, which really surprised me, that men are to have nothing to do with the raising of boys. When Bly is saying these things about the father in *Iron John,* all of that is completely destructive because women are completely peaceful as human beings, and if they had raised the sons alone, then the sons would never go to war. The fathers are all Pentagon murderers, and if you let them have anything to do with the raising of the sons, then there's going to be more wars. Now, that's an astounding idea when you look at it. Astounding.

It's astonishing to me that the women's movement, which has stood for so much consciousness raising among women, which has culminated in the United States in *Ms.* magazine, and which says a lot of true things, would be willing to publish something like this, which, if it's followed, if the fathers are continually sent out of the family, will create more gang murders, more terror for men and women. For example, in New Guinea they stopped initiation of young men among many of the tribes, and for the first time there are roving bands of two to three hundred young men moving around New Guinea. And in Kenya something similar has happened.

ABE : The women seem to have no perception of how damaging their behavior is at the point when the young man is passing from boyhood into manhood. If the young man starts to step away from the mother and begins to establish independence, it's as if the mother won't recognize that the son has the right, even, to make that transition.

ROBERT B : What can we say about that? First of all, one has to say that women have been humiliated by the Catholic Church and by the Supreme Court and by the old economic marriage in which the man had all the economic power. This humiliation has been going on for hundreds or thousands of years. And I think all men need to acknowledge that, and say that it's hard for us to understand how that would drive a woman into her own consciousness, so that she expects very little from the men around her. But then, when some of the anger that she couldn't express, for economic reasons perhaps, or physical fear, begins to be expressed by large groups of women, tremendous disturbance erupts in those women themselves, and yet they feel it as a definite movement towards sanity and health. I think that this ability to express anger and attack the patriarchy or attack men is the proper step to take in a movement away from centuries of timidity. But then an odd thing happens in that the ability to see becomes so disturbed. Is it that the woman is so deep inside her own consciousness that she cannot understand how different the boy is from her?

ABE: Yes, I see that.

ROBERT B: What I see is this absolute failure of consciousness, so that there is this possibility that many of the women simply cannot see how different the boy is from them. And that's a question of vision.

ABE: Any mention at all of any actual differences between men and women in the presence of the woman or the presence of the mother is denounced immediately as sexist or untrue or unreal.

ROBERT B: So that's a possibility. It's a genuine failure of vision. A second possibility is that during all of those years when the woman has very little economic power, but to some extent power to determine how things go in the house, a counterreaction takes place, so that she doesn't want to lose the boy, or at least one of the boys. This is not a matter of vision; this is a matter of power. She doesn't have power over the adult man because he can leave at any moment. That happened a lot in the sixties—turn on, tune in, drop out, or whatever. But she can have power over the boy, especially the favored boy. And then you'd have to adjust the whole thing and say that men want to have power over the area between houses, that is to say, they like empires. But women like to have power over what is inside the house. The idea that the female is the only gender without any power impulse is crazy. So what is happening is not a lack of vision, but its an actual presence of unacknowledged power, the desire that the life of one of the boys will be altered according to the way the mother wants him to be altered.

The third explanation is that what we're talking about here is knowledge. For example, the old initiators used to spend 67% of their time in Australia in initiating and working with the young men, which means that there's a tremendous amount of knowledge involved in helping a boy grow out of the female fetus that he was in the womb, outward, to be a boy, to be a youth and finally to be a man. Now both the men and the women have lost that knowledge. So that's a very different explanation. That the women don't see intuitively how different the boy is—that's one; that they want power over the younger boy in the house—that's another; but this third explanation is that there's been a vast disappearance of extremely important knowledge. And it's something like what happens in primitive tribes when you lose the knowledge of which herbs are useful for healing, when the trees are cut down.

I think it's more the third, that to change a boy, who is actually a female fetus in the womb—as you know, in the beginning all fetuses are female—to change that into a boy takes a fantastic knowledge on the part of the DNA, all of that fantastic knowledge we can't even imagine. And then for that boy to change into someone who, as they say, learns to disidentify with the mother, is very painful for him. He has to learn to give up Eden, which is the identification with his own mother, and then learn to identify with someone of a completely opposite gender (as it seems to him), to the father, and then to continue to go in that direction. Well, vast knowledge is necessary for that to happen. We are simply ignorant. So, if we agree with the third explanation, then I think that the women would have to say, "We need some humility here, in this situation." And the men would have to say to themselves, "How did we lose this knowledge? Were we too busy making money so we didn't bother about it? Did we expect the old men to do it?" Do men gain this knowledge when they get to be about sixty or sixty-five? Is that why the grandfather is so important?

ABE: It seems to me the First World War is the beginning of that. A European civilization that had been in the making for millenia, and that was actually beginning to humanize itself in a very interesting way, got wiped out during the First World War. All kinds of knowledge, for example, simple things that have now become clichés, got lost. For example, say I'm a suitor of your daughter, and it's before the First World War, and I say, "Can I have your daughter's hand in marriage, sir?" Well, the fact that I'm there at all means that I have a house, I have land, I have means, otherwise I wouldn't even dare to be there. So when you ask me, as the father of this daughter, "Are you able to keep my daughter in the manner to which she is accustomed?" what are you inquiring into? You're inquiring into the quality of man that I am, my spirit, my being. And everything represented by what I've just said was wiped away by the First World War.

ROBERT B: How was it wiped away?

ABE: The First World War wiped away a whole generation of human beings; it escalated the industrialization of Western Europe; it put women in the factories, and yet kept them at a kind of agrarian state of consciousness at the same time. And it bred a schizophrenia in Western womanhood that we're still reeling from. It wiped out a whole generation of men and their connection to their fathers. So you had the first generation of millions of fatherless males in the West.

ROBERT B: It's interesting that James Hillman mentions that when you used to go and ask for the daughter's hand, the father might say, "Ah, he's very well spoken." Well, that means that you were required to have absorbed some of this knowledge of rhetoric and careful speech and awareness of the sensibilities of others. And that disappeared completely. Even our politicians are not well spoken anymore. So, I think that's right. This is like what happens when all the shamans are killed all of a sudden, and no one knows what the herbs are anymore. That's what happened in the First World War. I agree with you.

ABE: Okay, here's a bunch of herbs, we've heard that some of these herbs used to be able to heal something, but we don't know which ones do what anymore. How do we rediscover this knowledge?

ROBERT B: Well, you have to try the herbs on yourself. That's the only possibility. And I also say that cannot be done in big groups. It's no use having two hundred people taking the same herb at the same time. So, I think that the knowledge of how boys can be changed to men needs to take place in small groups, in relation to the men recovering their knowledge, which is a different thing than the women recovering what they used to know, because women used to know a great deal about that. And you can still feel it in many mothers. I don't know how many women have written to me and said, "This *Iron John* was tremendously helpful to me in raising my sons, because intuitively I knew those things but I had never seen them expressed." So all of that is still present intuitively in a whole lot of women.

ABE: How are men to know how to go into the process of rediscovering the lost knowledge of authentic manhood?

ROBERT B: Men need to be together in small groups over a period of two to five years, where they can talk about what the absence of the herb meant to them, how a little bit of the herb they took at a certain age helped them. It's a very slow process. I don't believe in any of these men's groups taking place without 60-, 70-, or 80-year-old men in them. To give myself as an example, I was my mother's son, and my mother couldn't influence my father; my mother realized that my father would not change his way of life for her sake. I think that was the biggest shock of her life. So she chose me. I would change the course of my life for her, which I did. And in the course of that it separated me from my father and my brother, but it also pulled me into the whole world of feeling and poetry and all of those things. So there were great blessings given at the same time. But, when I was forty-five, it was very clear to me that men didn't trust me. The teaching that I do now I couldn't do then because the men would not have trusted my words. I was still talking in the old way, and what I'm trying to say is that, as I got older, as I got to be 55, 58—I'm 68 now—a certain kind of knowledge came into me about what it is that young men need and how an older man can be generous to them and can help defend them. I think it's a knowledge like that of herbs, and it came along as I got older.

ABE: What effect has that more mature knowledge had on your experience of yourself?

ROBERT B: When I began to receive some kind of old-man knowledge, two things happened. First, I had to give up the idea immediately that men and women are the same. That's step number one. The second thing that I felt was a tremendous compassion towards younger men that I had always felt towards younger women. I was chosen, in a way, to hear my mother's sufferings, which my father would not hear. And so I always had a lot of compassion for young women and their suffering. But it wasn't until I was sixty or so that I began to feel the same kind of compassion towards younger men. And it's obvious that as soon as that happened to me, I became a better father to my own son. Well, what else are you going to say? I mean, we're talking about the loss of this knowledge. It seems that when we left Europe for North America, one of the statements we made was that fathers are not important. The Fatherland is not important; grandfathers are not important. I think we said that, first politically and geographically, but then we began to absorb it all the way through our system.

ABE: And yet, peculiarly, we came to Turtle Island, the place where the elder, since the last ice age, had been and still is, in the Native communities, the highest office you can attain, in a certain respect.

ROBERT B : Well, we just shot them like we shot anybody else. But I agree. I heard Gary Snyder talking one day, and he said that among the Athabascan Indians they feel that the brain is not finished until you're fifty. So that's why the old men and women talk first, and the younger men keep their mouths shut. Well, I think that's true. I think the brain really isn't finished until you're fifty. So I think the women who are thirty-five have to be humble enough to say to themselves, "My brain isn't finished. I really don't know what to do with these boys. I have an unfinished brain." And the men have to say that, too. The fathers have to say, "My brain is unfinished, and that's one reason I can't deal with the woman. It's one reason why I don't know how to deal with my sons." I like the tone of the whole thing, and Native Americans are the ones who know that best.

ABE : On the one hand, you speak of the compassion for the daughter, and then you reach the compassion for the son. But what I hear you saying is that the man needs to have a respectful, compassionate regard for the woman, and at the same time have the capacity to disregard her opinions about what men and women actually are. Would that be close?

ROBERT B : I think so. Not completely disregard the opinion, but to say, "I don't know much about men, but I know that some of it is stored somewhere in my cells, maybe not available to me now. But it would be madness for me to accept the woman's opinions before I have gone to my own cells to find out what I think." So, I have to listen with honor to what she says, and then I have to use my own instincts about how I'm going to raise the boys. There's a lot of loneliness in that. One of the approaches that can be very helpful when a man is involved with a problem he can't solve, whether it has to do with a woman his age or a mother or father, or a conflict with a daughter or son, is to imagine an ancestor behind him, and to step backward into that hollow tree of the ancestor, and ask, "What do you think?" And wait until the answer comes. But, we don't do that. We immediately get into the fight with the woman. Isn't that right? We try to convince her or we try to fight off her argument. It's too naked. There's no protection. The whole line of defense of men is gone.

I don't think that regaining the knowledge means demeaning women or excluding women. I don't think of myself that way at all in the work I do. It has to do with the reconciliation of men and women. And it has to do with imaginative work on the part of men, of which this is an example. Imaginatively imagining one of your ancestors, and before you say another word, you step back and see what he might have to say about that. These are all attempts to rebuild something. Isn't that right? Because, at one time, you could go into the next room and say to your grandfather, "This is where I am. What do you think?"

Why don't men take this step backward? One, the man is so threatened by what the woman says that he beats her, and you're into wife-beating, which is horrendous. The second possibility is that he goes forward and says, "The woman knows better than I do, so I will repeat feminist doctrine, and that way she will approve of me, and I won't be in this terrible situation." What I'm saying is that neither of those two make any advance at all for the man, and certainly not for the woman.

ABE: I once entitled a little piece of writing "Never Trust a Man Who Claims to Be a Feminist." You know, you hear the feminist line come out of men, and you know it's bullshit. Men are very sensitive to other men's bullshit, but they get away with it with women.

ROBERT B: What I would like to do is tell you this story about John Rowan. John Rowan is English, and when I went over to England four or five years ago, they said, well, the only man we have in the men's movement is John Rowan. He wrote a book called *The Horned God.* So John Rowan is a classical example of the man concerned about men who has taken the feminist point of view. He believes the man should be a consort to the Great Mother. I was with John Rowan in a book recently about male spirituality called *The Choirs of Gods* that John Matthews edited in England. In that book Rowan described a ritual exercise that he had worked out. He has a woman who helps him, and this is the way it goes. He has about fifteen men and about fifteen women. His partner, the woman, takes the fifteen women, puts them in a circle, then they hold out their hands towards each other and they imagine female power and energy, until they get this circle all full of this energy. Then John takes the men and he goes to another room, and he tells them, "Now, what you have to do, first of all, is give up the male attitude towards work." So there's all this talk about workaholism, etc. Okay, I give up the male attitude towards work. "Now, I want you to give up the male attitude towards emotions." Okay, emotions are bad, they invade my body and that's wrong. Okay, I give up the male attitude towards emotions. So, it goes on like this, and you give up the male attitude towards love, and then you go on and you give up the male attitude towards spirit. I think the tenth one is that you give up all male aggression. The eleventh one is that you give up your testicles. The twelfth one is that you give up your penis. Now, when they've done this exercise, he brings them back in, they crawl under the arms of the women *[laughter]* and feel that the women have all the power. Here they are with no cock, balls, or anything. *[laughter]*

Now John Rowan recommends this as an excellent exercise to introduce men to men's work. How do you like that? Can you imagine a woman taking women off in a room and saying, "First of all, I want you to give up the female attitude towards children. Second, I want you to give up the female attitude towards beauty. Now I want you to give up your breasts, and now I want you to give up your..." I mean, women would kill that woman. No woman would say that as a way of introducing women to women's work. And yet, it's perfectly obvious that the women doing this exercise with John approved of what he was doing. And John approved of it. Isn't that amazing? It's been done in England a lot, printed in a book, and the editor prints it with no footnotes. So I think that's one thing that we're up against. And if a woman cannot see how destructive that is to everything that would produce a decent relationship, if she doesn't have vision enough to see that, then she has to at least ask, "Am I doing that to my son? Am I asking him to give up his attitude towards his male work?" Whoa! I think woman have to ask themselves a lot of questions along that line. Don't you think so?

ABE: The thing that emerges all the time is that women don't want power over men. And I speak from my personal experience with that. But almost all women can't help trying it. I think that's their way of finding out—and I think it's more instinct than knowledge—of finding out what you're made of. And at the moment that you are clear—not in a violent or hostile way—and you say, "Listen, there are some things that you are just not going to get to do with me," there's a smile that comes to their face. It's like a relief, like a weight that you've lifted from their shoulders, because now they're able to think, "Oh, okay, so you're the boy, I'm the girl. Great."

ROBERT B: I agree with you.

ABE: And yet, it's faith in that that the men in so many men's groups don't have. They don't understand that...

ROBERT B: That they could make any boundaries there.

ABE: Yes.

ROBERT B: I like that, because one of the things it's saying is, if the patriarchy is disintegrating along with the boundaries it created in terms of male power—and I don't think the women have brought that down, the industrial revolution brought it down—but, if that's so, that means that there's a power vacuum here. And what John Rowan is doing is asking women to start expanding out farther and farther until they're responsible with their arms raised for everything on the planet, and they're responsible for all of these men. Wow! That's damaging to women, to give them no bounds at all to their expansion. And so I think all feminist men have to ask themselves, "Am I encouraging women to expand their powers to a point where it will be extremely destructive to them?"

ABE: What do you think happened in America when the people elected Bill Clinton? It seems that some kind of shift in the psyche of America took place. Has there been a shift, and if there has, what is the nature of it?

ROBERT B: Well, you know, whenever you look at something you tend to look at it through whatever you've been thinking about. So, I'm going to answer partly in terms of the men's movement. In the workshops that Marion Woodman and I do together, there is something called the "false tutor," who is in connection with the "stepmother"—so it's men and women together doing it—who puts in the pin that puts the boy asleep. That pin was put in by Reagan and by Bush. A lot of destructive things happen when you're asleep, and being asleep allowed greed to move. So, what had happened was a terrible tragedy in the United States, an unbelievable amount of ground lost during these twelve years of sleep. People finally understood it, and Ross Perot helped with that. What happened was that the American people did exactly what happens in the "false tutor" story. They took a sword and cut off the tutor's head. Everything that Reagan was teaching and that Bush was teaching ended that night. The head was cut like that. Then, what happens next? Well, it's very interesting that Clinton made it clear at the convention that everything he got, he got from his mother, and from women. He defended women against the stepfather, which is a very good thing to do, and the women, his mother, Gennifer Flowers, and many others have given him many gifts. So he understands inclusivity; he understands something about the greatness of the female view of the world, to bring people in, unite them, not to split them and all of that.

Then, the more touching thing that happened is that he chose Al Gore, which was a brilliant move, and when they stood up there together, what we saw was a man with his first male friend. Now George Bush couldn't do that with Dan Quayle at all. In fact, he chose an inferior. But Clinton chose an (psychospiritually) older male, Al Gore, who possessed more of the kind of male knowledge gotten from his father, and he from his father. The *New York Times*, for example, printed an article in which it said that only two weeks after the convention an amazing amount of change had already taken place in the United States among the men, because basically it wasn't a fight between two machos now; it was a fight between Iron John and John Wayne, and that four years ago at a political convention you would never have seen men talking about their children who were nearly killed, or their mothers and alcoholism. But men had made enough changes in four years so that these men were able to do this.

And later, Gore said that *Iron John* had been tremendously helpful to him, especially with his son. So, we were actually watching a change of consciousness there, from the stagnant one of Bush with those lies and that dubious connection with the banks, to the human sphere of Bill Clinton, who has a good root in the mother, and a good tutor in Al Gore connected more to the father.

the process
is the message

JEAN SHINODA BOLEN
in conversation with
ALEXANDER BLAIR-EWART

Jean Shinoda Bolen, M.D., is a Jungian analyst as well as Clinical Professor of Psychiatry at the University of California, San Francisco, and a board member of Ms. Foundation for Women. A Fellow of the American Psychiatric Association and Diplomate of the American Board of Psychiatry and Neurology, Dr. Bolen also teaches and leads seminars throughout North America. Her four most recent books include Goddesses in Everywoman *(1985),* Gods in Everyman *(1990),* Ring of Power: The Abandoned Child, the Authoritarian Father, & the Disempowered Feminine *(1992), and* Crossing to Avalon: A Woman's Midlife Pilgrimage *(1994).*

ALEXANDER BLAIR-EWART: The women's movement in the West in a way found its roots in the birth of America. If we go back to the late 1700s or early 1800s, America led the Western world in the establishment of women's educational centers and that kind of thing. By the 1960s it took a sociopolitical form, and by the beginning of the 1980s you have the Goddess really appearing in mass consciousness. There is a sort of chicken and egg question here, if this doesn't sound too absurd. But do you feel that those early glimmerings in women's suffrage, and the breakthrough in feminine consciousness in the West, is something that was already moving out of the depths, out of the archetypes, and that it just took us a while to catch up to it?

JEAN SHINODA BOLEN: I think they are related. I would say that, first of all, the United States and Canada have by and large been settled by immigrants who were adventuresome, who set off on one of those great journeys beyond the known world to settle over here. So that the very archetypal nature of the people who came to the Northern Hemisphere included the impulse to define their own space, to break with tradition, and the need for a certain real autonomy in defining themselves and their experience. Most of the people who came over were Protestants, at least in the case of the United States. And so there is a shucking off of patriarchal, established, institutional authority sort of built in to the folks who came over and settled here. I think that spirit had a lot to do with the suffragette movement and the women's movement of the sixties. When pioneers start to settle a new country, the men and women who come over struggle to establish themselves on a much more equal level than is the case in their original home with traditions that go back thousands of years. So there's a sense of equality and an "I define myself" archetype. Finally there is the meeting with the return of the Goddess that is one of these morphogenic field phenomena.

ABE: Something that is beginning to really penetrate into mass consciousness as well is the phenomenon of the Madonna, the Virgin, the Goddess at places like Medugorje. What impression does that phenomenon make on you?

JEAN B: It seems to me that it's a part of a global return of the Goddess in different forms. The return of Mary, not only there but in Mexico and in Ireland, around Knox, shows increasingly in the experience of the apparition of the Virgin. It is an outer-visionary experience that is in my way of thinking the same as the internal mystical experience of the feminine aspect of divinity.

ABE: So we're talking about living in a period now where the barrier, if you like, between the inner world, the subjective world, and the objective world is collapsing. One of the things I've been wondering about, particularly in the light of Julian Jaynes' book *The Origin of Consciousness in the Breakdown of the Bicameral Mind,* is what does that mean for us now, with the Virgin at Medugorje and these other places? I mean, that's an objective phenomenon. Five hundred people at a time see the sun dancing, or whatever it is. It's almost like a total reality shift, as if miracles are reappearing in the world.

JEAN B: Well, miracles are reappearing and they are being objectively contemplated as well. Julian Jaynes would say that there isn't a pause between the feeling and action and the experience of divinity right there. So that "I do this because Athena standing behind me directs me to do it."

ABE: But it's something a little different from that, isn't it?

JEAN B: I think it is. I think it has to do with a probable time when divinity was hallucinated or experienced inwardly in a very real way by people who had not developed a linear, left brain, and who didn't have a sense of separation, didn't have a sense of "I think therefore I am," but rather "I'm part of everything, including this apparition or this hallucination which is just as real as this tree or this animal or me." Because we are all a mix of spirit and matter. And that then shifted into a much more rational mind separation from environment and from mystical experiences. But now we have in place a developed thinking apparatus, an observing apparatus, and at the same time increased access to the archetypal, the mystical or the eternal realm, with the right brain as receptor of that realm. So we seem to be able to cross back and forth between the two worlds without obliterating them.

ABE: That's one of the primary issues, isn't it, that here we are functioning in this postindustrial, technological world, at least in the West, and yet at the same time a mystical reality is breaking through into a world that was originally constructed in such a way that its goal was to keep that out? So in a way it looks as if there is something in humanity, or something in our primal reality, that is reasserting itself in the face of that. Or is it that people feel the loss of something in this technological world, and at some level or other open themselves to mystical reality?

JEAN B: I can see we've got a chicken or egg situation here.

ABE: I don't know, is there an answer to that yet? Maybe there isn't.

JEAN B: There probably isn't an answer to it, and yet there does seem to be an accurate spiritual tradition that's been present all along as the left brain has been developed. By the time Christianity emerged, it had that sense of "seek and ye shall find," "ask and it…

ABE: …shall be rendered unto ye."

JEAN B: Yes. That sense that you as an individual entity, which is a left brain experience—"I think therefore I am"—begin to intuit that there is a higher order, a divinity, that might be accessible if you are open to the experience. And you can't make it happen. It isn't something that you can do through your will alone, but something you can only do by invitation and receptivity. There is some shift when you go into a contemplative or meditative experience that invites in that other mystical reality, and whether within the Christian tradition through prayer, to invoke the deity or the sacramental experience through which grace would come, or whether through a more Eastern tradition of meditation, there is a voluntary suspension of pure left brain functioning to open up to the right brain as the receptor organ of this other reality.

In psychology, especially so in Jungian psychology, that increased openness includes an appreciation for the dream realm, and that means you start to consciously remember your dreams, or try to remember them, write them down, think about them, amplify them, work at perceiving the symbolic language. And when you're doing that, you're clearly doing that with your intelligence. You are putting your intelligence to work on receiving that which is possible to receive through that right brain perceptive organ that presents us with images and affects, that nonverbal language. As soon as we start paying attention to the dream world, then it's easy to start viewing the outer world as if it were also a dream, and through that way of looking at outer reality as if it were a dream, noticing that synchronicities are always happening, and that there are symbols to interpret. When you do, as when you interpret a dream, you find the meaning of the experience that you're living at the moment. You find some coherent way of making your way by listening and trying to find the inner equivalent of landmarks on the journey.

ABE: One of the criticisms that is leveled at the Jungian approach by its critics is that here you have something that is purely subjective. So, if someone tells me that my dreams are significant, then by suggestion they'll become significant, or if somebody tells me that archetypes are significant, then by suggestion they'll become significant. And yet, coming back to the experience of the Goddess at Medugorje, it seems as if the archetype acts quite independently of human wish fulfillment. We're talking about five hundred people at a time experiencing something together.

JEAN B: Of course, they are standing there wishing and open for the experience, too. So there is no difference in relation to your other example.

ABE: Then are the archetypes independent of humankind?

JEAN B: Yes, that's what Jung was maintaining all along, that the archetypal level of the psyche, the collective unconscious, is objective, it's not personal, and it has its own life. It's there in place. We get in touch with it.

ABE: The whole thing sounds very much, then, as if it's pointing at a Neoplatonic or Platonic view of the universe, where you have your nine hierarchies of archetypal beings, you know, gods, goddesses, all the way back to the Godhead.

JEAN B: Except that that's a systematic viewpoint that is not necessarily right. I name archetypes by goddesses' and gods' names, and that's in some way an equivalent. The archetypal world is like the world of nature. When we come into the world we look around us. We can put everything into phylums. We can define the different categories of animal, mineral, etc. We can say that there is an order because we have a need to make order in our psyches. But whether there really is such a thing, or whether it is just helpful for us to impose some sort of hierarchy, is another question altogether. And the systems that are essentially hierarchical, that come out of a hierarchical mentality, are reflections of a left brain tendency.

ABE: I can see how they can be perceived in a left brain way. But I think the original idea of those hierarchies was that the hierarchical aspect of it was simply that awareness or human consciousness, as it came into an authentic relationship with the different characters or archetypes in these hierarchies, would grow or expand. You're talking about, not so much a vertical hierarchy, but more that these things are almost like symbols or directions to show you that you've come this far, you're aware of this much, but that there's more.

JEAN B: Well, that's certainly true. It's like entering a forest, or entering the ocean. You start wherever you start and you go in, and there's all the rest of it to discover. Is that how you're using it?

ABE: Yes. And that each one of the archetypes has distinct characteristics. They're recognizable in the sense that if as a man, you're in Zeus consciousness, that's a whole modus vivendi that is a very different kind of experience from, say, Hermes or somebody else. Or, if it was Aphrodite or Persephone or Demeter, that it's actually a different experience of yourself and of the world in relationship to that archetype, to that state of consciousness. How many years ago was it that you published *Goddesses in Everywoman?*

JEAN B: It was 1984.

ABE: That book has had an absolutely phenomenal affect. People are still picking it up for the first time. People are reading it for the tenth time, and the language that is in that book has become part of culture in a certain respect. The whole goddess movement has grown and is developing, and from where you're standing as one of the primary enunciators of that consciousness, where do you see it at the moment, and where do you think it's going to be in the future?

JEAN B: Well, it's interesting to track myself as an example, because I start out as a woman influenced by the women's movement and someone who knows about Jungian archetypes. That leads me to write something that is intended primarily as a psychological book, a book that defines psychological patterns in us, and how the outer world encourages or discourages the expression of those particular archetypes. At that point it is still quite psychological. But what then happens with me and especially with women who read the book is that the spiritual dimension starts to move into the psychological dimension, which I think is only fitting because psyche does come from the word "soul," and it really is about the soul level of the person. But the book ends up being a text for women's spirituality, and I find myself participating in some of the first women's spirituality conferences that are being held.

What I did for many women was provide words for an experience that they were already having. I'm a highly intuitive word-making person, and a lot of women are not. I meet them and discover their realms and it affects me. I understand now how much more embodied and nonverbal and energetic are the archetypes than how I described them in *Goddesses in Everywoman*. So the realm gets bigger, and yet the labels of the goddesses are large enough to continue to fit. Then there is the synchronicity of these times in which goddess literature and goddess archeology starts to emerge, and it meets a spirituality-oriented psyche in thousands of women who are receptive to what is literally being dug up, and understanding something about the nature of divinity having a definite feminine quality that we never were told about. So there is a movement into that whole realm of goddess spirituality, which, unlike sky god divinity, isn't monotheistic and isn't all full of theological premise. And it starts to see divinity by all kinds of names, which was always traditionally so when there really was goddess worship. Each goddess in a particular place had her own name, which was different from the goddess's name somewhere else. And yet everyone really was worshipping or experiencing the same archetypal entity.

ABE: So a bridge, in fact, has occurred, because I recall you were here in Toronto a number years ago, and I had the very interesting pleasure of being at your seminar as one of three men in a hall with about six hundred women. That was an experience in itself. And I recall at that time wondering, Well, where is the bridge from this into the spiritual? It seems as if the spiritual, in fact, has made its move from the other side; the bridge has come from there into the psychological.

JEAN B: Yes. But it's almost like a landmass starting to come up out of an ocean; it may come up at one point and look like just a little piece, but in fact the whole landmass is moving up. It really is all connected under the water, and we just don't see it initially. And then you see another piece of an island, still part of that big landmass, and that is, say, a new archeological find. And then there's another island that comes up that is some kind of wiccan tradition that has been rediscovered, or a combination of rediscovery and emergence. Then there is the whole feminist, Christian theology that is emerging, and there is Carol Gilligan writing about how women have a different ethical way of looking at things. At first it looks like they're all just disparate islands of thought, but then, as it emerges more and more, it becomes obvious that this is the top of a much grander landmass that is what might be called "the Goddess" coming back up into the culture. So it isn't so much a bridge, but rather a recognition.

ABE: The whole process continues and it looks as if we haven't seen all of it yet.

JEAN B: I would certainly agree. It really does seem as if more is happening, and much of it has to do with the whole connection between feminism and ecology, seeing the Earth as a sentient being, and acting as if it had a consciousness. And then there is the affection that is growing in people towards the Earth. To me, this represents a major shift in collective consciousness. We so often talk about the collective unconscious, but there really is a collective consciousness that also makes major shifts.

ABE: If you were to rewrite *Goddesses in Everywoman* this year, would it include more of the spiritual aspects?

JEAN B: Well, it would be different in a couple of ways. I think there would be another archetype that I would have emphasized. I would have added the wise woman, the crone, Hecate. I didn't before because I was too young to really know it intimately enough. The other reason is that it wasn't emerging into the culture quite as much then.

ABE: Say more about Hecate. What's Hecate all about?

JEAN B: Well Hecate was a pre-Olympian goddess. She isn't emphasized very much in Greek mythology, and yet every single one of the major pathways of development in the Greek goddesses has a maiden form and a mature form. As it turns out Hecate is the last shared form. So if you're looking at the schema of the moon divinities, you go from Artemis, who is the virgin goddess, to Celine to Hecate. And you go from Persephone to Demeter to Hecate. And you go from a virgin form of Hera to Hera to Hecate. So Hecate ends up being the wise-woman crone version of what is known in all other cultures as "The Triple Goddess." The wisewoman crone in Western civilization especially got obliterated with the witch hunts. As the women's movement women, who have tapped into this archetypal layer, are growing menopausal and postmenopausal, they're tapping into this archetype, and they are getting a sense of an initial fear of it, because to claim it is to also claim the history that went with it, which was that you got burnt at the stake for having this kind of wisdom of nature, of bodies, of seasons. It's an earth wisdom that comes from having lived long enough, having suffered enough, having gotten through enough lives to have a perspective on it.

ABE: So does Hecate have a much more embodied spiritual consciousness out of her life experience?

JEAN B: Yes, there's much more a sense of the sacred dimension in everyday life, and a being present at the time of birth. She's the midwife, she's a presence when life begins and when life ends. There is something awesome and sacred and archetypal about these major transitions in life that people know who are present with a receptivity to the experience. They're in the presence of something that could be called sacred or divine, which should be presided over with some kind of priest or priestess attitude.

ABE: And this awareness is cutting across many different cultural, ethnic, and theological boundaries, it seems.

JEAN B: It really does seem to be doing that. What I see it doing is bringing up what was repressed and dismembered. It's a remembered part of the human collective psyche that comes up again to be side by side with that more left brain, linear, objective observer part. So there's a possibility as this whole archetypal realm becomes much more real to people in any form, whether it be Jungian psychology or goddess spirituality or Eastern meditation, that whatever the form it takes, it then carries the other half of our human nature. I happen to think that Jungian psychology is one of the most accessible ways to go for people who are intellectually curious and psychologically minded. There are different strokes for different folks, but if you are kind of introvertedly oriented and you've been educated in literature and other things, and you have a questing mind, then to delve into this realm I'm speaking of from a Jungian perspective is a nonthreatening way in.

ABE: Year after year, I've been watching this phenomenon right here in Toronto through being at the desk of *Dimensions* magazine, and watching how much Jungian awareness is finding its way into many aspects of culture. One would have to imagine that there must be something that is either intrinsically valuable and/or intrinsically needed by people at this time in Carl Jung's work. Twenty-five years ago, when I was a younger theosophist living in England, the joke that used to be made around occult and spiritual circles was that Carl Jung was the mystic's psychologist. But out in the mainstream Jung was very peripheralized at that point.

JEAN B: What I saw in San Francisco was that in the sixties Jung became much more accessible to young people, and this was the psychedelic period, the antiauthoritarian, anti-Viet Nam period. A whole generation of people had come into contact with this, mostly through the drug culture and through the altered state of consciousness that rock music alone provided. And during that same period, because of the Beatles, there was this whole interest in the Maharishi Mahesh Yogi and the whole Eastern meditative movement with people like Richard Alpert moving east and becoming Ram Dass, etc. So from the sixties onward there was an anti-industrial revolution happening, and Jung fit into that. Jung still doesn't fit into mainstream psychiatry. Jungian ideas and thoughts are much more pervasive in the culture generally than they are in the scientific establishment. He is still a sort of mystical, nonscientific person from their point of view.

ABE: So there's *Goddesses in Everywoman*, there's *Gods in Everyman*. You also wrote a book called *The Ring of Power*. Could you talk a little about what you're exploring in that book?

JEAN B: The book is about rejected children, their authoritarian fathers and dysfunctional families. It came out of getting totally engrossed in Wagner's *Ring of the Nibelungs*, and seeing that the characters in that story are more complex, more human forms of the great divinities that I was writing about. So Brunhilda is an Athena that has really grown in depth and conflict as a result of being moved by compassion. Wotan is a Zeus who has literally come down off the mountain to wander amongst the folks, and who, in his effort to rule the world, turns out to be a terrible father, and suffers from the difficulties he has balancing his relationship to his children with being number one in the universe. So, first of all, it was like getting immersed in figures that I knew very well from writing about gods and goddesses. And then, within *The Ring Cycle* there is this whole deeper mythology that begins with the notion that there was once a world ash tree which linked Heaven and Earth and there was harmony and there was a spring at the bottom.

ABE: Iggdrasil, with the serpent gnawing away at it.

JEAN B: It's not named that in Wagner's *Ring*. He calls it the world ash tree. And a figure that is like his version of Wotan comes and tears a branch off the tree in order to make the spear with which he will rule by law. It's right on the shaft of the spear, the contracts and treaties that will bring order to the world. When he takes that branch off the tree, the tree withers and dies, and the spring dries up. It's a whole commentary on the cost of the attempt to rule the world with law. Anyway, that's just one glimmer of it. And because I was just captivated by the music and the message, I began to want to write a small book on this. Well the trouble was that I can't write a little small book. *[laughter]* It emerged as a much more profound book than I had intended.

ABE: Do you have anything to say about "following your bliss" and psychological health?

JEAN B: Well, I think the healthiest people do follow their bliss. It sounds too light-sided, just "follow your bliss," but if you follow your bliss there is a sense of deep meaning in what you do, and it also means that you have this sense that you are living the life that you are meant to, that you're doing what you came for. It may take you through real depth and difficulties, it might estrange you from other people. So it's not all sweetness and light to "follow your bliss." If you're doing what you love, even if it's hard to do, there's a joy that comes from engaging it, and I think that psychological health does not have to do with being well adjusted in the world so much as it has to do with living from authentic depths.

ABE: One of the other things that was been widely discussed in new age and parallel circles is the emergence of a spiritual Brotherhood. I'm hearing that from so many different men now, the desire to bring together heterosexual men who are aware of what women have been going through for the last twenty years, have gone through their own stuff with that, and are now at a place where they feel that they can positively and in a very yang sort of way interact with that. I'm very happy to see that emerging and I think that's going to be a very large part of what the nineties are going to be about. I hope the dance is actually going to begin now, in that sense.

JEAN B: Oh, I think it will. And it's time for the fathers and mothers to exit and leave it to the sons and daughters. It's really a different archetype for culture when it's brothers and sisters, or sons and daughters, rather than mothers and fathers. That seems to be what's happening.

6

eastern
traditions
western
challenges

GEORG FEUERSTEIN

RAM DASS

spiritsex

DR. GEORG FEUERSTEIN

in conversation with

ALEXANDER BLAIR-EWART

Dr. Georg Feuerstein has written over twenty books on
spirituality and is a foremost scholar on the Yoga tradition. He
is a contributing editor of Yoga Journal *and* Ecstasy *magazine,*
editor of the anthology Enlightened Sexuality *(1989), and*
author of Yoga: The Technology of Ecstasy. *His two most recent*
books are entitled Sacred Sexuality: Living the Vision of the
Erotic Spirit, *(1992), and* Holy Madness: The Shock Tractics &
Radical Teachings of Crazy-Wise Adepts, Holy Fools, & Rascal
Gurus *(1992).*

ALEXANDER BLAIR-EWART: Because of the Judeo-Christian tradition
in particular, we have a lot of apprehension around the idea of a healthy,
holistic, and completely integrated sexuality. Do you think that people are
ready to rethink sexuality at this stage?

DR. GEORG FEUERSTEIN: The short answer is no. You always hope
that more people will be reached at this point than perhaps before the
sexual revolution occurred. And considering the immense number of
problems that people are facing in their sexual lives, from the guilt that we
have inherited from our traditions to performance anxiety to all the rest of
it, one would hope that by now people are looking for something that is
deeper and not simply a gimmicky technique or some good advice from a
marriage counsellor. Sex has very much to do with the rest of our very

fragmented lives. And if people want to put their lives together, sexuality certainly is a large element in that.

ABE: In the book *Sacred Sexuality* you talk about sex, love, and transcendence, and you talk about spiritual breakthrough in sex. How could that actually take place and what is it that people have to realize about sexuality that they don't currently?

DR. FEUERSTEIN: I think a whole bunch of things. Sex, for most people, is unfortunately and sadly little more than one or two hops in the hay a week. It's a very perfunctory kind of thing for most people, and the little thrill that comes with it seems to be enough compensation for many. If people want to repair their lives—and that's really what it boils down to—they have to look at all aspects of their existence, and see to what degree they live their life in a mechanical way. And then, hopefully, understand that there is quite another way of living that includes higher dimensions of existence. I'm very hopeful that more and more people will be dissatisfied with the way they obtain their sexual thrills, and understand as time goes on perhaps that they are shortchanging themseves, that there are profounder experiences of, not just thrill, but blissfulness, blissfulness beyond pleasure. And as there is more of a felt need for this kind of experience, I think people will happily reorganize their sexual lives, as well.

ABE: Would sacred sexuality represent a different approach to relationship altogether?

DR. FEUERSTEIN: Well, certainly it would. If our relationship to the ground of existence, to God if you like, is straight, all other aspects of our life will fall into place naturally. If my relationship to the ground of my existence, my higher self, is in order, then I will be a kinder person, a more compassionate person, and a person who doesn't feel separated from others.

ABE: Is there anything inherent in the worldview of sacred sexuality that would allow a man and woman who have lost their passion, engagement, and love to go through a process of rediscovery of each other, or does there have to be really intense chemistry there in the first place?

DR. FEUERSTEIN: You see, you can't repair sexual relationships on the basis of sexuality alone. I think this is a mistake some sexual counsellors make. Something much more comprehensive has to happen. The man and the woman first have to be truly intimate with one another. And they have to know each other's needs, know each other's abilities in terms of responding to each other's needs. They have to know each other's fears and hopes and so on, and have to have a basic desire to be together and to *grow* together. I think it's the commitment to growth that is important, and if the sexuality is dormant in a relationship, usually the relationship is dormant. The man and woman don't talk to one another anymore; they don't excite each other anymore; and maybe the only real interest revolves around work or children or whatever. But they are not alive anymore as people to one another. And so the relationship can't be repaired simply by saying that maybe they should consider looking at sexuality in a different way.

You can always doctor things to try to fix it, and for a while it may work out. But ultimately we are isolated beings if we don't connect up with that larger reality. So you can't start from sexuality and work towards harmony. You have to start from the disposition of harmony in order to make a change in life that includes sexuality.

ABE: In *Sacred Sexuality* you discuss various traditions including the Tantric traditions of India. Those traditions seem to be very old, and according to your account of those traditions it looks as if there are quite a number of misconceptions in the West about what Tantra actually is.

DR. FEUERSTEIN: The single most important issue here is that there is a mighty difference between Tantra, original Tantra as it is taught even now in remote areas in India, and Tantra as it is propagandized in the West. And I know there are some people out there who will hate me for this, but I make a very significant distinction between Tantrism and what I call Neo-Tantrism. Most of the Neo-Tantric teachers of whom I'm aware have not had the benefit of a teacher-disciple relationship in the way it was established long ago in India, and the way in which Tantra has been handed down for hundreds of generations. Most people learned it either from other Westerners or from books, and I think we need only look at the literature of the Neo-Tantric movement to realize that it is a very thinly disguised movement that seeks to magnify pleasure rather than recovering the bliss which is an innate aspect of our transcendent self, or the identity that is anchored in the divine.

ABE: Does the distinction have to do with the role of physical sex?

DR. FEUERSTEIN: For me, Tantric sexuality has originally been a minor aspect of Tantra. It is made into the single most important thing in Western Tantra, and I think that has to do more with our predisposition, our sexual obsession, than any spiritual orientation that is rooted or derived from original Tantra. There are many Tantric schools that recommend strict celibacy, where the whole sexual issue never even arises. The emphasis is placed entirely on rituals and ceremonies that awaken the inner power, the kundalini power, guiding it to the crown of the head, as in the tradition of Hatha Yoga, in order to accomplish what we can metaphorically describe as the sexual union between the feminine and masculine principles in the Universe. In what are known as the left-hand schools of Tantrism—there were very few of these—this union was understood in a literal sense, and the feminine aspect was manifested or was embodied by an actual human Tantric partner, a woman who was initiated into the Tantric secrets and who was in a way used for that purpose by the male initiates. Of course there were also female Tantric initiates who would use male counterparts who embodied the divine male principle in the same way.

ABE: In Western neo-Tantrism, then, the embodied sexual tendency is dominant?

DR. FEUERSTEIN: Yes it is. That seems to be the main preoccupation of Neo-Tantrism, judging from the literature and the reports I hear from different schools. I've never myself been involved in any of it, mainly because of my impression that what seems to be moving those people is the sexual interest, and it's just unworkable for most Westerners. My own recommendation in the occasional talks I give on Tantra is always that anyone who really is overly eager about finding a Tantric group or finding a Tantric sexual partner should first very carefully examine their own motivation. It's very likely that the people who want to have Tantric sexuality the most are the ones who should perhaps practise a period of celibacy for six months to find out where their sexual energies are coming from, what emotional roots there are, and whether there are other problems that should be handled first.

ABE: It's interesting to note that most people appear to react to the idea of any period of celibacy with absolute horror. Even people who are purportedly working at a spiritual way of life feel that if they don't have sex for a month something awful is happening to their lives, and if it goes on for longer than that, it's a major catastrophe.

DR. FEUERSTEIN: I think most of us are sex addicts. We wouldn't necessarily use that term, but I think that's what it boils down to. We have become addicted to that thrill, that very momentary thrill of orgasm. It's a habit, and like any habit it is very hard to break. So we suffer when we have to be celibate, especially when we are forced by circumstances—our partner dies, or we break up, or we feel guilty about masturbating—and then we experience a lot of emotional trouble. We are not used to feeling our body filled with energy. If it is our habit, say, to have two orgasms a week, which seems to be the average for North American people, and then we abstain from sexuality for a period of time, we don't know what to do with the energy. We run around like chickens with their heads cut off. Not a nice image, but that's about it. And we want to blow it off. So, given that, how could we handle the delight and the bliss that comes with a higher realization, with samadhi ecstasy? We wouldn't even know what to do with it, because it fills the whole body; it's not somewhere in the head. It's when your entire body feels utterly pleasurable and blissful.

ABE: So you're basically saying that celibacy, in the context of a person who has a reasonably good psychological balance to start with, can lead to health rather than sickness.

DR. FEUERSTEIN: Absolutely. In fact, I would say more than that. I would say that anyone who is addicted to sexuality or orgasm, in the way that most people are, is not healthy to begin with. What we consider normal is not necessarily healthy. I think the traditions are very clear on this point. There is so much psycho-energy involved in sexuality that any orgasmic discharge literally pours out vast amounts of energy that we could use to repair ourselves if we are not well, to invest in creative projects, and so on. And so we live a life that is energetically flat. We can't take, for some reason, the tremendous turmoil, which is what it would be for most people, the pressure, as Freud would say, of the libido in the body that looks for an outlet. In Freud's own case—and maybe we should learn from this—he was a tremendously creative person; he obviously was a sexually highly charged man. But most people don't know what to do with this energy, and our culture provides very little guidance. What people do is usually discharge it twice a week.

ABE: And that's true of both the man and the woman?

DR. FEUERSTEIN: Both the man and the woman. Especially now, with the small amount of liberation that has occurred through the sexual revolution, women feel that they're entitled to their orgasm as well, that something is wrong if they can't have it once or twice a week.

ABE: As a basic tenet of Tantrisms, at every level that whole obsession with ejaculation, orgasm is just completely bypassed. What's on the other side of that barrier?

DR. FEUERSTEIN: Well, let's first talk about what that energy means. For the ordinary person it manifests simply as nervous tension that has to be released to feel some kind of semblance of balance. The traditions teach us that this energy is something that goes beyond the physical body. It is a psycho-energy that wells up within us, comes from very distant regions, and it manifests as different things, from our breath to nervous energy to sexual energy. And what we have focused on culturally is sexual energy. In Tantrism and similarly in Taoism and other traditions, a different wisdom prevails. They say that if we assume that this energy is a sacred energy, we relate to it differently. For us, it's a nuisance, almost, that we have to throw off. For them, it is something very sacred that can be worked with to find our way back to our true identity, which is the higher self, that spark within the divine.

ABE: So sexual energy is rediscovered at its source. Then what happens?

DR. FEUERSTEIN: The energy that manifests on the physical level as sexuality, which is in the lower center of the body, is used, magnified even, in certain Tantric schools, either through stimulation such as looking at a naked woman, or contemplating a naked woman in her absence, or the ingestion of alcohol and mead, which are all forbidden to the Tantric practitioner in the normal course of things. And then this augmented energy is systematically guided up through the body by way of meditation and concentration, first of all to the heart center. When that energy reaches beyond the sexual center to the heart center, something happens to it. We realize that it's not sexual energy we're talking about; it is a psycho-energy, a sacred energy that simply manifests in the lower centers in a certain way.

Once we have gathered it at the heart center, we realize that this energy is something much bigger and much more valuable than sexual energy.

When it opens our heart there will be compassion, there will be all kinds of other intuitions, high-level realizations, and then we can find the wisdom to guide it beyond the heart center into the higher centers of the body, which are in the head. And there, the energy again reveals itself differently. The idea in Tantrism is to ride that energy to the crown of the head, the crown chakra, where it pierces through the head and unites with the energy that is surrounding the body and the cosmos at large. This is the marriage of what they call Shiva and Shakti, Shakti being the feminine energy within the body, Shiva being the static energy that is surrounding the body, and also of course interpenetrating it. Once this happens you realize that the entire notion of sexual energy was really an illusion. It is simply a lower level manifestation, a lower vibration of the same cosmic energy that sustains our bodies, sustains everyone's life.

ABE: So it is an essentially transformative process. You take the whole human being into this state, whereas there are other schools where you leave the body behind.

DR. FEUERSTEIN: Right. I see two major orientations within any spirituality, any tradition. First is the vertical tradition, which consists of an ascent of awareness. You identify with the higher reality while forgetting the body, forgetting in two ways. First of all, you're no longer aware of it as a separate thing. You can forget it insofar as your priority is union with that higher reality, and so the body itself is no longer given any value, and you begin to neglect it. And so you have ascetics in India who live in a high state of consciousness, but have to be fed by their disciples because otherwise they would die from hunger. The second spirituality is a much more integral spirituality. It has that ascent, but it also understands that the body and the physical world as a whole are a manifestation of that same reality that is reached or experienced through that mystical ascent. And so there isn't that separation anymore. This kind of spirituality is holistic spirituality, and is far more palatable to us moderns than the vertical type of spirituality which was very much a feature of past eras.

ABE: That holistic sexuality as you've defined it would seem to be more suitable for the kind of culture we are in where we don't have an antagonistic attitude towards the physical plane.

DR. FEUERSTEIN: If we are materialists, we have a mistaken

appreciation of it, because we regard it as *the* ultimate reality, but we can learn from the traditions that say that the physical realm is like the outermost peel of the onion, and that there are deeper and deeper layers of reality, and that, as human beings, we have the potential to discover them.

ABE: Can you say more about what is on the other side of the ejaculation orgasm sydrome?

DR. FEUERSTEIN: In orgasm, essentially, if we are honest, what we feel is a kind of tingling sensation in a very limited area. If we are more relaxed, and very few people seem to be, we can have that pleasurable sensation spread through wider areas of the body. If we are even more relaxed or particularly attuned to or in love with our partner, we might find that for a moment we have become unself-conscious in that pleasure. And very occasionally, one experiences a kind of mystical blowout in sexuality, where pleasure suddenly becomes bliss, where the body's boundaries melt, where we are no longer aware that these are our genitals having these sensations, but suddenly all these feelings and sensations are thrown wide open and we feel connected, not just to our partner, but to all of life. And the bliss that wells up inside us is the same bliss that exists forever outside us.

ABE: One reads in Tantric literature of the man and woman reaching a point where they simultaneously attain kundalini awakening through the practice. Are there many documented cases of that?

DR. FEUERSTEIN: No. I think a lot of the stuff that is reported, especially in Neo-Tantric groups, has nothing to do with kundalini awakening. Prior to kundalini awakening, there is what is called the prana arousal, where the life force in the body—not the mammoth energy of kundalini, which is a very distinct thing—but the life force that circulates in the body, that maintains the body, starts streaming. And a lot of this streaming is confused with the kundalini. For instance, you could have prana streaming, say, from the tip of your fingers up your arm, or sudden burning sensations in your hands, but that doesn't necessarily mean that the kundalini is awakened. It's a local phenomenon of prana flow.

ABE: So, is the kundalini awakening something that is so absolute, in a way, that you couldn't mistake it for anything else?

DR. FEUERSTEIN: Yes. You see, you could compare the prana streamings to an ordinary chemical bomb, whereas the kundalini is a nuclear device that's triggered by prana. In fact, in certain schools in Hatha Yoga, the idea is to focus on the lower center and also to guide the body's prana there through breath control, and then the prana acts like a stick that keeps hitting the snake, which is the kundalini. And then the snake gets angry, and what does the snake do? It rises up and hisses, which is exactly the sound that is described by people. I've never had an awakening in that sense, so I can only repeat what I've read and heard. The kundalini hisses and rises up the central channel like a snake.

ABE: There obviously are many people out there who have these experiences, but we don't hear much about it.

DR. FEUERSTEIN: In my book I give descriptions of what people have experienced in those moments. And it can happen spontaneously to people who have had no previous experience with any spiritual tradition. Very often they don't know what to do with it. They think they're out of their minds, or they're very anxious about concealing it, because they think, well, what will my partner say, what will my family say? And so we have what I call a conspiracy of silence around spiritual experiences in sexuality, and spiritual experiences generally. Very few people, even now, talk about the experiences they've had, and many people have had some amazing ones.

Just recently I made the acquaintance of a man who had a fairly full-blown kundalini experience some thirty years ago and ended up locked in a mental hospital. I was the first person he talked to about this, and the symptoms he described were very classic kundalini symptoms.

ABE: The tragedy with those symptoms is that, in the Western psychology books, a lot of them fit in rather too neatly with the description of "deluded," "paranoid schizophrenic," etc. So you have this major problem where there are many people, I think, institutionalized in mental hospitals, whose initiation has become pathologized by the surrounding culture. We victimize people who are in the process of authentic enlightenment.

DR. FEUERSTEIN: Absolutely. And that was, I think, R. D. Laing's great contribution, to suggest that maybe some of these psychotics are not just psychotics, but people undergoing genuine spiritual experiences.

ABE: Stanislov Grof has helped to evolve the Spiritual Emergency Network, an agency that helps these kinds of people. So there appear to be some glimmers.

DR. FEUERSTEIN: Yes, and in fact it's the beginning, I think, of something that will one day, hopefully not too long in the future, be recognized as a very ordinary fact, that there are some people who seemingly have psychotic breakdowns, when in effect they are spiritual breakthroughs.

still here now

RAM DASS

in conversation with

ALEXANDER BLAIR-EWART

Ram Dass (formerly Richard Alpert) has been at the forefront of the new consciousness movement since the early sixties when, while on the faculty of Harvard University, his explorations into consciousness and intensive research into psilocybin, LSD-25, and other psychedelic chemicals, in collaboration with Timothy Leary, Ralph Metzner, Aldous Huxley, Allen Ginsberg, and others, brought him controversy and a dismissal in 1963. In 1967 he travelled to India, where he met his guru, Neem Karoli Baba, who gave him the name Ram Dass. Since 1968, he has pursued a variety of spiritual practices, including devotional yoga, various Buddhist meditation practices, and Sufi practices. In 1974 he created the Hanuman Foundation, which organizes his lectures and workshops, as well as developing projects such as support for conscious dying and spiritual help for prison inmates. He is currently cofounder of the Seva Foundation, an international service organization dedicated to alleviating suffering in the world community.

Ram Dass has authored a number of books on spiritual topics, including: Be Here Now, Remember *(1971),* Journey of Awakening *(with Daniel Goleman, 1978),* How Can I Help? *(with Paul Gorman, 1985),* Grist for the Mill *(with Stephen Levine, 1987), and* Compassion in Action *(with Mirabai Bush, 1992).*

ALEXANDER BLAIR-EWART: Like so many people, I read *Be Here Now* numerous times and I still look at it occasionally. But you've come a long way from there over the years. How deeply held are your original Hindu inspirations at this point in your life, and how are those inspirations affecting what you are currently doing?

RAM DASS: When I first opened to spiritual dimensions of consciousness through psychedelics, I found the experience ineffable. I looked around for metaphors, and the metaphors that were available and very helpful to me were originally Buddhist, through the Tibetan Book of the Dead. And then that opened up into the Bhagavad Gita, the Upanishads, and the Hindu tradition. Then, of course, I went to India looking for some cartographers who could read those maps, found my Hindu guru and explored the practices of Yoga. I don't think at that point I became a Hindu. I just used those practices, and I think, as time has gone on, I've broadened the scope of my practices to embrace a lot of different traditions. I would say that the universality of the truth that underlies spiritual traditions daily infuses my life with meaning. But I wouldn't say it's primarily Hindu any longer.

ABE: There was a point when you were seen by millions of people as a major spiritual guide. Just the fact that you existed and who you had been was a very powerful thing for a lot of people. I imagine that you've gone through various stages in the evolution of guru-consciousness, and I know there are a lot of people out there currently who are reaching a sort of teacher/guru stage for the first time. What do people need to watch out for on the path to being a spiritual teacher or guru?

RAM DASS: I think that when people feel the need for spiritual growth, if they recognize that yearning as coming from an intuitive wisdom within themselves, and they seek the deepest truth, then they should just stay open to all of the things around them and keep running things by that intuitive wisdom. Each individual is unique and in that sense has to find a path and guidance that is absolutely suitable to their unique predicament. Therefore, they can't respond to somebody else telling them, "You should do this," or "This is your way," or "I did it, so you should do it." I think a person has to look at the smorgasbord of opportunities and then find that one which feels intuitively right. Once you find one and you start to do it, it doesn't mean you can stop using that intuitive criterion. You've got to keep using it. Sometimes you start on a path, you've joined the club, and everybody around you says, "Aren't you wonderful, you're one of us," and then it doesn't feel good somehow. You've got to trust that intuitive feeling, even if the situation is very pure. I think the response "This method/person/ technique and I have no business with one another at this moment" is the statement you'd make. You don't have to judge that the method or the guru is impure or anything. You just say, "In my intuitive heart I don't feel there's any work here at this moment." And if you trust that, that's a good protection.

ABE: Is a guru or teacher essential?

RAM DASS: In India they say, "God, guru, and self are one." Whether you follow the path of devotion to God and study the Word of God, or whether you follow the path of finding a being who reflects the ultimate truth and then form an emotional relationship that helps you mirror your own impurities, or whether you go deep within yourself, you can get spirituality through all kinds of methods. So, if you don't have an external guru, you certainly don't have to worry about it. It's not going to slow you down. It's wonderful to have a being that is a good mirror, but you certainly don't need it.

ABE: A lot of people, including Ken Wilber and Dick Anthony, have looked at the transpersonal psychological stages that the ego of a Westerner goes through in the process of becoming "enlightened" and then becoming a spiritual source for other people. And there definitely seem to be stages of ego-inflation involved in that. I'm wondering if I can get you to talk about that process, and how you came out the other end of it, which you obviously have.

RAM DASS: Well, I don't think I've come out of it completely. I don't think, until the last gasp before the moment of full enlightenment, is one ever free of some ego in the way in which one pursues one's spiritual path. At the beginning of spiritual seeking, the choices we make are very much in the service of our ego structures and needs. But as the practices work, one begins to extricate one's awareness from identification with the structures of ego and starts to connect to the deeper truth that lies within one's awareness, or behind the phenomenology of self. So, in a way, you're using leverage to push against the actual structure that got you into the game in the first place. And it's really fascinating to see that. I mean, I may have been chosen, or was attracted to, and dropped into the slot of being a chela or disciple to my guru because of my need for that kind of a father figure, psychologically. But as the process goes onward that particular motivation becomes somewhat irrelevant, and what you're left with is the purer and purer essence of what that connection is.

ABE: I wonder to what extent it becomes possible for people to be able to take a reality check on their ego at a stage where they feel that it isn't really that present?

RAM DASS: I'll tell you what I do. First of all, I surround myself as much as I can with people who bust me, who are *satsang* (speakers of truth), or *sangha* (holy family), a community of beings, whether they're teachers in various traditions or the people I work with. And the nature of the contract that I have with the people I work with is, "Look, I have lots of ego. When you see it getting in the way, and me not seeing it, would you point it out to me? I'll hate you for doing it, but I still want you to do it. And let's be good enough friends so that you can withstand my lashing out at you for doing it." Then, of course, when I go and study with a teacher, I open as far as I can to what the teacher's technique leads me to, and often that shows me my own way of manipulating the game for my ego protection, because the ego dies very hard. You're not trying to kill your ego; you're just trying to kill the power it has over you.

ABE: A number of thinkers and writers have said that the primary sickness of the West is ego-sickness, that there is this tremendous isolation and a sense of unwarranted competitiveness among people at levels where it just shouldn't be. Do you see that as being the reality of the Western world at this stage?

RAM DASS: I do. I think I would phrase it slightly differently, though. I would call it individuality, that which we represent which is separate and unique, in terms of the multiple planes of our identity, and that which is also part of the whole. When the balance gets out of whack we get so preoccupied with our separateness that we lose that part of our consciousness that is one with all things. And once we get into the separateness, which is the ego of boundaries, self versus other, we get very frightened, because that separateness is very little and the forces around us are very great, whether they be parents, culture, floods, or whatever. So we build a whole structure of life based on that fear, or based on trying to ameliorate that fear. Once we come into the balance, where we are rooted in our interconnectedness with everything, in terms of community and in terms of unity with spirit, we can then honor our uniqueness without being frightened, because we are never away from home; we're always still part of it all. And that balance is, to me, where the full human potential is realized. I think that the way we've screwed up in terms of ecological issues has been through our separateness, not realizing that we're part of a symbiotic community.

ABE: Do you see the rise of spiritualized feminism, if I can call it that, as being an actual and real healing force in the face of that collective condition?

RAM DASS: Well, there have been certain kinds of mythic structures in our society that have identified men with rationality and women with intuitive wisdom. I see the rise of the recognition and acknowledgment and respect for intuitive wisdom as an incredibly valuable asset for us. My sense is that ultimately all of us have all of it, and on the social level I think women have been kept by cultural structures from contributing and being respected, not allowed to bring in their full potential to make society richer. And I'm delighting in the way in which women are finding a voice, and that wisdom, if it is respected, enriches the culture immensely.

We got out of hand. We got to thinking that our prefrontal lobe and the science and technology it spawned would be our salvation. I think there's an awareness now that our minds just keep screwing things up; we don't get out of it through our mind.

ABE: The earlier Baba Ram Dass, or Richard Alpert, was very strongly associated in the minds of millions of people with "non-ordinary realities." I'm wondering to what extent that other side of life is a part of your life now, after what must be nearly three decades of meditating and engaging in many diverse spiritual practices?

RAM DASS: I would say that the past thirty years have been an attempt to integrate planes of consciousness, or altered states, with normal waking consciousness. At first my earlier work was involved with going out into these altered states, these other planes, astral, causal, whatever you want to call them. And then I began to come back and slowly figure out how to integrate them. At first one does it all sequentially. But over the years I kept working at it by going in and out and in and out through all my practices, to try to find a way to have it all more or less simultaneous.

ABE: Does an example of this integrated awareness come to mind?

RAM DASS: Yesterday I was with somebody who was dying of AIDS—he died last night—I knew and had worked with him for a number of years and I loved him very much. So, at the emotional/personal level, my heart is hurting because I'm losing a friend, and at the deeper level of my being I'm watching the beauty of the Law unfolding and the transformation happening. At a deeper level still, it's all empty form. And all of these things are true at the same moment. When I've stopped needing to alight with my awareness in one place or another, it's all there all at once, and it's kind of a gestalt that integrates the planes of consciousness. It's far out to feel the pain of loss and the joy at the same moment. At first you think something's wrong; you're supposed to be feeling one or the other.

ABE: Do you, then, feel that there is some sense of personal immortality, or that whatever God bit that we are simply goes back into the All or the One?

RAM DASS: Well, there is certainly a part of us that has never left the One, that is just the One manifested in a unique form on certain planes, in which, when you identify with that uniqueness, you lose sight of that part that isn't so identified. So, in one way, nothing's happening, and there's no time, and so it's all a hype at that level. In terms of where you go after you die, I really experience transmigration as a function of the level of karmic evolution, and so there are beings who carry from birth to birth a kind of unique psychic DNA that probably projects them because of their thoughtforms into a continuity of uniqueness for many many rounds, until it gets so subtle and so light, and there is no karma being created, that at that moment when they drop their body there's no grabbing towards something else. At that moment the awareness is just back being the same awareness that is in trees and rocks and earth. If you stand outside of time that whole evolutionary cycle, which could take, in Hindu terminology, Kalpas and Yugas...

ABE: ...fifteen figure numbers, right?...

RAM DASS: Yeah. It happens in just a blink of the eye, and in the final sense nothing happened because there's no movement. So, I'm playing at all those levels all at once.

ABE: We have the insight that the ego is limiting, and at the same time, out of that awareness of the One, something that we could call compassion begins to germinate in us. And I wonder if it's from that perspective that you have arrived at what your current life is about?

RAM DASS: Well, my book *Compassion and Action* autobiographically is just about that issue, spelling out that transformation. And I think it's absolutely true that as you experience that which lies behind your separateness and other people's separateness, you ask not for whom the bell tolls; you realize that the hurt in the world is our hurt, and you find yourself drawn more and more towards those actions which release suffering wherever it is. You feel, as you're being an instrument for that, constantly dissolving into deeper and deeper harmonious ways of being in the world. Now, when you look at me from the outside, you say, "Isn't he a good, compassionate, kind, serving person?" because all I do is serve. At another level that has nothing to do with what is going on inside. Inside I'm just getting off on it. *[laughter]* It's an incredible rush. I just love it.

ABE: That's an important distinction you're making there, because in the West, particularly since the time of Kant, the whole idea has been to do your duty, regardless of how you feel when you're doing it. So you're saying that the love and the enthusiasm for what you're doing has to be there or it isn't quite real?

RAM DASS: I think that there are stages. In the early stages you do acts of compassion, partly out of righteousness, to be a good person, to see yourself as a good person, to do your duty—my *dharma*, my obligation. But I think at the levels where the surrender gets deeper there is none of that left. It's merely just a part. It's just like trees giving off leaves and rivers flowing downstream. The river isn't saying, "Aren't I good to flow downstream?" or "I must," or "It's my duty."

ABE: A lot of people feel that they would like to do some kind of service. But on the other hand, they're afraid of being gullible or maybe being taken advantage of. How does discrimination play into this highly enjoyable act of compassion?

RAM DASS: Intuitively, when you're quiet enough so that you're allowing intuitive wisdom to guide you, rather than linear, analytic, intellectual discrimination, there is a sense in which you understand the gestalt of the existential moment, which includes all of the forces acting upon you, historically, physically, socially, psychologically, spiritually, and you couldn't ever rationally weigh all that stuff. But you can intuitively, out of that, arrive at an act that feels appropriate, harmonious. And that may include setting boundaries on what you can do and what you can't do. At certain stages the ego needs to be fed, and at other stages it's more or less irrelevant. And you can't make believe it's one when it's the other. You can't get a model of "I wish I were Christ or Buddha, and therefore I will act as if I am and it will all be all right," because you might end up as what I call just a "horny celibate" *[laughter]*, somebody busy *not doing* something. So there is a timing for different levels of compassion, and you've just got to know, you've got to listen again and again to know what boundaries you set, because it doesn't pay to burn out and get angry and then get to hate everybody you're serving. I mean, that obviously isn't "healing the world."

ABE: In terms of meditative states in relation to discrimination, do you think there really is a state where, as the mind clears and you become more centered, more in touch with the reality of the One, it becomes possible to actually comprehend other people's motives?

RAM DASS: Oh, I think absolutely there is. The quieter you are, the less you are identified with any time/space locus you're standing in, the more you are everything around you and you are their motives as well as your own. Once you get out of the trap of time and space and into those planes of awareness where you are one with everything, then the ability to focus on any point would tune you into their motives, and if you have the power to bring it into consciousness, you would know that you knew their motives. Or you can leave it at the intuitive level, where you just respond from an understanding of their motives without knowing that you know it.

ABE: Which is the wiser course, do you think?

RAM DASS: I think the wiser course is to respond without knowing you know it. The whole issue of having "powers" is tricky business, a very risky game.

ABE: The *siddhis* (psychic abilities or powers).

RAM DASS: As my guru said in his charming and rascally way, "Siddhis are pig shit" *[laughter]*—he, out of whom miracles poured continuously. But he wasn't busy doing them. They just were there. That's different.

ABE: And yet, as you know, in the new age movement, for instance, and in a lot of contemporary spiritual movements, this pig shit seems to mesmerize an awful lot of people.

RAM DASS: But that's all ego. There's a huge amount of ego in the new age movement. It's everybody enjoying the "powers." I mean, if you move from powers of, say, psychology to powers of astrology, and knowing stuff about people because of their astrological profile, you feel you've got more power than you had before. Power is the third chakra; it's not that interesting. I think Westerners are obsessed with power because they feel so tiny, because they got caught in their separateness.

ABE: When we speak of compassion and service in the West, what is triggered for people is our Judeo-Christian past, which was a very romantic past—I think it was Nietzsche who described Christianity as "Platonism for the masses"—so that we have these romantic feelings about having an ideal society. What would be the distinctions between this approach that we're speaking of here, and that more traditional romanticized idealism about how society should be?

RAM DASS: I think the romanticized one that you're speaking about is product-oriented, and what we're doing is process-oriented, that is, you end up being what you are, and out of it comes what comes. You don't do it necessarily to bring about a certain end. You do it because it is appropriate action. But you don't know how it's all going to come out, and you don't even know whether how it comes out, which isn't the way you think it should come out, won't be better. So you're not holding a model of the end product and then manipulating things to get them there, which is a way of turning everything into an object to be manipulated.

ABE: We tend to think about social change as activism that has a goal. Now, you are highly active and what is in the book *Compassion in Action* is about action. What is the difference there?

RAM DASS: I think the difference is in the stance and the investment. For example, when we went to Guatemala we had enough money for four villages. But there were thirteen villages that were starving. And we just didn't have the money for all of them. So we said, "Well, we'll give to four this year and we'll give to the other nine next year, if we can." And the Guatemalans said, "Well, if you give us for the four, we're going to divide it up among all thirteen." And we said, "Well, that isn't necessarily the wisest strategy for people to stay alive." And they said, "Well, you don't understand. In our holy book, it says that when you're walking along and somebody falls down, you help them up and everybody walks a little slower."

ABE: How do you resolve those differences?

RAM DASS: What we've learned over and over again in our work with other human beings is a listening, collaborative approach, rather than having a fixed model of how it's to come out. In Nepal, where we work with blindness, we say, well, we'll put in educational systems because a lot of women in the villages don't realize that there is cataract surgery available, and they could see again. And as we go into education programs, we find out that a lot of people think that when you get old you go blind and that's fine, and they don't want to do anything about it. Do we say, "You've got to do something about it, because we have a model that seeing is better than blindness"? Or, maybe, as they go blind, they find a new role in the society, and what the hell, that's no worse than anybody else's life. So, it teaches us, in a way, a humility about our own models of reality that I think is extremely important for us. At the same time you do aim to eradicate needless suffering, and you can have a model that says "blindness is suffering," but you can't have it so rigidly that you force everything into it.

ABE: You spoke a moment ago about the ego that has been in the new age movement and the immature involvement with "powers." Do you see that as being a natural process, in the sense that people become first involved at an ego-inflated level, but that because they have gotten involved, they will go through these changes and become more mature spiritual beings?

RAM DASS: I think that's absolutely true. There is a confrontational moment that we are facing currently in this period of the nineties, where the uncertainty about lifestyle and longevity that's created by ecological imbalances, economics, political and social instability is forcing people to see the way in which part of their zeal to get into other planes has had a denial root in it. And they realize, I think, the same thing that I felt, that getting high isn't the same as getting free, and that finally you would like to be free more than you would like to be high. And you just can't push anything away. I think the "la la land" world of spirituality is giving way now to a much deeper kind of karma yoga, or groundedness. You know, the pendulum flips back and forth, and when it's reactive it often has a negative component. People can say, "Oh, all that spiritual stuff was bullshit, and I've got to get back to what's real," which is just as much a mistake as saying, "The spiritual dimensions are everything and the rest is an illusion." I think you've got to see these as all relatively real and also relatively not real.

ABE: In the aftermath of a collapsed culture, which I think we are in and have been in for a long time now, we seem collectively to be wandering around in a kind of no-man's-land, looking for pathways across it, but mostly going around in circles. In a larger collective sense, do you see us as already beginning to cross over out of that sense of lostness into a new reality? Or is it that we are just at the very beginning of going into the valley of disillusionment?

RAM DASS: Oh, I think we're at the beginning. It's going to get much more colorful, and that's why these are very exciting times. We've got to go a long way to find a new balance that allows us to be perfectly poised between life and death, between future and no future, between lifestyle changes and holding on, between chaos and cosmos, between the formless and the formed. In all these tensions, we have to find our balance, so that we're not trapped in one and therefore frightened by the other. And I feel that it has to do with a kind of cultural readiness, as well as the purity of the message. If a culture is ready, I don't know whether there has to be a traumatic opening or just some moment, some little window of opportunity, through which that message of purity, that new journey, can sweep through collective consciousness. And I think we're just beginning on that journey now.

who are we?
what are we?

ADAM CRABTREE

ELISABETH KÜBLER-ROSS

JEAN HOUSTON

multiple man

ADAM CRABTREE

in conversation with

ALEXANDER BLAIR-EWART

Author of Multiple Man: Explorations in Possession and Multiple Personality *(1985), Adam Crabtree has been a practising therapist for more than twenty years. A frequent guest lecturer and teacher, Crabtree has written and narrated radio programs for CBC's* Ideas *("The Enchanted Boundary"), as well as produced a series of seventeen programs for educational radio entitled* Mysteries of the Mind. *His most recent book is entitled* Magnetic Sleep: Mesmer & the Roots of Psychological Healing *(1993).*

ALEXANDER BLAIR-EWART: One of the issues that has certainly come up for a lot of people exploring the new age movement is the relationship between channeling and multiple personality disorder, and the fact that since Freud we have been progressively finding out that the human being is more and more complicated than we used to think.

ADAM CRABTREE: For me, the history of this goes back long before Freud. It actually goes back to Mesmer, who developed animal magnetism, and out of that grew hypnotism as an art. That was really the uncovering of an unconscious or subconscious world and multiple streams of thought in that subconscious world. Freud came in after about a hundred years of that investigation had already taken place and he really didn't add anything significant in terms of the architecture of that. What he added was a way of understanding the unconscious in terms of emotional conflict and so forth, which is, of course, extremely important.

ABE: He had a tremendous aversion, didn't he, for anything on the hidden side of the human being, the occult or whatever you want to call it?

ADAM C: To my knowledge he avoided it. Some people have surmised that he had an interest that he could not follow partly because he was already engaged in things that were controversial enough.

ABE: If the human being is functional or living on many levels of awareness, and there seem to be more and more levels opening up all the time, our view of what a human being is must be undergoing an incredible assault.

ADAM C: Yes, that's right. That assault was already taking place in the 1870s and 1880s and Pierre Janet was right in the middle dealing with it, because he actually said that there can be many streams of consciousness, of subconscious processes of thought, unknown to the person, and they can all be going on simultaneously. That was a huge statement to make because it certainly breaks down the notion of our being simple beings with a mind, and that we know what's going on in it.

ABE: What would be an example of that?

ADAM C: Well, he dealt with quite a few women who had disturbances of consciousness that today we would call dissociation, and he invented the word dissociation actually out of those experiences. These were people who would alternate back and forth between states of mind. In some cases they were multiple personalities and those states were different personalities. What was pretty clear from the point of view of our interest in channeling or anything related to that kind of phenomenon is that these streams of consciousness were not coming and going one after the other. They were actually existing side by side or simultaneously within the individual. He found in his experiments with people who had various personalities that each one of these personalities had a mental life. In the last ten to fifteen years of multiple personality disorder work, this is one thing that becomes very obvious, that there are simultaneous streams of consciousness, one for each of the operating personalities.

ABE: And each one has, for instance, different handwriting?

ADAM C : They can, yes.

ABE : It is also suggested that they tend to originate, as far as the person herself is aware, or the personalities themselves are aware, either at the point of this lifetime's birth or at a later date. If I understand this correctly, that's one of the ways of telling the difference between multiple personality disorder and, say, someone channeling an entity. Yet it doesn't seem terribly reliable to me.

ADAM C : There is a problem here. In my work with multiple personality disorder usually it is quite possible to trace the origin of a personality to a specific moment in the individual's history. Now, they often begin around age two, three, or four, and then continue to be formed for any length of time and sometimes throughout life. A person can have many, many personalities. You can trace the origin, and it is often the case that the new personality was formed to handle a difficult situation, a specific trauma, sexual or physical abuse. But you haven't really solved the problem, unfortunately. You still haven't solved the problem of: is that personality something that is then created from scratch within the individual in some mysterious, unconscious way, or is it a pre-existing personality, let's say a past-life personality or even, heaven forbid, a personality from, let's say, a wandering spirit of some kind, not previously involved with the individual? I say "heaven forbid" because this is so hard to accept in our conventional thinking, but I have seen a couple of instances that make me really take that possibility seriously. You would probably be interested to read Chris Sizemore's book called *A Mind of My Own* because in this book, Chris, who is Eve of *The Three Faces of Eve,* says something that really struck me. She is now one personality. She has been integrated, but she has come to the conclusion that these personalities were with her at birth.

ABE : What does that mean for her?

ADAM C : In other words, it looks like her own personal experience of her multiplicity is that these are past-life personalities. For someone to say that in this field is pretty startling. Even though she is not a doctor of psychiatry, she has a lot of stature in this field. People do listen to her.

ABE : In the mystical schools the person who is undergoing spiritual development is told there will come a point when they will start to remember or experience feelings from other lives, and that the biggest problem at that stage will be to hold yourself all in one piece, because you will be assailed by emotions from different parts of time. You will have this experience of being pulled into several pieces and that only through training in personality integration is the neophyte likely to survive that level of initiation. It seems that a lot of people who are diagnosed as schizophrenic, for instance, seem to be having a very mystical kind of experience, but are unable to hold their integration while they are going through it. Are there parallels there? Is the gap closing between what we are finding through Western research and those older traditions?

ADAM C: As of yet, in terms of the conventional workers in the field of mental health, there is still quite a gap. There is a comparison to be drawn here in what's happening in the investigation of multiple personality disorder and what you were saying earlier about Freud, in that the people who work with multiple personality disorders have had a very hard fight over the last ten to fifteen years to get the disorder recognized and accepted as a real disorder. There has been an amazing, very strange resistance on the part of the psychiatric and psychological world to accept this disorder even though the evidence for it is undeniable.

ABE: Why do you think that resistance is there?

ADAM C: Well, I have my own personal theory about that. I think it is because there is an unspoken, unconscious fear that to accept multiple personality disorder is like accepting multiple souls or spirits in a person, rather than just accepting multiple parts, which is the way psychiatrists who work with it present it.

ABE: So there is a kind of identity crisis there?

ADAM C: I think so.

ABE: As in, who is the real Adam Crabtree and who is the real Alexander Blair-Ewart? Well, who knows?

ADAM C: Yes. You have that problem no matter which side of the fence you stand on. That is, no matter whether you accept the personalities as parts of one individual or from other lifetimes, or spirits, you have the same problem of who the real one is. Because even if you accept these things as parts, it is hard to say sometimes who is central or who has the inside track on the identity of the individual.

ABE: Psychology was originally rooted in metaphysics, wasn't it, and it sort of got moved away from it and pushed more in the direction of anthropology and so on, and because there is no metaphysical underpinning that's agreed upon in any way in psychology and psychiatry, we have a kind of crisis now.

ADAM C: Yes, I think that is true. I think that this condition more than any other disorder challenges our view of what human beings are. That is actually why I wrote the book *Multiple Man*, because I felt that multiple personality disorder is a window into human nature that is unique and challenges a lot of things we don't ordinarily think about.

ABE: It is interesting that what personality means now is different, and that the personality has undergone an incredible revolution in the last hundred years through, for instance, the media. There are vast numbers of people all around us who wish they were actors and who actually are acting a lot of the time. So we have a culture that encourages this and in looking at channeling there is a level there where it is almost as if human beings are turning into a form of media.

ADAM C: Yes, that is right. My attempt to understand the phenomenon of channeling has been, in my own estimation, only very partially successful. The way I explain it to myself is that if others, let's say, who are not part of my own personality or part of my own past lives, but others outside of that line of experience, are going to talk through me or somehow manifest through me, then there must be something in my very nature that allows me to do this. There must be some way that I am so malleable that I can, at least temporarily, become somebody else and do it very well. It is as if a part of me, analogous to a past-life personality, can become an outside personality, at least temporarily. That's the closest I have been able to come to try to say something about what is going on in the structure of the human psyche with channeling. It's complicated by the problem that we can act from our own unconscious. In other words, it is possible and I believe that it does happen, that we can form personalities, or let's say, become actors in a certain persona because of something unconscious that wants to express itself, and not necessarily because of another existence or because of an outside entity.

So there is the problem of credibility, or how does one judge the credentials of the purported entity who is coming through? It might be that the individual who is doing it doesn't have any doubt, but for those on the outside it seems like to a large extent they have to rely on cogency and maybe even, let's say, predictions coming true, evidence of that kind, or some paranormal productions that all add up to conviction. And maybe that's good enough for most people. For me, I have difficulty with this. But I don't at all deny the possibility that channeling, or some channeling, does have something to do with another outside "entity" expressing or manifesting through an individual.

ABE: I am completely convinced of that myself, that that phenomenon can happen and does happen, and is probably happening a lot more than we publicly acknowledge.

ADAM C: The problem lies in judging any individual case. Every case becomes somewhat problematic.

ABE: Yes, because we are dealing with human beings. So you can't standardize.

ADAM C: Yes, that's right.

ABE: So we are saying here, then, that possession, if that isn't too sensational a word to use here, is possible and that there is some evidence to point to the fact that it can happen and that it does happen.

ADAM C: Yes, definitely.

ABE: What does it mean for us if our culture develops an interest or sympathy towards something like channeling, where the possibility of possession is opened up?

ADAM C: I don't know, because that requires a judgment on the culture and society today. I think there have been cultures in the past who have certainly accepted this fairly easily, the notion of "possession" and "prophecy." But I think the fact that we are accepting it today, I hope in addition to whatever degree it arises from insecurity and looking for answers more ardently than before, that it also means there has been some progression towards self-exploration on the level of the psyche. When I read things from earlier sources, let's say, a century ago in the area of psychotherapy and psychology and so forth, I do believe that there has been an advance in inner awareness generally in the world.

ABE: Oh absolutely.

ADAM C: Maybe part of the reason that about 25 or 30% of the population actually believes in these things is that to some degree we are becoming more experientially aware of the depths of our psyche.

ABE: I am quite aware I am making a value judgment when I say this, but one of the criteria that I have used to orient myself towards the phenomenon of channeling is the criterion of integration versus disintegration. The more integrated somebody is, the healthier they are, the more disintegrated, the more unhealthy they are. It seems to me that channeling encourages a disintegrative process.

ADAM C: It seems to me that it does, too. I don't see how it could be any other way.

ABE: In that sense channeling worries me. What I mean by channeling is deep-trance channeling, where someone is unconscious and another entity is using their body in some way or another to communicate with other people. I have this deep sense that in a way it doesn't matter what that entity is saying, that something that shouldn't be happening is happening, namely possession. At the same time I am aware that I am deeply conditioned by a Christian background.

ADAM C: Yes.

ABE: One of the questions is where does the channeler go while the channeled entity is using their body?

ADAM C: A question that has never been answered to my knowledge at all satisfactorily. When you study the equivalent of channeling a hundred years ago, one of the most interesting parallels to modern channeling, I think, is

William Stainton Moses. William Stainton Moses himself felt a little bit uneasy with these entities who expressed themselves through him. He questioned them, wondered if they were really who they purported to be, and so forth. But when you read what they had to say, they are in about the top 5%, I would say, in terms of quality, because so much of the outpourings you got a century ago and what you are getting today is pretty poor. You are not really learning that much and some of it is sort of silly.

ABE: Pious pablum.

ADAM C: Yes, and so you don't feel a lot of confidence. To me, this is one of the problems that I have with channeling. I find it hard to get interested in the content. The phenomenon I have an interest in, but the content very often isn't enough to hold my interest. I get better content from people who are living. And so why would I be drawn to this? I think that one of the reasons that people are really interested in channeling perhaps hasn't as much to do with the content as the fact that it is happening.

ABE: Yes. There is some miraculous or mystical process going on.

ADAM C: Exactly. Now with regard to the business of where somebody goes when they are channeling, the very same problem happens with most cases of multiple personality disorder. When another personality takes over, the host or original personality goes away and is not aware of what is going on, and when it comes back, it is not aware of having been anywhere. This is one of the reasons why many do not know they are multiples, because all they know is there is a blank in time. They haven't been anywhere else. There is just a blank. Now that's the case only for the birth personality. Usually the other personality—and there can be ten, twenty, thirty other personalities in an individual—will be aware of what's going on when others are out, or they can be if they want to, if they want to bother to pay attention. They have the sense that they are somewhere all the time. Inside they have their spaces and their places and their activities.

So there is a parallel in multiple personality disorder in that the earth personality or the host personality has the same kind of "Where do I go when these others are in control?" that many mediums had, like the nineteenth-century medium Leonora Piper, for instance. She was not aware of being anywhere, I believe, when she was channeling or someone was talking or writing through her. To my knowledge that has never been satisfactorily answered. Why should it be, for instance—if you can use multiple personality as a way of looking more deeply into this—why should it be that only the central personality has the blank? With the many multiples that I have worked with, that is a question I have not been able to answer. Now, there are exceptions. There are some multiples where the one who appears to be the birth personality also has awareness when others are out. These are very highly developed multiples, where they are functioning quite well, and the personalities cooperate with each other, and so forth. But there could be a question there of whether you are really dealing with a birth personality at all, or whether the individual thinks they are because they go back a long way. There is a question there and in my mind it is still completely unanswered.

ABE: If I sit down to meditate, I'm pulling my awareness away from all my worldly concerns, away from everything to do with other people, in a way, and focusing myself on, say, a very, very deep level of relaxation. The interesting thing with that is the more I do it, the more I feel integrated, the more I feel well, and the more I feel I have access to all of my memories at every level. I don't see that process working in channeling, for instance, where there is simply a blackout, really, on the part of the human being and then this other thing happens. What I find distressing is the apparent lack of curiosity on the part of the channelers themselves about the psychology of what is actually happening to them.

ADAM C: Yes. And that corresponds to multiple personality disorder, too, because people who dissociate easily in this way often don't have much curiosity about it. They just accept it and don't explore it as a phenomenon.

ABE: Which again is a very strange thing, that on one hand you have people claiming that through these means they are able to reach deeper levels of reality, understanding, knowingness, and life wisdom, and yet at the same time there is a sort of aphasia towards the actual functioning of the process. Why have human beings reached this stage now where the critical faculty is not working?

ADAM C: Well, I think that the critical faculty has always been not working. [laughter] I think that it just depends on who you are talking to. For instance, mediums have always been remarkably uninterested in looking at themselves.

ABÉ: So the question arises then—is channeling dangerous?

ADAM C: Is it dangerous? I don't think so. I don't think I could call it dangerous. I think it runs the spectrum from being an obstacle to having a full life, to maybe for some people actually being a positive experience. I don't know enough people who are engaged in it to judge that, but from what I have seen and have read of it, from what I know about people who dissociate, that dissociation can be present in degrees in people's lives, but I don't think it is dangerous. I haven't heard of cases of possession that are really destructive, and this surprises me because I still work with people who have very bad possession experiences from, say, the Ouija board and automatic writing. But I haven't had anybody come to me yet who was one of these bad cases from channeling. Now if that were happening from channeling, then I would say it can be dangerous. In regards to my own particular bent as a psychotherapist and historian, my main interest has always been dissociation in all its forms, and I think this is a really interesting recent type of dissociation, and that we can learn from it. I am sure we can learn from it by studying it.

on life
after death

DR. ELISABETH KÜBLER-ROSS
in conversation with
VALERIE ELIA

Over the past twenty years, Dr. Elisabeth Kübler-Ross has studied more than twenty thousand people who have had near-death experiences. Her book On Death and Dying *(1969) became an international best-seller and her cutting-edge work in the field of death, dying, and transition has brought her both acclaim and intense criticism. She is also the author of* To Live Until We Say Good-bye *(1987),* AIDS: The Ultimate Challenge *(1987), and* Questions and Answers on Death and Dying *(1974). In her book* On Life After Death *(1991), she draws from her experiences with her dying patients to talk about what happens at death and how that knowledge can change how we live.*

VALERIE ELIA: After helping thousands of people face death and the process of dying, what comes after is no longer a mystery to you. You describe the distinct stages of shedding the human body, the ability to perceive everything happening at the place of dying, and you suggest that we don't die alone. And you say it so definitively. I wonder how you answer your critics who see this as fantasy.

ELISABETH KÜBLER-ROSS: Well, it's the difference between believing something and knowing something. I have done research on this for fifteen years, and I know it beyond a shadow of a doubt. Every step that people experience in near-death experience you can verify.

VALERIE E: How can you do that?

ELISABETH K-R: Well, to find out that people are whole again when they shed their physical body, we interviewed blind people who had no light perception for ten years or longer. We asked them what they saw during their near-death experience and they could tell you what kind of clothes people were wearing, what kind of jewelry, wristband, glass frames, everything. Then, when brought back to life, they were again blind as a bat.

VALERIE E: And what about this concept of meeting your loved ones at the point of death?

ELISABETH K-R: That is the easiest to verify. I checked with children who were involved in family car accidents, in which most, but not all, of the people had been killed. And children who are seriously injured are always shipped to trauma units, burn units, or ICUs, and they're not told who was killed at the scene of the accident. I visit them about two or three days before they die. At a certain point psychophysiological changes take place in them. For example, when they're in a coma, they wake up; or when they have been very restless, they suddenly become very peaceful. And then I sit with them and I ask them, "Can you share with me what you experienced?" And they look through you, not at you. It's like they're checking you out as to what motivates you to ask that question. Then they say, very calmly and with incredible serenity, "Everything's good now, everything's all right. Mommy and Peter are already waiting for me." In fifteen years I have not had a single child who did not somehow know when a family member had preceded them in death.

VALERIE E: So this child knows that members of her family have died, and that information is not known to you?

ELISABETH K-R: That's right. The children were not informed. Everybody keeps it secret, because they're afraid that if the child knows that mommy died, they may give up hope and not fight to stay alive.

VALERIE E: You once said that children who are dying are different from healthy children, and also different from adults who are dying.

ELISABETH K-R: Only children who have been ill for a long time are different because in proportion to how many years they have been sick or suffering, their spiritual quadrant opens up much earlier than in healthy, average children, where this cannot occur (normally) until they're teenagers. But, if you have a nine-year-old boy who has had leukemia since age three, two-thirds of his life has been spent in that hospital, missing school, his friends, a lot of suffering. And that enhances the premature development of the spiritual quadrant. That's why dying children who have been ill for a long period are very different kinds of children from those who are hit suddenly by a car and die quickly.

VALERIE E: You talk about some of these children having out-of-body experiences. Do they share those experiences with their parents?

ELISABETH K-R: It depends on the kind of parents they have. Most of my children have been able to share their experiences with their parents.

VALERIE E: Is this not threatening to them?

ELISABETH K-R: Well, for some people it is, but I think they're also prepared by the illness of the child, and they're open to different things that they would not have been open to before.

VALERIE E: It's so difficult to contemplate the death of a child. Why do you think that some are born to spend only a few years on earth?

ELISABETH K-R: I think little children who die young come to planet Earth as teachers. And the death of a child is an incredible teacher. People change totally, like 180 degrees.

VALERIE E: And do you see them as "the chosen," then, and not the unfortunate ones?

ELISABETH K-R: They're not the unfortunate ones. They only have to stay in "school" for a short time, while us old bags have to learn for fifty, seventy, ninety years. *[laughter]*

VALERIE E: So, in fact, they have learned so much that they can leave quickly.

ELISABETH K-R: Yes. Or, they come for one specific purpose, to help a parent grow compassion, love, or understanding.

VALERIE E: What do you feel about the never-born? How do you view abortion?

ELISABETH K-R: As though it's a part of God, and God has all knowledge. Do you think a soul would be so ignorant as to pick a womb where they know that they'll never have a chance for a physical life? Life on planet Earth is nothing else but the school where you learn to grow spiritually and to enhance your chance to eventually return to God. Abortion is the destruction of a temple that is being prepared to house the soul. No child with all knowledge of God would pick a womb where they know the parents are planning already to get rid of the temple which is being prepared for that soul.

VALERIE E: It's also through children, I believe, that you have learned about guardian angels, certainly a Sunday School fantasy for many people.

ELISABETH K-R: Millions of children talk to their playmates. And then when they go to first grade, a mom or a dad says, "Don't talk to these imaginary friends. You're a big boy (or a big girl) now." And that shuts them up. But then, when they're dying, they again become aware of these beings and they continue to talk with them.

VALERIE E: Does each person have a guardian angel?

ELISABETH K-R: Yes.

VALERIE E: What is the role that they play in our lives? Obviously they don't help us avoid tragedies.

ELISABETH K-R: No, but see, what they're not allowed to do is to interfere with your free choice. Free choice is the biggest gift God gave to us. But we are responsible for all our choices and their consequences. Tragedies are opportunities to grow and to learn while you're in the physical body. Would you really want a life where everything is served to you on a silver platter and there are no wind storms?

VALERIE E: And the guides are there to console us?

ELISABETH K-R: They're guiding you, they're connecting you with the right people at the right time at the right place. They're literally guiding you to keep on the main track, so that you can fulfill the mission or purpose that you chose before you were born.

VALERIE E: If we connect that to Carl Jung's concept of synchronicity, could we say that the guardian angel is helping us to acknowledge that synchronistic event?

ELISABETH K-R: Yes. There are no coincidences. I call them "divine manipulation." If you check nothing else in your whole life but the so-called coincidences, then you will know how you are guided and directed and loved.

VALERIE E: So everything has a meaning?

ELISABETH K-R: Yes. Positive meaning.

VALERIE E: All periods of history have great tragedies; war and suffering is endemic round the world. Closer to home we have, for example, the AIDS epidemic. What is the purpose of this kind of suffering?

ELISABETH K-R: God, if I would know. We are in the midst of a period of spring-cleaning of Mother Earth, because Mother Earth is also having AIDS, is also dying due to our pollution and our neglect. But I think the whole of planet Earth is in a period of being reborn and made new, and my hunch—not my knowledge—my hunch is that these few heroic souls chose to have AIDS to enhance that spring-cleaning of planet Earth, so that people can become less nasty, less mean, less rejecting, less discriminatory, and have more compassion, love, and understanding.

VALERIE E: So they are suffering for us and for Earth?

ELISABETH K-R: Yes. And it is an enormous natural enhancement of their own soul growth.

VALERIE E: I think of Nietzsche's concept of "amor fate" (to love one's fate or destiny), but I think it can be difficult to accept your fate when you're starving or dying of AIDS.

ELISABETH K-R: One of my guides said to me that he wants to come back to Earth one more time. He wants to die of starvation as a child. And I said, "How stupid can you be? Why would you pick such a lulu?" And he said, with great love and great serenity, "It would enhance my compassion."

VALERIE E: As a scientist and a doctor renowned in your field, you've certainly gone out on a limb to say some very controversial things. And now, to speak of your own guides, I think that takes a certain strength and courage. How have you gotten that courage to speak out?

ELISABETH K-R: You see, thirty or forty years ago, if any of my patients wanted to talk to me about life after death, I said, "Listen, I'm a doctor and I'm a psychiatrist. Ask your minister." I always passed the buck. And then for the first time in my life I met a real minister who practised what he preached, and I had hours and hours of hot discussions with him. He would say, "Medicine would be wonderful if only we could answer one question: What is death?" And because he always, from his pulpit, said, "Ask and ye shall receive," I challenged him. I said, "I'm going to ask God now to help me to do research in death—not dying—death, to help me come up with an absolutely accurate definition of death." I felt that if we could know what death is, it would save a lot of the suffering, headaches, and problems of families and patients. And so I pointed my finger up to the ceiling and said, "I'm asking you now to help me do research in life after death." And five days after, I had my first patient with a near-death experience. This was long before Raymond Moody's research was published. And so every time I asked something, I got an answer. But only things I needed, not things I wanted. There's a big difference between the two.

And then I asked my helpers, after Moody's book came out, to please help me go beyond Moody's book, so that I would know how to continue this research, not just to have near-death experience, but to know what is beyond. And within a short time, a few days, I had a case of an American Indian who was hit by a hit-and-run driver on a highway, and left on the side of the road with severe internal injuries. So she was not visibly injured. Now, it's not normal for a woman to lie on the side of the highway. But not one car stopped to ask her if they could help. Only one man—a Good

Samaritan—stopped and asked her if there was anything that he could do for her. And she said with great serenity, "There is nothing else anybody can do for me." But he did not leave her. He sat with her on the grass and about fifteen or twenty minutes later she looked at him, suprised that he was still there, and said, "Maybe one day there is something that you can do for me." And the request was that one day he would visit her mother who lived on an Indian reservation, and give her a message. And the message to the mother was, "Tell her I'm okay. I'm not only okay, I'm very happy because I'm already with my dad." Then she died in the arms of this stranger. Well, this man was so moved that he went out of his way and drove seven hundred miles to visit the mother of this victim, who was not upset that her daughter had died, but very attentive to the message, because she said her husband, the accident victim's dad, died one hour before the car accident seven hundred miles away.

VALERIE E: So that confirmed in your mind this concept that at death you meet those whom you loved?

ELISABETH K-R: Not everybody, but if there was real genuine love...

VALERIE E: ...and they preceded you in death...

ELISABETH K-R: Yes. And that led me, then, to investigate accidents after Labor Day, Memorial Day, Fourth of July, and to talk with children whose family members have been killed.

VALERIE E: Is it the bulk of this experience, then, that has given you the courage to speak of these things? There is a local doctor here in Ontario who had a near-death experience in a plane crash and she began to collect case histories and wished to form a network of international physicians so as to acquire more information on this near-death experience. And she states that, as an intellectual and a doctor, she had to go through a period of silence before she could speak out, because she, I guess, feared the criticism. Where does your courage come from?

ELISABETH K-R: See, I have been so abused and rejected, called the "death-and-dying lady" and other things, that talking about this was nothing new to me. I went through all this a long time ago when I started to work with dying patients. So when the time came and somebody in the audience asked me, "What happens to a child when he dies?" I knew that this question was raised at the right time and at the right place. So I went public for the first time. But I wasn't lynched, you know, I survived. I do get some nasty letters and some people say, "What a pity, she used to be a scientist and a good physician, and now she's flaky." That's other people's problem, not mine. If we know something, and we can prove it and verify it, I think we have the obligation to share it with people.

VALERIE E: And you yourself had an out-of-body experience, which gives it some credence.

ELISABETH K-R: I've had several such experiences.

VALERIE E: Were they frightening?

ELISABETH K-R: No, they were delightful. Absolutely delightful. When you're having such an experience, you often don't want to come back. I knew my work wasn't finished so I had to come back.

VALERIE E: I wonder how you see death and what follows, compared to, say, the Tibetan Book of the Dead. Do you think that we go through a purification process after death, whereby we have to experience whatever pain we've inflicted on other people, sort of a karmic reenactment?

ELISABETH K-R: Every human being does this when they do their own review. You have to review every deed, every thought, every word you have ever uttered.

VALERIE E: We ourselves are entrusted with that?

ELISABETH K-R: Everybody has to do it themselves. And then you also know the consequences of every deed, every word, every thought. And that is, symbolically speaking only—not literally—going through hell, because by then you know about all the help you received during your lifetime, how so many people bent backwards to guide you onto the right track, how they helped you left and right, and how little you appreciated.

VALERIE E: So, there is a review, a type of purification, and there is no hell, then?

ELISABETH K-R: There is no hell except the hell you make for yourself. I mean, when I wanted to adopt twenty-eight babies here in the boonies in Virginia, hell broke loose. They shot bullets through my bedroom window. I had to go back home with a police guard surrounding my car.

VALERIE E: They did this because you wanted to adopt...?

ELISABETH K-R: Yes, I wanted to adopt twenty-eight babies. I wanted to use my farm here as a place where children whose parents died, or who didn't know their parents, would have some place where they could be raised with love and healthy food. I grow vegetables enough for a hundred people, and I'm totally self-supporting. I have my own boat, my own wood, my own vegetables, and I live all alone on a three-hundred-acre farm. So I thought, what better way to use a gorgeous farm than to adopt those twenty-eight babies and give them a chance to live. But when I put in a request for rezoning the farm to have these babies, all hell broke loose. They threatened me with Ku Klux Klan cross burnings; they wanted to burn my farm down; they shot bullets through my bedroom window; they made my life a living hell. But the art of living is that when things are rough and people are really nasty, you don't become negative. I knew this was a test, and that if you can keep your sanity and keep on living without being afraid that a bullet will come for you any minute through the forest, then you can grow. And I'm learning that gradually and slowly.

VALERIE E: You've said that once we know death we'll never be afraid again. I think, often, that death is very remote, and that it's life that can be very frightening. How does this knowledge of what death is change our living experience?

ELISABETH K-R: If you know that death is only a transformation into a different form of life, then nobody disappears, nobody vanishes into nothing, and we continue to grow and we continue to learn with no end to it. It's like going from first grade to second grade, or from seventh grade to eighth grade. You live very differently when you know you have to continue to learn and to grow.

VALERIE E: Can you give an overview, then, of what our time on Earth is about?

ELISABETH K-R: Our time on Earth is the only place where you can learn to give and receive, where you can learn to love others as much as you love yourself. It's a place to learn "Thy will, not my will." This is ultimately not too difficult to learn. But what they never taught us is "Thy time, not my time," because we want it right away. So you have to learn patience. You can't learn this on the "other side."

VALERIE E: I wonder, in your profession, with this ground-breaking work that you do with the dying, whether or not you've been faced with the temptation of ego-inflation, and possibly being led astray in that way?

ELISABETH K-R: Dying children keep you very humble. If you make a mistake in the interpretation of their symbolic life, they say, "You're stupid." I mean, they're so blunt, so honest. If you are ever a phony baloney, they tell you straight to your face.

VALERIE E: Have children been your greatest teachers?

ELISABETH K-R: Yes. Even more than adults, because they carry less phony baloney. They don't worry about what the neighbors think. They are very blunt and straightforward. And if you work with them for fifteen, twenty years, you become a bit like them.

VALERIE E: If death is such a positive experience, as you describe it, how will that affect the grieving process as we know it?

ELISABETH K-R: We miss them terribly; we miss their presence; we miss their laughter; we miss them reading a book to us; we miss a thousand moments. But we also know that if we have really unconditionally loved them that we'll be together again for much longer than here on the physical plane. And that will help us a little bit to overcome the biggest fear and the biggest pain. Losing someone you love is a very sad thing. And if you have learned in childhood to shed your tears and know that with tears and time you can heal, then you do much better as a grown-up. But if you are raised with "Oh, you're a sissy, there you go again, crybaby, and if you don't stop crying, I'll give you something to cry about," then when you lose a loved one, you keep your stoical face and you do not grieve, and the grieving process takes much longer.

VALERIE E: So your grief is for the remembrance of what it was like to be with that person on Earth. But it surely is tempered by the fact that what they're passing through is so much more positive than what, for instance, mainstream religions have led us to believe.

ELISABETH K-R: Yes, but you see, I think, in about twenty years from now, when everybody knows this, we're going to celebrate when somebody graduates, and we're going to be sad when somebody is born. I'm exaggerating a bit, but not much.

VALERIE E: When you say graduate...

ELISABETH K-R: To me, death is a graduation. That means you have learned what you came to learn, and you have taught what you came to teach. And then you're allowed to graduate.

VALERIE E: It sounds like you believe what Carl Jung would say, that our time here has to become more conscious, and that when we have succeeded, if we do succeed, then it's time to graduate.

ELISABETH K-R: Absolutely. Jung is my favorite teacher. He was my neighbor. I loved him and adored him, and I avoided him like the plague. I thought, If I ever go and talk to this man, I'm going to become a shrink. *[laughter]* And that's the last thing in the world I wanted to be.

VALERIE E: What did you learn from him?

ELISABETH K-R: I avoided him! I never talked to him.

VALERIE E: Did you read his books?

ELISABETH K-R: Naturally, but much, much later. In the last few years, I knew I couldn't avoid it, in order to do what I had to do. But I was led through a very zigzag road to get into psychiatry, because I avoided it like nothing else in the world. I had to lose a baby before I ended up in psychiatry.

VALERIE E: Your own child?

ELISABETH K-R: Yes. My first pregnancy.

VALERIE E: And then, in a roundabout way you came back to Jung?

ELISABETH K-R: Yes. Naturally you always end up where you're supposed to be. Some people climb the mountain straight up and others go around the mountain seventeen times.

VALERIE E: You've had a great deal of exposure to grief and suffering. You were a happy country doctor in Switzerland, and then you worked in a dreadful state hospital in Manhattan.

ELISABETH K-R: It was a nightmare. They experimented on their patients with LSD, mescaline, psilocybin. Those patients were fighting it like the dickens and yet nobody listened to them.

VALERIE E: But all these experiences have brought you to where you are today.

ELISABETH K-R: Yes. They taught me a symbolic language that dying patients use. They taught me a lot.

VALERIE E: Any final words before we say good-bye?

ELISABETH K-R: Just tell people that we're going to go through a big turmoil, a spring-cleaning of Mother Earth, and if they can keep their head in the clouds and their eyes on where they're going and where they come from, they don't have to be afraid.

myths for
the heartlands

DR. JEAN HOUSTON
in conversation with
ALEXANDER BLAIR-EWART

For more than twenty-five years Dr. Jean Houston has lectured and conducted seminars and courses at universities throughout the U.S., Canada, and Europe. She has served on the faculties of psychology, philosophy, and religion at Columbia University, New York University, and the University of California. She is past-president of the Association for Humanistic Psychology. In 1985 she received the National Teacher-Education Association's award as Distinguished Educator of the year (USA).

Dr. Houston is director of the Foundation for Mind Research and author of Life Force *(1980),* The Possible Human *(1982),* The Search for the Beloved *(1987),* Godseed *(1987), and* The Hero and the Goddess *(1992). She is also coauthor with her husband, Robert Masters, of* Mind Games: The Guide to Inner Space *(1990) and* Listening to the Body *(1979). She has written numerous articles and created hundreds of instructional audiotapes in the field of human capacities.*

ALEXANDER BLAIR-EWART: In your book *The Search for the Beloved* you define the human being in terms of a "this is me," "we are," and "I am" framework. This certainly echoes the older ways of viewing the human being, as in body, soul, and spirit. Why do you prefer this approach as a way of talking about the human being rather than the right brain/left brain paradigm?

DR. JEAN HOUSTON: I think it's because there is so much of the right brain/left brain paradigm that simply isn't true. This paradigm originally represented Sperry and Bogan's split-brain research—all about what happens if you sever the corpus callosum resulting in a separated brain. It was put forth in the fifties and gained a lot of credence in the sixties. And it was dealing more with pathology than with the whole brain. From this research it was shown that different hemispheres of the brain clearly have different kinds of emphasis and function. But the fact of the matter is that the brain is infinitely more complex than that. When you talk about the fully functioning brain you have to talk about it as an orchestral instrument, just as you cannot talk about the harp or the drum carrying Beethoven's Symphony no. 5. We are so much more than our brains. And it isn't a case of there being no critical and immensely valuable research and results of research that have come from split-brain theory, but that the more one delves into it, the more one realizes that to try to define human existence by only that kind of paradigm is like listening to the earth with a stethoscope.

ABE: The trouble I've always had with the left brain/right brain paradigm is that I see it as materialism sneaking in the back door of the new age.

JEAN H: Yes, and it's kosher, you see. It makes people feel good because it serves the current mythos, which is scientism. This is very quickly dying, but we still have the last dregs of it. And even some of its arbiters are the first to say that it is like the tip of an iceberg which is a much vaster phenomenon. Also, if you want to speak of neurological kinds of definitions, what about the midbrain? What about the mammalian brain? What about the old brain, the limbic system, the reptilian brain? So maybe we are rather the triuned ones, and the problem is that two of our brains don't even talk because they have no speech. *[laughter]* We exist in this marvelous state of a kind of schizophrenia of brains.

ABE: At the risk of sounding as if I'm suffering from conspiracy theories, do you think that the left brain/right brain paradigm was being deliberately pushed by anyone?

JEAN H: I think it's more unconscious than that, an unconscious urge, a kind of will to power. And people who are in an entropic mode are utilized by these forces of entropy. Now, whether you call them demonic or whether you call them Gaia's natural homeostatic function, *[laughter]* I don't know. I myself don't necessarily adhere to either the conspiracy theory or the illuminati theory. I do think that you see entropy everywhere in all kinds of forms and it looks to the untutored eye or to the paranoid eye certainly as a force of conspiracy.

ABE: Why do you find it so absolutely essential to use a threefold way of looking at the human being rather than just working with the left brain/right brain paradigm which seems so popular?

JEAN H: Because I don't wish to be popular and I don't mind being inaccurate. But I want to be true—true and inaccurate. I think the left/right paradigm is accurate but not true. It's just that we have to keep a certain level of—well, I don't want to say vagueness—but let us say a softer outline, a softer boundary between things. When you begin to constellate it in brain, the boundaries become much more rigid. And also the use of the metaphors that become applicable to "I am," "we are," "this is me" allow for a much larger application of metaphor and feeling, whereas the brain tends to close it down. Also, to be perfectly honest, this is merely one of many, many different kinds of processes and metaphors that I use.

ABE: I found it interesting that you included the gods in your "we are" aspect.

JEAN H: What we are calling gods, which are the great patterns and paradigms that exist in psycho-spiritual forms, get constellated around particular cultural archetypes and particular feeling archetypes, and that belongs to depth development. I do believe that the depth realm exists. Now, whether it is part of the psyche's continuum I do not know. I suspect that it's both, and plus much much more.

ABE: You go beyond that and you seem to say that the "I am" is monotheistic, it's unity oriented.

JEAN H: I wouldn't say "mono". I would say it's the integration of all these parts. It is the integral reality rather than the monotheistic reality. I'm not particularly monotheistic in my psychology.

ABE: It appears to be in the "I am" that you cross the bridge from psychology to the mystical.

JEAN H: I think I cross it earlier. I cross it probably in the bridge between the "this is me" and the "we are," because sacred psychology more often than not deals with archetypal and mythic structures, symbolic structures that illumine the other two parts of the continuum.

ABE: I was wondering if you are prepared to describe your current favorite way of articulating things, in the sense that an artist, for instance, will go through different phases.

JEAN H: I'm in one of those great transitional periods, which means that I will use everything that I have ever learned. And I'm yearning at another thing—this whole membrane theory, the theory of correspondences. I had a very, very important dream. Did I tell you about it?

ABE: I don't know if you did.

JEAN H: I had known Joseph Campbell for many years, since I was in my early twenties. I had done eight or nine seminars together with him, and I owe a great deal to his work and theories. Two weeks after he died in November of 1987 I woke up one morning having had a dream, and having been so physically distressed in the course of the dream that I woke up with muscles strained and stretched, barely being able to move. I hadn't torn anything, but by golly I'd come awfully close. I limped out of bed and felt this great weight on me, and I couldn't figure out why.

This was the dream: Joseph Campbell had just died, or was about to die, and he called to me to come over to him. His face was gray and he said to me, "Jean, help me finish the correspondence." Now I knew that Joe was about eighteen years behind in his correspondence. *[laughter]* He said, "Come to Upper Riverside Drive and help me finish the correspondence." I was trying to think, well, what is Riverside Drive? Riverside Drive is the upper west side where I had gone to school at Barnard College in Columbia. But it still didn't make much sense. And so, in the dream I said, "Joe, I can't, I've got all these things I've got to do, I've got all my relatives coming, and I've got another book. Joe, I can't, but I'll send one of my close associates who is much more efficient than I am." So I sent him my associate and he sent her back saying, "You have to come and help me finish the correspondence." So

I went, and then I woke up. Well I couldn't figure out what the dream was about, and why I was in such a deep state of distress about it.

About a week later a colleague of mine came to visit, and I told him the dream. He said, "Well, of course, it's about helping him finish the correspondences, the correspondence between things." And wham, there was one great breakthrough revelation! Of course, that's what it was about! Joseph Campbell had guarded, had harvested the mythos of just about every region of the world, and what was not in place yet was the correspondence between these mythic symbolic understandings—the myth and ritual structure of so much of our brain, our psyche, and the relationship of this mythic/symbolic structure to economics, to history, to science, to art, to literature. Part of the basic matrix of the human condition is the weave of a template of the mythic/symbolic structure which is such an incredibly indigenous part of our being, and which helps to illuminate so many patterns of correspondence. So that's where I am, whether I like it or not. *[laughter]* Those are my marching orders.

ABE: Those correspondences first began to emerge in a serious way in the nineteenth century at the point when comparative religious study developed as a field of scholarship.

JEAN H: Yes, with Frazer, with his great gargantuan smorgasbord of correspondences. But it's as if the world has truly turned a corner since then. I'm as familiar as anyone with all that massive amount of work, but it's as if there is a whole other thing present now. For example, when Joe and I would work together, the way it would work was that he would tell me a myth, say *The Odyssey* or the search for the Grail, and then I would say "Stop" every five minutes or so and I would create or project a form of ritual or psychophysical process that would illuminate that stage in the story. Then we would do some of these exercises together. The audience seemed to lap it up. And he used to say to me, "How can you think of those things?" He always found it quite amazing, and I used to think to myself, How could you not?, *[laughter]* but I never said it. For me the myth was something not just to be enacted, but to be *done*. For the ancient Greeks—"the things done and the things said"—they always had to go together.

ABE: That work certainly enriched the experiential work that you have been doing with drama and storytelling.

JEAN H: Oh yes, very much so. In many of my seminars I take a very great story or stories and they become patterns in which these experiential processes illumine the mythic structures. We've lost, and probably rightly so, the ancient, ancient cultic significance of many of these mythic structures. Take for example *The Odyssey*. *The Odyssey* contained an enormous amount of very primitive material—e.g., the death of the solar king who goes down into darkness with Xerxes and then is resurrected with Penelope. *The Odyssey* is filled with these ancient matrilineal cultic rituals. But all of what Homer changed, although he did not recognize it (he changed much for aesthetic purposes), became an extraordinary story. Then, of course, it's a mystery play, it's a series of rites of initiation, at a time when the other mysteries are really deepening all over the place. So my doing it as a mystery play, as a mystery rite, brings it now to a kind of consummation of all these stories that contain a loadedness, almost a genetic code of unfolding on every possible level, as it was for the ancient Greeks. The great ancient Hellenes essentially got their education by going over and over *The Iliad* and *The Odyssey*, because their coding evoked the latent drama of the glory that was Athens, because it contained the story of the birth of high civilization, and a partnership with the gods rather than a dependency.

ABE: It's interesting that we are naturally to some extent genetically coded to respond to those myths, which in turn are coded to natural rhythms and cycles and experiences of life. But somehow we've lost the connection.

JEAN H: Yes, very well said. I see a certain amount of my work as keying the coding. And that's why, when I work in all these countries, what I look for is the root mythos to see if it contains the coding that can uncode that society for its next stage.

ABE: That points to something else, Jean, which is what we are doing to ourselves collectively in this society in the way of education, and in the way that popular culture is handled, which is that we are perversely and probably unconsciously withholding from ourselves the one thing that we need individually and collectively, which is to get re-membered. Do you see any positive signs of change there? Do you think the educational system is going to change?

JEAN H: Yes, I do. I think that just being exposed to so many people who are in a state of either breakdown or re-membering is almost a reweaving, to take you back to *The Odyssey,* whose main metaphor is weaving. It's a reweaving that happens when you have the critical conjunction, the crisis of consciousness, of necessity and of the earth changing itself. Because we are not just the latest product of the metabolism of the galaxy. We are the neuronal network of the planet, which I believe at this critical point in history is changing. I cannot buy into, let us say, the early twentieth-century despair about the lack of progress. First of all, the idea of progress is such a dopey idea anyway. There is no such thing as progress; you can only *talk* about progress. But in the process of the planet where we are now, I think that we are not the only ones minding the store, that, if you will, our genetic coding is not just latent in our organism. It is extended. We are not just encapsulated bags of skin dragging around dreary little egos. We are symbiotic with many fields of life. And when those fields are being charged, then I think that we are being charged accordingly. I think that although you can talk about very deep cycles and patterns of unfolding, you can also talk about extraordinary catalytic jumps that occur from time to time. Darwinism of the steady state growth is certainly not true. We know that the jump phenomenon is more the rule than the exception.

ABE: So you're essentially saying that life, in its totality on planet Earth, contains within it the capacity and even at this point the urgency to right itself and become well, having been unwell.

JEAN H: There is so much pathology on the planet. You only have to fly over the Earth to see these great yellow mushrooming clouds of pollution over the cities, with so much pathology and erosion. But there is also an immense yearning for health and this is also carried to the messenger circuits of the self, to we as individuals, who are the neurons of the planet.

ABE: This is in the long term quite a positive and optimistic picture of things.

JEAN H: We are the people. I mean, I realize that other times in history thought they were it. Well, they were wrong, this is it! *[laughter]* I mean, why are so many movements coming to a kind of head? What is trying to happen in the world? There are factors such as planetization, the new technology, but also the rise of the archaic, mythic structures trying to reweave and regrow themselves. How does a culture reweave itself? It's almost as if the root myth bears the seeds of its own unfolding, of the next stage of the social forms.

ABE: On the other hand, is all of this evidence of a dying away?

JEAN H: It's both/and, not either/or. It's a dying away, or let us say a transduction, a transforming of parts. I think it's more like alchemy than death around the world. There is a very interesting theory that is moving in scientific circles that we have spent too long looking at the DNA structure of things. But DNA may not be where it's at, that tradition that says it's in the cell. It is really in the *cell membrane*, because the cell membrane gets to a certain point of expansion and then it has to multi-cell and become something else. And it's as if the nucleus of many civilizations is dying, or undergoing profound change, while the membrane is "out there." I think a lot of the new age movement, not everything by any means, is essentially a cell membrane phenomenon, of this jump to a next level. And this is happening in societies as well as in individuals.

ABE: How is all this going to show up, for instance, in economic transition, political transition, all of those kinds of things? Because if there is going to be a new age, then there's obviously a transition phase from this age to the new age.

JEAN H: That could take some time because, you see, instead of moving to a planetary culture, a kind of ecology of cultures, we could move into a very long interim period in which the tactician, the tactical artist gains the...

ABE: ...upper hand?

JEAN H: *[laughter]* And thus all the management consultants all over the place. New age, of course, is a term that is on the American dollar—the Novum Ordum. It's a term that recurs in one form or another about every seventy-five years. And what is different about this one is that never before have we had so many factors that are unique in human history literally endemic all over the planet. So that the ante has been raised and the complexity is much greater than it has ever been, and thus the shift or jump phenomenon can be more profound.

ABE: Are you saying that there are certain tendencies in human beings that may hijack the alchemical process, hijack the revolution?

JEAN H: Yes. There's the sense of homeostasis which has always been in us—business as usual, only more so. Another is a loss of the great patterns of connection to most of the great stories. It is the great patterns that are in eclipse for many people. And again, because of the fact that you have so many factors that are unique in human experience, people often have lost the vertical dimension in the pursuit of the horizontal. On the other hand, you also have an awful lot of good news. On the physical level never before have you had so many people interested in their own health, and interested in the extension of their body and by corollary their mind. On a psychological level the emphasis on a kind of reflection on what it is to be human is something that I see as happening all over the world in ways I think are unique. It's not a collective interest in the tribal identity as much as it is the personal identity, and mythically I think the great stories are rising. Spiritually the Zeit is getting Geisty. *[laughter]*

ABE: What is the relationship between anxiety, as normally defined, and the quickening, as spiritually defined?

JEAN H: At a certain point I think that they overlap each other, and they may look very much the same. Then, you see, "By their fruits you shall know them," and anxiety will often become narcissistic, cannot get out of its own puddle.

ABE: Is the rise of the mythic, or what you call the great stories, the alchemical agent that turns anxiety into the quickening?

JEAN H: Yes.

ABE: So is anxiety a sort of entropic quickening, where the individual hasn't made contact with the mythic?

JEAN H: Yes. I think that's an excellent perception.

ABE: I think I'm beginning to get some sense of what you're about. I've noticed a lot of people who appear to be very progressive in postpsychological thought, neo-Jungian and post-Jungian and new age, who seem very reluctant to take the plunge and describe what that bridge is that takes one from the more academically respectable psychology into the mystical. You don't seem at all afraid of that. Why?

JEAN H: It *is* a fear and trembling, because you are literally going where—

not where angels fear to tread—but where angels don't tread. *[laughter]* And I think that one has to expand the metaphors. To me it is not so much the leap between two disciplines, or into an unknown discipline, as it is an extension of metaphor. Living as I do in so many metaphors, and having worked for so many years with the human psyche and with what beings can be, it becomes very blurred between one level of discourse and the other. Now, I lived for many years as a college professor. I grew up in that world and it has a great deal to offer, a certain kind of discipline, and a recasting and harvesting of the past. But the fact is that we cannot indulge in that exclusively. It is a question of having many frames of mind, frames of reference.

ABE: Free thinkers had to have the wars of the town and gown to form Oxford and Cambridge. And now we have universities which have, according to Canadian philosopher George Grant, turned into multiversities—they just produce for and serve the technoculture. My pet theory is that new age universities now have to emerge as a new point of growth, largely from people who've left the university plus a wave of fresh, new, raw geniuses coming up out of the ranks. Do you see that as happening?

JEAN H: Yes, it is happening. It started as a trend in the sixties with the creation of a very large-scale adult education program. I think that there is the multidimensional, not just the multi-university that is emerging. In the United States there are programs at union graduate school that offer legitimate credentialed degrees, but of which the exploration is truly an exploration into one's own capacities and depth, as well as offering very innovative studies in the particular disciplines that one is pursuing. So I think that what you're talking about is happening almost by default. I wish that it had more conscious and conscientious direction. I would take it right to grade school. We're being educated for about the year 1915, not the immense complexity of the multicultural world, which is what we're emerging into in the next millenium.

ABE: We're struggling with nineteenth-century political and social paradigms, like left wing/right wing, capitalist/communist. Obviously this emerging mythic-world consciousness and nineteenth-century polarized, political paradigms are not going to make very comfortable bedfellows. Do you see the political/social sphere adapting or absorbing this new material, or do you see it as being washed away altogether in due course?

JEAN H: Let me just speculate in certain ways. I'm thinking that in the fourteenth and fifteenth century there was something that was well known, called "Fortuna's Wheel," and it was a wheel that represented the stages and cycles of life. The wheel would turn and another cycle would come up. I would say that we are gradually beginning to move out of homo politicus and economicus, where economic paradigms are central to the understanding of self and state, which we've been in since certainly the nineteenth century. And that because of the complexity of world change, it is almost as if another kind of human—homo ecologicus—will emerge in this shift to another mode. In no previous civilization did you have economics at the core of the human curriculum. Economics is only one image among many—politics, the religious life, the artistic life, etc. This is the first time in history that we have economic issues colonizing the psyche and the society. I think that we're going to be moving from that into either another emphasis, or a much more balanced structure of emphases. It is not unlike what happened with the human ego. If we were in the minds and bodies of our ancestors of six hundred years ago, we would not recognize their psychology at all because they did not have the dominance of ego. Ego was but one image among the multiple images of the psyche. And I think, similarly, in society, economics is one image of the multiple images. The world is too complex to be strained through the lens of economic structures. I'm speaking almost biologically here, that biologically it's a very bad match right now, and it just can't sustain itself.

ABE: All right, so there's a revolution in world consciousness which is evident. Who is leading that revolution?

JEAN H: I feel, ultimately, that it's a depth phenomenon, so that you cannot speak of a leader, General this or that.

ABE: I'm talking in terms of a cultural, metaphysical leadership. What we're talking about here, Jean, is our baby—Western humanity's baby at the moment, isn't it? Because there certainly isn't a ground swell of this "breaking through into a new consciousness" happening in China, and much of what was the Soviet Union is still trying to get itself into the early twentieth century.

JEAN H: Now there I would disagree with you. I think that a lot more is going on in the former Soviet Union. It's not there up front yet. We sort of perjure that area of the world by talking about it as a kind of backward, donkey culture. But I think what has happened is that here you have one of the most religious cultures in Europe, and then after the first Russian Revolution it seemed as if the icons of the saints were replaced with the icons of Marx and Lenin.

ABE: Which was in itself a state of cultural slavery.

JEAN H: And then the theology went underground and emerged as a very complex and brilliant science fiction. Those things are true. But in those countries you also find that there is an intensity of focus on depth issues and depth aspects of the psyche to such a degree that you'd have to go to the United States to find a comparable emphasis. So they may be backward in terms of the way we look at things, but I'm not sure that something very profound isn't happening. I was in South India a couple of months ago, working, and I asked a man in a village, "What is it that you'd like to learn?" He said, "I must learn how to improve my mind, so that my soul and my people can deepen." I've heard this everywhere. And the images of the language that they use may not be new age, but they are, if anything, even older. They are the perennial philosophies.

ABE: What I'm getting at, Jean, is that unless something is out there and up front, in that larger sense, it doesn't really exist!

JEAN H: I'm not sure of that. But when you ask, "Where is the leadership?" I think that it is not seen yet, but it is emerging. I think it should not be seen too overtly too soon because then it will be polarized, become a celebrity, and that's the worst thing that could happen. You see, it has occurred in some ways in the twentieth century but it became very demonic because people simply had not done their human homework.

ABE: Are you talking about the Third Reich?

JEAN H: I'm talking about the Third Reich as a demonic mythic form. I'm talking about what happened in Italy as a demonic mythic form. Certainly Stalin was a member of an old Gnostic cult (and so was Malenkov), and that was a demonic form as well. I would hope that we have had a catharsis of these forms so that these deeper things can happen. What happened in the sixties was a kind of jubilant celebration of the sense of this renewal, but there again people had not done the depth levels of their homework. I think that has happened in the ensuing thirty years, and it has involved coming to terms, not only as a people, but also as social entities, with, in my own metaphor, the "possible human," trying to create a possible society.

ABE: Certainly in any large gathering there will be X percent of people who are on the brink of some kind of breakthrough or breakdown. I feel that that is a phenomenon which is only going to grow, that in the latter half of the nineties more and more people are going to "lose it" within the context of mystical experience.

JEAN H: Well, this is a very interesting and important phenomenon, and it is one that has always been known throughout human history. You know, Francis of Assisi was one of the most disorganized human beings who ever lived, but he broke through or broke down, as his family believed, and actually came through incredible fevers. He had an enormous series of fevers for six months, then went into a state of utter limbo and numbness that went on and on. And it was like he'd fallen into a vacuum. It was only later that it came back. He prayed, he yearned for it. He had also had a pattern in his culture that said that spiritual experience might just happen to look like this, and then *this* happened. If we want to talk about Teresa of Avila, if she had lived today, she would have been considered really quite neurotic. The point is, what is the mode of the lens of diagnosis? A great deal of the mystical experience or of the experience of the losing of one's boundaries by present pathologizing language is really very crazy. Part of the problem is not a question of the distinction between what is pathological and what is mystical, but a sense that there are certain times and places within the psyche in which they look, and indeed may be, identical. But the point is found in the guidance and the patterns that are then engendered. They are like supersaturated solutions; everything is available, and what is the seed crystal that one is going to drop in that is going to create a new crystalization of the psyche? We almost need halfway houses for people who fall into the vacuum.

ABE: Yes.

JEAN H: And that is what we do not have. I think that so much of our psychotherapeutic treatment is based on models of pathology and not models of...

ABE: ...the entire human being.

JEAN H: Yes.

ABE: What is *The Search for the Beloved* a metaphor for?

JEAN H: It's a metaphor for the search for that connection within the depths of ourselves that is a kind of partnership. This is a very ancient form of belief, that we are sitting on the icebergs of ourselves and the depth of that is that god/self, that entelechy, and the relationship is often very powerful and positive when it is experienced emotionally. I am interested in the therapy of cultures. *Therapaia* is the ancient Greek word, whose root meaning is support or caring, and whose secondary meaning is *thea*. I think that there is a more ancient meaning which is doing the work of the whole, doing the work of the god. And what is the therapaeia of cultures? Cultures can in a sense be looked at as a person can be looked at, because culture is the person writ large. I worked with the Institute of Cultural Affairs all over the world trying to work on many levels of society to begin to evoke in a therapaeic—not therapeutic—manner the elements that can lead to whole system transition instead of a systemic breakdown, which is much more, unfortunately, the prediction. See, I come out overtly as an expert in the human capacities, but my covert agenda is the evocation, the eliciting of a culture to its next stage, without there having to be so much breakdown.

ABE: So you're sort of a priestess of the possible.

JEAN H: In heirophantic language I suppose I am. I would use the term midwife or evocateur. I don't know that it's priestly.

ABE: Do you think that part of the need for a mythic reawakening in people is due to the exponential intrusion of technology into every aspect of our lives?

JEAN H: You see, it's happening in places which are essentially non-technological societies. I've been on almost every continent in the world and worked in many bioregions. And I see that the fascination with this is virtually universal, so you can't just say high tech. However, if we go deeper into your question, there is a chestnut I heard from Paul Tillich many years ago that "history may be the shadow cast by eschatology," meaning not just that there are events at the end of history that are pulling us forward, but that they are being bled through or seeded through by the great patterns of creation, by the evolutionary impulses, and now it's as if they are so intense at this particular point that we are experiencing their shock waves, and the only thing that gives us enough pattern to understand these radical transitions that we are going through faster than at any time in human history is a mythic structure. We are living in mythic times and so we look at myths to try to get some kind of sense of who and what and where we are, some cartography to guide us.

ABE: What comes to mind is Toynbee's concept of archaism. When humanity is at a certain crisis point, you have a polarity, archaism to futurism, and he talks about how both of these lead to tyranny and fragmentation. What is there about this reawakened mythic consciousness that frees it from the double bind of this polarity?

JEAN H: Well sometimes, of course, it's not freed; Hitler would be a supreme example of that. A big leap backward into the future. But I think that what is unique in the mythic structures is the other alternative, which is connected to the Greek term *palingenesea*—the continuous birth. The hero, the heroine, the mythic being who decides to take on the larger life is generally born in a time of dying, in which he or she lives in an outmoded situation and has to travel, journey, search, quest beyond the outward situation, either to ingress to the great "causal zones" within, or to exgress into another realm. Now I think what is happening, what the new mythic imagery is suggesting, is that we are heading upwards to heaven, into outer space, or downwards onto the earth into paradise. It's either heaven or paradise. They are the only logical alternatives. We cannot have cities like Tokyo or Los Angeles or these megalopolises like Sao Paulo, which are heading towards thirty million people by the end of the century. The earth cannot support that. Now this is not to say that technology is bad, but it may be that with the incredible conjunction of technology with the human imagination set free, some of us, not all, but some of us may not really be appropriate for this planet anymore. *[laughter]*

ABE: Yes, a different kind of human adventure.

JEAN H: Yes, the mythic time that we are talking about and the new adventures, but if we have to go out, we go out with elegance and grace and with a very different kind of consciousness. Not with what science fiction writers suggest, you know, the essentially archaic, baronial, feudal consciousness that they describe.

ABE: Can I pull you back into the concept of palingenesea? Toynbee talks about the concept of palingenesea as maybe being the thing that rescues one from all these dangerous byways and then he points directly at the figure of, I suppose, what we would call the "Cosmic Christ." The human individual as an "I am" who has the power of rebirth in him and who has inherited the Earth.

JEAN H: You also have in the East very similar thoughts about Buddha and the Maha Buddha, the Maitreya. There are other end-of-history archetypes. I could pick at least ten or fifteen of them.

ABE: Do you feel that's where we are now, at the end of history?

JEAN H: Let's put it this way: I think we're at the end of ideology.

ABE: Oh yes, absolutely!

JEAN H: We're certainly at the end of ideological history. History has been the contention of ideology, contention of villages and nations and ideological states. I think we are truly coming to the end of it and we will certainly see the petering out of it by the twenty-second century.

ABE: When you look at deep ecology and what that means politically, you see every ideology in the world crumble before that, because all of our political structures are going to be determined by ecology.

JEAN H: Ecology is the ultimate leveler of all of these ideological forms. When you start talking about deep ecology, you're also by the way talking about the deep psyche.

ABE: Yes. A whole Earth culture, a different sense of time.

JEAN H: So that psyche is being activated, ecology is being activated. The cosmic person is being activated, you know, the Purusha of the old Vedas, the person who is both organism and environment, symbiotic with worlds within worlds within worlds, both within and without themselves, who has access to the "I am," access to these depths that they could not have access to as long as they were having to spend all their time keeping their metabolism going and having to contend with ideological forces. So when you get beyond metabolic maintenance and/or sustenance and you get beyond ideology, it means that the human brain/mind spiritual system is available for much much more and then those pulsings and mythic codings start coming in.

ABE: Beautiful. So now what's arising here is a pair of opposites. A yin force and the yang force. Let's say the yin force is deep ecology because it embraces everything.

JEAN H: Yes. That's the paradise center.

ABE: And we also have the "I am" within the mythic.

JEAN H: Within the mythic within the psyche.

ABE: Yes.

JEAN H: The "I am" as being itself.

ABE: And the "I am" in each individual is fully awake within the yin force of a deep ecological awareness of the Earth. What is the bridge between the "I am" and deep ecology?

JEAN H: I think the bridge may be the mythic itself. I think of the Sanskrit notion of the *yidam*. What is the yidam? The god, the goddess, not God. Not God itself, but the amplified persona of the psycho-spiritual pattern and archetype that allows you through identification and extension the way to access "I am that being." Now obviously there are many religious traditions that do it directly like Zen Buddhism, where you polish or hone yourself into "I amness," where you do not need the archetype in between. Most religions and all popular religions require the yidam as the beloved, that amplified extended self, the archetype of the larger self to which you connect. I'm not saying that we're necessarily moving into that, but I think a great deal of what we call the "channeling" phenomena is essentially a modern way of trying to access this mythic structure that brings you directly to the "I am," that allows you leakier margins and more opened and fluid boundaries which you don't have in your ordinary everyday existential self.

ABE: Yes, but...

JEAN H: Many yes buts. *[laughter]*

ABE: Let's raise the yes but of the fact that the phenomenon of channeling means that for one thing the person doing the channeling is unconscious. I'm talking about deep-trance channeling, where the individual who is doing the channeling is pretty well in a coma and some other aspect of them or some other entity is speaking through them and often not saying terribly enlightened things.

JEAN H: My husband and I have read literally tens of thousands of pages of this material coming out of people in deep trance. And when people started to publish this stuff we couldn't understand it. We said, "People pay to buy books full of this?" *[laughter]* But it gets beneath the surface crust of consciousness and the automatons of the creative unconscious are happy and willing to present entire automatous realities.

ABE: So are you saying that channeling is an expression of the unconscious in a Jungian sense?

JEAN H: Yes, but the unconscious can shade into much more because we are organism *and* environment. It shades into another environment, which is lensed through, I think, the personal unconscious. For some people that's all it is and for others it may be much more of a lensing and focalization.

ABE: Where does the "I am" emerge from that phenomenon?

JEAN H: I think the "I am" is always there in the midst of it. There are all the classical mystic texts of Meister Eckhart, saying, "The 'I' by which I see God is the same 'I' by which God sees me," and he got into a lot of trouble with the Pope over that one. Or Saint Francis saying, "What we are looking for is who is looking." So I think it's a permeation, not necessarily a hierarchy. We hierarchicalize it so as to understand it, but that's purely a mapping. It's just a question of the releasing of the lensing.

ABE: I agree with that completely, but then there's this difficulty of unconsciousness involved in channeling, if indeed what is occurring is that God is becoming aware of Itself.

JEAN H: Yes, I would say what we call gods or "yidams" or archetypal structures certainly grow themselves in part through us. I would agree with someone like Kazantzakis that we become the saviors of God to the degree that we allow for self-reflection. When we get to the realm of "I am," I am the first to say I don't know. *[laughter]* We can't assume and speak for the gods. I don't know that we can speak for Being itself. Perhaps Being itself does put us out. Let's say I'm looking right now at a figure of a monkey. If I were to be comical about it, I would agree with someone like Terence McKenna who says that "we are not monkeys but we are in monkeys." *[laughter]*

ABE: Ah yes, I see what you're saying.

JEAN H: And maybe we are God-seeded primates. How did that brain develop so very fast? Those frontal lobes? Transcending all kinds of evolutionary expectation. Could it be that we are quickened? That was part of one of the great turnings of prehistory when the depths, the energies, and the need to propagate all of the Earth was such that something occurred so that these primate species suddenly were activated by this deep pulsing from the Earth's unconscious, the Earth's psyche, or from an even larger metabolic structure. Part of our problem is that we do exist in brains that in part are very primitive. Two of them don't even talk to each other anymore, so that our finest ideas get caught in ideology, and that's monkey business. Read the newspapers. Take somebody like Christ, you know, who comes in the old traditional mythology to redeem the old Adam, meaning the old primate. He gets caught up a tree.

ABE: In relation to ideology, the only way to protect yourself from being swallowed by an ideology is to keep the big questions open.

JEAN H: Yes, quite.

ABE: And coming back to the mythic, how does myth keep questions open?

JEAN H: Because it requires palingenesea. It requires this constant shock and the big turnaround. It's always the road of trials or the road of challenges. It speaks to our deepest yearnings. It is, as I've often said, a coded DNA of the human psyche so that you can't get really stuck or caught in it. It's also like a force field that keeps lighting up new arenas of our mind. It's a kind of potent coded-symbol system that releases some of our own coding. We're in mythic times because we're in times in which our coding is being released.

ABE: What's causing that release?

JEAN H: Well, remember *2001: A Space Odyssey*, that great picture where you had that funny rectangle? *[laughter]* Every time they touched it, they'd go whoop! Clearly, coding got released. We're being uncoded through the sheer uniqueness of our time, the fact that we are moving towards planetarization with an awareness of the planet being alive; we are moving towards whole systems transiting positions all over the world. We are moving to the rise of women to full partnership with men. A radical technology in which imagination joined to computers, electronics joined to biofacture, joined to genetic engineering, joined to whole new energy bases. Joined to the accessing of the spiritual mythic in symbolic systems of the whole world, so that they're not insular anymore. They're bleeding through. We are creating virtually a second Genesis. This, you know, to all effective purposes, is releasing a coding. Haven't you felt yourself being progressively uncoded over the last twenty or thirty years?

ABE: Oh yes, indeed. I'm about as uncoded as you can get by now. *[laughter]* In your experience of doing seminars and working with people at so many levels, can you talk about the process? How does it work?

JEAN H: There's a great deal of telling of the mythic story and of one's own story as it relates to the myth. So already the personal-particular is elevated to or moves into the personal-universal within a broader context. There are many exercises that serve to release habituated structures—brain exercises, physical exercises, mental exercises.

ABE: Do those exercises emerge out of the myths themselves?

JEAN H: No. The way I work them is that I look at the myth and the exercise presents itself.

ABE: Mythic creativity in the moment...

JEAN H: Yes. If I were, for example, to look at Odysseus getting out of the cave, dealing with the cyclops, well, he uses phenomenal intelligence. Now, we might enact that, yes, but then we would look at what is the nature of this phenomenal intelligence. So we would study Odysseus' mind and discover that he had craft, cunning, wit, and he was able to entertain a variety of possibilities. We'd then create an exercise to engage that. You see, it relates both to Odysseus and to the person's own life.

ABE: By talking about Odysseus, you just plugged into the awakening mythology that arises around space visitors or extraterrestrials.

JEAN H: Yes. He was one of the world's first spacemen. *[laughter]*

ABE: Do you have any thoughts about that whole phenomenon, people like...

JEAN H: Whitley Streiber?

ABE: Whitley Streiber and the impact that he's made, Jacques Vallee's books, etc...

JEAN H: Well let me tell you what I truly think. I don't know if we'll have visitors from outer space. I cannot speak for that. I live in a county—the Hudson River valley—where everybody sees them and I'm the only person who hasn't. I feel that a lot of it is eschatology casting its shadow. When you look at the phenomenology of mystical experience . . . take someone like Hildegard of Bingen . . . she was seeing behind her closed eyes flying discs, whirring vortexes, lenses of light. And there's a lot of this that's in the psyche to herald an annunciation, to announce another possibility. I'm just wondering if this isn't part of the world psyche waking up, in which we begin to see these things, because what I think is happening is so overwhelming and so utterly beyond our expectations that it is safe to think of these phenomena as being "out there." "Out there" we can deal with. But if it's part of the whole collective psyche, a cocreation, then it's scary.

ABE: What is the role played by myth in the creation of your own reality? Because obviously if you're trying to create your reality out of seminars for success, there's a certain lack of real richness there.

JEAN H: There is something wrong with a great deal of so-called new age thought and also new thought—Christian Science and that kind of thing—which assumes reality without shadows, without a constant holographic reverberation of the people. I do not believe that I by myself, as some kind of insular encapsulated being, make my own reality.

ABE: One is constantly encountering the world?

JEAN H: Well, I think we are more of a "we are."

ABE: Yes, "we are" is balance.

JEAN H: I think of Doris Lessing's wonderful point in the *Shikasta* series where she talks about how the original great society had the suchness of "we," and the suchness of "we" I think is what creates reality; it's the ripples, you know, cascading.

ABE: In that sense of the modern human being working at reality, working at deepening on one side and on the other trying to be more functional in the external world, what sort of things are people needing to get hold of in order to nourish that process?

JEAN H: Well, I think a great deal of it has to do with meaning. When you are living at the time of the death of ideology and the end of history in that sense, you're also living in a time of the ending of traditional meanings. So it's the question of meaning, the understanding of one's own depths as they shade into others' depths, in relationship. How does one stop long enough to become attuned to these great pulsings that are occurring, the rhythms of awakening? Then how does one transduce them in terms of the vehicle of one's own self within history, and then transmit them? Just the other day I came up with: Stop, Attune, Transmute, Transmit.

ABE: Yet there's a lot of fear attached to the breakdown of ideology. It's not terror, but it's the realization that a bridge is being burned. I look out into the world and I see that there are millions of people who are not only unable to burn that bridge, but who are fighting very violently against this process. We have Islamic and Christian fundamentalism. We have all of these fanaticisms. How long is it going to take to work itself out?

JEAN H: Who can say? Certainly we're looking at the next hundred years, because phenomenal ideologies are going down that have thousands of years in the matrix of history. But I also feel that so much is coming up, so much social invention and spiritual possibility. There are new ideologies and subcultures coming up within these so-called fundamentalist forms.

ABE: So in the place of ideology, which is linear, rigid, and falling apart, you have the rise of the mythic.

JEAN H: The rise of the mythic always attends the end of ideology, any ideology. This is true for the end of any age. We are in no ways unique in any of this.

ABE: What are the major examples of that?

JEAN H: All right, let's take the sixth and fifth century B.C. Look at China, let's say the end of the Chang dynasty, during which the country broke into many feudal warring states. In the midst of this chaos in China, who rises within decades of each other? Lao-tzu, Confucius, with his deep empathy and heartfulness, all these people who are looking for alternative ways of dealing with the end of history.

ABE: Toynbee comes to mind again. He talks about how a period of violence is often followed by a very peaceful renaissance.

JEAN H: You have Lao-tzu who is really looking at the naturalist's way of being, and Confucius tuning into nature as a way of getting back to the source. Down south you have Mahavira, the Jain, and of course Buddha. Buddha's great invention, which Toynbee says is one of the greatest inventions of human history, is the Sangha community.

ABE: The holy family.

JEAN H: The holy family. To the west you have the Pythagorean communities, communities based on sense and number, logic, music, and mysticism. And I could go all over the world to show what's happening in that extraordinary sixth century B.C. But in every case it is the breakdown of the feudal states that forms the context for these developments.

ABE: When you talked earlier about living in this very unique time within these mythic rhythms, what came into my head were the words myth under pressure...

JEAN H: *[laughter]* Hothouse myth.

ABE: Yes.

JEAN H: You're quite right.

ABE: We also have nuclear power in the world. The myth which is holism, of the unity of Earth and humanity, still has this deadly challenge before it and maybe that's also part of what is fertilizing or firing myths to awaken from inside us as we encounter the shadow side of technology. In that sense there's a time pressure, isn't there, at this turning point, and the uniqueness is that it's happening planet-wide all at once?

JEAN H: That is my experience literally all over the world. All over the world you find pictures of the whole Earth tacked up, in huts in Africa, down in southern India. This whole Earth image is everywhere. And at the same time the old mythic structures are arising to be remythologized.

ABE: Are those old reawakened mythic structures and the emergence of the planetarization of consciousness going to merge?

JEAN H: Well no. I think we're moving towards a planetary myth, but it is not something that is exclusive and it does not swallow its own children.

ABE: A really new cosmic and planetary myth, with ancient roots.

JEAN H: I think it is. It's a family of mythic structures with an overarching planetary myth that will start in our time. We will probably have a pretty good idea of its true nature, I imagine, by the middle of the next century.

8

stalkers
and
dreamers

TAISHA ABELAR

FLORINDA DONNER

JEWEL

the sorcerer's crossing

TAISHA ABELAR
in conversation with
ALEXANDER BLAIR-EWART

In the long years since Carlos Castaneda first informed the world of the wonders of American aboriginal spirit knowledge, many recognized that a tradition of great significance had begun to reveal itself to the world. Over the years Castaneda has progressively shown the all-engulfing worldview of the Toltecs in its reformed state as a work of spiritual art, shaped by the new seers who have survived the devastating encounter with European colonial civilization. Taisha Abelar, author of The Sorcerer's Crossing: A Woman's Journey *(1992), is one of the new seers whose designation "stalker" balances the world of the "dreamer."*

ALEXANDER BLAIR-EWART: Can I get you to talk about the complex subject of "stalking"?

TAISHA ABELAR: There are two ways of approaching this. First, a general definition is that a stalker is someone who has made an art out of being unobtrusive. That is, he puts himself in the background, and there's a certain training that is involved in order to become unobtrusive. Also, stalking is designed to give the sorcerer or the practitioner a jolt, and by a jolt we mean a push or a slight burst of energy so that the "assemblage point" shifts ever so slightly. The stalkers are aiming to move or shift the assemblage point, and through that to change their perception of the world. Perception, of course, can be changed through dreaming, but stalkers do it while they're awake. The way sorcerers perceive the world is that they say that everything we see while we are awake in this reality is a question of the position of the assemblage point. I'm sure you're familiar with Castaneda's books, and you know what the assemblage point is, but let me just describe it again. It is the focused awareness point of luminosity on the luminous cocoon (also understood as the aura).

We believe that the human being's energetic body is a mass of fibers of light of infinite number, and each one of those is a specific awareness. They're not the light of, say, electricity, but they're actually the light of awareness. On the luminous egg shape that makes up the energetic body there is a point of extra luminosity where the concentration of the person, his awareness, is assembled, and that point of luminosity is about the size of a golf ball, from the point of view of the "seer" who sees the person's luminous being. But it can change size; it can also change position on the luminous body. And where it is located determines what is perceived, because there's a matching of the fibers that are lit up within the luminous body with the fibers that are out in the universe at large. Sorcerers maintain that the universe as a whole is composed of an infinite number of energetic fibers, some of which are perceivable, and others which are absolutely beyond our capacities as human beings to perceive. So when the position of this assemblage point, this lighted-up area on the luminous being, matches what is outside, then perception takes place.

ABE: Would this apply to everyone?

TAISHA A: We all have our assemblage point at pretty much the same place, because as an infant is born, by virtue of the fact that he is going to be a human being, a social person, he has to match the location of his assemblage point to that of other human beings in the world so that he can interact with them, perceive the same world. Because our assemblage points are in the same place, we can have language, we can talk about trees and cars and solid walls and floors, and we can have a spatial and temporal continuity; we know that there was a yesterday, there'll be a tomorrow. All of that has to do with the position of the assemblage point. Time, our conception of everything we know, is determined by where that heightened point of concentrated awareness is located. And if by some anomaly it is not in the place where the human assemblage point ought to be, then these people are either sorcerers, (and we'll talk about that in a moment), or they're a candidate for mental illness. You find these latter kinds of people in asylums because their assemblage points are not fixed at the position where other human beings have theirs. Therefore they don't have this intersubjectivity in terms of perception and they don't have agreement as to what constitutes reality. There's a biological mandate that says that all human beings should have their assemblage point at this particular position so they can be what we call human. Animals have it at different places, and that's what fixes their species of animal. Trees have their assemblage point at a certain place in their luminous shell, and that makes them trees.

ABE: So could we also call the assemblage point the position of collective persona reality agreement?

TAISHA A: Exactly. It's our persona, it's our person. Now this person, sorcerers say, is not all that we are humanly capable of being. We can be more than just a social person. In order to be more than what society, or what our birthright, has given us, we have to move or shift the place of the assemblage point. We have to move it out of the position where it is stuck. So, not only is the assemblage point capable of moving elsewhere, but when it does, other luminous intelligent fibers of awareness are lit up and matched with the universe, and therefore other realities are constituted. These other realities are as real and solid as the one we are in now. And it's all based on the fixation of the assemblage point. If it moves—and it does; it moves in dreams, by itself—we call that dream reality, to be separated from the waking state. We acknowledge that there are other realms of experience, but we always refer to them from the position of everyday reality. Sorcerers don't do that. They say that you can move the everyday reality while you're awake. You don't have to do dreaming. Dreaming, of course, is the control of the movement of the assemblage point in sleep, in dreams, and the fixation of it elsewhere.

ABE: And you can do it without being insane.

TAISHA A: Absolutely.

ABE: That in itself is an enormously revolutionary statement.

TAISHA A: Yes, because our agreement says that crazy people out there have hallucinations, see monsters and what not, and that they're somehow deficient from the point of view of the social order. Yes, they're deficient in the sense that they have not stabilized their assemblage point where everyone else has. Somehow their assemblage point is in flux, it's constantly shifting. They're crazy because they're hallucinating, and they don't have the energy to maintain their assemblage point at any one given position. If they did have that energy and the control, they would be sorcerers, because they would be stalking that new position.

ABE: Yes, I see that.

TAISHA A: So what this all really boils down to is a question of having the energy to perceive more than what we are allowed to perceive given the fact that we are born as human beings. Our social order doesn't allow us to venture into other realms except through insanity or dreams, which it doesn't really count as real anyway. So those are two avenues that are open, but they're not really viable avenues. Now, sorcerers say you can move the assemblage point, provided you have enough energy to fix it at another position, because you don't want to end up crazy and absolutely lost in these worlds upon worlds that they maintain exist out there like the layers of an onion. So what is needed is control, energy, and fluidity, and what they call "unbending intent." Fluidity enables one to shift the assemblage point, to move away from the given spot that makes us persons, gives us a sense of self. And that's where self-importance has to go out the window because as long as we maintain our allegiance to the self, what we're really doing is maintaining our allegiance to that particular position of the assemblage point. We'll never be able to perceive anything beyond what is the taken-for-granted reality. We're allowed only to perceive what is permissable by our given position within the social order. So we need fluidity to move the assemblage point elsewhere, and then we need the stability, the concentration, the energy to fix it on another position. And this is what sorcery really is.

ABE: Does your essential beinghood, your essential humanity, survive this transition into worlds of alternative reality?

TAISHA A: Your luminosity and your awareness, which is the assemblage point, stays intact elsewhere. But it's not human. It doesn't have to be human, and there's the error that we don't want to make. No, you leave everything that's human behind.

ABE: Most people would not really want to do that.

TAISHA A: Exactly, no, they don't. There's a lot of interest in our work, in Carlos Castaneda and don Juan, but they don't really want it. What they have is an intellectual curiosity about the possibility that there is something else out there, because we all have that as human beings.

ABE: If we acknowledge that this sorcerer's path is really for the very few people who will actually walk it, why then did you publish your book?

TAISHA A: One reason is that Carlos Castaneda and Florinda Donner, myself and Carol Tiggs, are the last of don Juan's line. They didn't know at the time we were being trained that Carlos was going to be the next Nagual. And they trained us in dreaming and stalking and many of the techniques we're talking about. But then it turned out that Carlos is not at all a four-sided Nagual. A Nagual is one who has four energetic compartments. But he's a three-sided Nagual, meaning his mission is different. One of the major differences is that the Nagual woman who traditionally goes with the previous Nagual's group—in this case Carol Tiggs—first went with don Juan, but then one day she came back. The Nagual Carlos's intent, or Florinda Donner's and mine, literally held her back in this reality. In other words, her assemblage point shifted back so that she is now with us. Now that's absolutely unheard of in all the generations of Naguals and seers in don Juan's lineage. And because Carol came back she gave us that energy to actually write about our experiences.

ABE: What does this unprecedented change mean?

TAISHA A: The designs of the Spirit are absolutely different from what they were for don Juan. His group followed the rules, they had a certain training procedure. Although they were abstract, they were in this sense very concrete. They were practitioners of the things that were handed to them by the previous group, and they handed down these things to us. But what we actually keep are only the most abstract methods such as the recapitulation, the idea of impeccability, the idea of doing or not doing, which amounts to the total negation of practices or procedures.

The Nagual woman Carol Tiggs gave us this extra energy to bring these things out into the ordinary reality. Otherwise, they would forever have remained ideas only. And because we practise them, we are the ideas. There's no difference between what we say and what we do, and that's why we are able to move our assemblage points, because they're not only abstractions. Our bodies actually embody these things.

Yes, there are millions of people reading these books and any one of them could practise and succeed in finding the way. And the reason I say this is because you don't need a teacher. Being abstract, the way all of us are in this last generation, we can see that all you need is a minimal chance, an idea. So if a person does the recapitulation, the not doing exercises, etc. , the Spirit or the Intent itself will guide them and teach them because that's already built into the exercises and into the books.

ABE: What are some of the methods by which one can foster and cultivate stalking energy?

TAISHA A: There are techniques or devices that sorcerers use, and they include "not doing" techniques and "recapitulation," which is the fundamental technique of enabling the assemblage point to move off its normal position. There are also methods such as "losing personal history," which also enables one to move away from what our fixed idea of the self is. But losing self-importance is the key because, as I said, as long as we have this idea of a self, a strong self, an ego, a personality with which we interact with others in terms of intersubjective agreements, then we are held. You see, the strength of the world of the social order is so gigantic because of the agreement of billions of people holding that assemblage point at that particular spot.

ABE: So, at a really crass level, you could call it "peer pressure," and at a universal level you could call it "the spirit of the times."

TAISHA A: Yes. At a very individual level you could call it "self-indulging," or one's idea of the self, or bowing to peer pressure. And then at a larger cultural level there's language, the family, fundamental barriers you have to break through—individual, peers, family, culture—and then some gigantic collective unconscious that holds everything in place. A sorcerer has to jump out of all of that onto a different level. And then even behind this collective unconscious you have the biological mandate that we're really trapped in this "ape mold." We have our biological drive, we need to be social, gregarious beings because we're social animals. Solitude is something that frightens people to death. I mean, that's one of the killers of neophytes, the idea that they have to have a solitary journey, a solitary quest, because the recapitulation is done in absolute solitude. People think, well, they can meditate together, do things together, as long as they still have a group consensus. But you see, it's that very group concensus that prevents the subtle movement of the assemblage point. So you do have to get beyond that force, and you have to have the energy, and the energy comes from all the things that I mentioned before, including impeccability, and also using your death. You give a death, because you'll end up giving a death anyway. If you follow the sorcerer's path, if you wish to move away from the self, from that given position of the assemblage point and venture into the unknown, then it is like dying. The self has to capitulate, and it's a horrendous feeling, emotionally, physically. It is like, you know, man against the universe.

ABE: And that death is protracted, isn't it? I mean, it doesn't happen in one miraculous moment. It is something that progressively occurs. It could take years. When do you know you've really done it? When do you know that you've finally died to that old self, or become what is called in the literature a "formless warrior"?

TAISHA A: You have to be formless. You have to not have a self. First of all, like you say, it's not a sudden process, although it can be. The movement of the assemblage point can be in some anomalous cases sudden. A great shock all of a sudden moves it elsewhere and a different reality is constituted in front of the person. But that usually doesn't last because it comes from an external force, and it usually shifts back. If it does last, the person won't know what's happened, and those are the cases for the asylums, the institutions. So, a gradual change is best because you have control.

ABE: I take it that drugs, power plants, can also induce this?

TAISHA A: Yes, exactly. Under the influence of psychotropic drugs you see different worlds, and the assemblage point is absolutely blasted out of its position. But you are not doing that, you don't have the control. Again it's an external agent. The sheer presence of a Nagual moves the assemblage point, too. His impeccability can move the assemblage point in his students. He doesn't have to give them the slap on the back or anything like that. Sheer energy can cause apprentices to assemble different worlds. But you see, there again, whenever we were in the presence of don Juan and his people, their force made us do fantastic things. Those things I write about in my book. But when I came back to Los Angeles and they weren't around, there I was with the force of the social order on top of me, and my assemblage point moved back into the "first attention." The tragedy is that unless you move your assemblage point back to the places where it was under the influence of don Juan and his people, you barely remember what you did or what those worlds consisted of. They're like dreams. You have to store the energy to allow it to move into heightened awareness, so that you can maintain it there on your own and venture. And then you move it further. So it's a gradual shift.

ABE: How do you store or keep the energy to move your assemblage point?

TAISHA A: The "recapitulation" is the major method. I just want to mention that another way of moving it is sheer impeccability, by intending the movement. Intent is really a line, a force that connects one directly with the energy out there at large. And because it has an intelligence, a guiding order of sorts, they call it the Spirit, the Eagle. But when man links his personal energy to the energy out there through impeccable acts, the Spirit itself moves the assemblage point for him, because in a sense he has relinquished control. He has relinquished himself, his ego. He has let go and is allowing the guiding force of Intent to move him. And all of these sorcery activities that I mentioned, the recapitulation, all the not doings, have the sorcerer's intent already linked to them. So a person just has to do these things and let the Intent take him, and his assemblage point will move, because these are ancient techniques that have been handed down for generations within don Juan's lineage, and they already have that link to the Spirit inherent in them. We already know of the necessity of storing energy, because that's the only way to get out of the mold that we are born into as humans. We always like to talk in terms of the human ape, because it really puts man in a proper perspective.

ABE: I accept the ape metaphor very well. But the theory of evolution has never managed to explain to me how come we have these other capacities in us.

TAISHA A: What sorcerers say is that we are continually evolving. Therefore we should not limit ourselves to that ape-like position of the assemblage point. Within the luminosity of human beings is the potential for an infinite number of other possibilities. Yes, from the point of view of evolution we have sort of stopped, encrusted ourselves at the current position. But the force of evolution continues. Sorcerers are beings who at one time were human beings. But they have evolved to something else. They are no longer human beings in the strict sense of the word, because they can move their assemblage point elsewhere and maintain those positions, and actually change their form. They don't have to maintain their human form. They can move downwards, shift down to the animal level, so they can change shape into animals, into crows, into birds, or any other animal or entity. Or they can shift into inconceivable realms that have no physical counterparts, but are abstractions.

ABE: The literature speaks of two kinds of seers, old seers and new seers. Can you talk about the difference between the two?

TAISHA A: There is a distinction between the old sorcerers and the new sorcerers in don Juan's lineage, between his teacher the Nagual Julian and don Juan's apprentice, the new Nagual Carlos Castaneda. These latter are modern-day sorcerers, and what they're interested in is this evolution towards the abstract, away from any of these downward shifts that are so easy to do in dreaming when the assemblage point by itself finds these positions. And for that reason all of the people associated with Carlos Castaneda are university graduates, educated, clear thinkers (hopefully). I mean, that is one of our tasks. An actual sorcery task is to be able to think coherently, to think clearly, to see where we are as human beings, and to see what our potential is. We try to get to this level of actual truth by using reason in its strictest sense, not in the shoddy sense of reasoning something and then acting in some other totally contradictory fashion, which is what human beings do.

ABE: One meets people who have abandoned reason and logic, and the natural functions of the mind, and who end up in a kind of twilight zone of not really being able to derive any clarity about anything.

TAISHA A: Yes, and that was one of the major pitfalls of the old sorcerers, who emphasized dreaming techniques to shift the assemblage point, and who did not have the stalker's technique to balance that out. It's a question of balance, because unless you have the sobriety and the control, what's the point of moving the assemblage point? You move it and you get lost in those realms and you're never able to return to this level. Stalkers have that control. In stalking you create the reality wherever you are by creating structure, by imputing order, by reasoning. You can reason even if you're in a totally different realm. You can still maintain your awareness. You try to bring order to the inconceivable perceptions, the chaos that is the universe, and the prerequisite for shifting into different realities is the ability to summon the energy needed to keep your awareness intact while in them.

ABE: Can you talk in a more specific way about the "recapitulation"?

TAISHA A: Recapitulation is a very ancient technique handed down by the old sorcerers in don Juan's lineage, but it was sort of forgotten by them because they were more interested in power, in dominating people. The furthest thing from their mind was the idea of losing self-importance. But the new sorcerers revived this technique and we now consider it really the most fundamental technique in sorcery of all the techniques we learned for moving the assemblage point. And you don't have to be a "sorcerer's apprentice" or anything like that. Anyone can do it.

It is a technique for erasing the idea of self in terms of all the memories and associations with people that one had during one's lifetime. When one interacts with people energy is exchanged, and through deep emotions it's left in the world and in people. So the strategy is to regain that energy so that you can have it all with you now, in the present. Why leave it floating around in some mysterious past that holds you fixed in the place where you now are?

What you do is you find a place of quiet and solitude, an enclosed space preferably—the sorcerers used to have their recapitulation boxes where they would bury themselves, or go into caves—a place that encloses the energetic body so there is some pressure put on the luminous self. But before you sit you make out a list of everyone you've ever encountered throughout your life—your family, associates, etc. This takes some doing, some remembering, which in itself loosens the assemblage point. And you work backwards in time. Actually, you make two lists. You start with your sexual experiences because sorcerers say that's the fundamental energy that's lost out there, and if you retrieve that, then that will give you the boost to do your other people.

So you have your two lists and you sit in your recapitulation box and start the breathing. This third element, the breath, is very important because the breathing is what disentangles the energy. Our interaction with others is done with our energy body and the breath moves the luminous fibers. You start by putting your hand on your right shoulder, and when you have visualized perfectly the scenes of people and places in your mind, then you place your chin on your right shoulder and inhale, turning your head to your left shoulder. You then exhale moving your head back to your right shoulder, and then bring your head to center. It's like a sweeping of the scene. You sweep the whole scene, person, place, whatever, and you pull back whatever was left out there on the inhale, and exhale whatever of that other person's energy was left in you. So you detach yourself from that particular encounter, and you do this with everything.

After you've done this for your whole life, you've detached pretty much from your remembered past. This is not meant to be a kind of self-analysis, but you can't help seeing in the way you act and behave and what is expected of you a pattern forming. And with the breath you break that pattern. So what you essentially want to do is move into formless, patternless behavior, which is the way a sorcerer acts. He's absolutely fluid. Which brings us back to stalking. A stalker is someone who makes himself unobtrusive. He has no pattern, nothing to assert, no point to make, no demands, no desires. And all of this is eliminated through the recapitulation.

ABE: There is also something called "stopping the internal dialogue" in this tradition. Can you talk about that?

TAISHA A: The way these patterns are ingrained in us is through the internal dialogue, in which we keep repeating certain things to ourselves like, "Oh, I'm no good," or "They don't like me," or "I have to be like this to prove myself," this constant flow of thoughts or reaffirmations of the self. The sorcerers say that you need to put a stop to that continual reinforcement of the self, which fixes that position of the assemblage point.

When you begin to elongate these moments of silence by shutting off the internal dialogue, then you have the power that comes from sheer silence. That in itself will allow the assemblage point to move from your everyday state into heightened awareness.

So, by doing these techniques the seer within us gets to break out. There are lots of techniques like these in Carlos Castaneda's books, for example, certain gazing techniques. You can do a match technique where you just hold up the flame for a moment, gaze at it, then douse it, but not completely. Then turn it upside down and hold it in your left hand and look at the flame as it burns the bottom of the match. This quiets the mind. You can do any sort of minor meditation techniques to accomplish this, but I wouldn't recommend that you go heavily into Oriental meditation techniques because you're already doing the recapitulation and you don't want to get fixed into any form. All we're doing now as abstract sorcerers is a minimum of technique so that we can get away from the self. We don't want to get into the area of ego enhancement, i.e., "now we're meditators," etc.

ABE: So you don't want to build up an image of yourself, even as a spiritual person?

TAISHA A: No, you don't want to add to that, and when you look at how much you have to get rid of, you'll be kind of careful not to add more. *[laughter]* And that's where impeccability comes in. You want to maintain your daily behavior on an impeccable level, and that means you just do your humble best. We're no longer interested in reasserting the ego or the self, or defending the self. The brunt of our daily energy really goes into defense of the self because it's attacked left and right, and the mind rallies like lightning to try to patch up the ego's wounds. But the sorcerer lets it go. Don Juan had a good adage. He said, "Eliminate the self and fear nothing." If you don't have a self, there's absolutely nothing to fear, because all of our fears and disappointments come from our idea of the self, whether positive or negative.

So the only thing that the modern sorcerer or stalker is really dependent on is something so abstract that he calls it the Spirit, the Unknown. By getting rid of the self, they give the self to the Eagle as a token. They give themselves in a symbolic death, and in that sense the Eagle, they say, allows the impeccable warrior to escape.

ABE: And the old sorcerers were not able to do this?

TAISHA A: That's right. When the old sorcerers did dreaming, they had very heavy ego and so they got lost and trapped in different levels of dreaming. They had their ideas of power and they became obsessive, so they weren't able to move out again, because they were too heavy.

The modern-day stalker is not obsessed with anything. He treats the whole world as "controlled folly," which means that there's order, there's structure, but it's not to be taken seriously because there are other orders, other structures, an infinite number of layers to this onion of reality, and he can go elsewhere. But wherever he is, he creates his order and his structure, and when the Spirit moves him, something moves the assemblage point and he moves elsewhere. He's impeccable in his dreams and in this everyday reality if and when he's here.

ABE: Would you say it's a major accomplishment on the part of the would-be seer when they reach a point where they are no longer concerned with whether or not they are liked?

TAISHA A: Yes, that's a major accomplishment. The sorcerers have a theory about the energy you were given at your own conception. If the parents liked each other, sexually I mean, if they had a very grand time, a great sexual experience, when that child is conceived it will have this great burst of energy. And he may not care whether or not people like him because he has this intrinsic sense of energetic well-being. But, if one of the parents is bored—don Juan always called them "bored conceptions"—or if they just went through the motions of having sex because they were married and it was the thing to do on Friday night, then that child will come into the world with a real disadvantage. He will always feel that something is missing. He wants his peers to like him, he wants mama to like him, and she may not even like him at all.

Sorcerers can see how energetic a luminous being is. They can see how the energy moves. In some people it's very sluggish, stagnant, and of course that expresses itself in a very meek or low-level zest for life. In others it's strong. Everything to them is a challenge. They dominate people naturally, have this charismatic, almost mesmeric effect on others, and they are not as needy as other people.

ABE: Of course, then that person who has all that energy will attract all kinds of needy people who want to suck on it. *[laughter]*

TAISHA A: The sorcerers say that the self is really a metaphorical dagger that we stab ourselves with. But it's all right as long as we bleed in company. As long as there are others bleeding with us we're okay. *[laughter]* And I have to include myself in that category because absolutely I was not a product of a zestful union. And you see these demons in the recapitulation, which is never really done, because it has to be tried and tested in the everyday world. You can't just escape into the desert and do it, and then feel good and that's the end of it. Get back with your mother, your father. What do they do to you for you to react like the little girl, the little boy that wants mommy to do his laundry, to take care of his tummy? We still have those feelings. So, recapitulation just by itself is not enough. Stalkers stalk the Self, and so when they're with people in the world, they're constantly stalking themselves and seeing what's happening.

being-in-dreaming

FLORINDA DONNER
in conversation with
ALEXANDER BLAIR-EWART

Florinda Donner is a longtime colleague and fellow dream traveler of Carlos Castaneda. She is the acclaimed author of Shabono *(1982),* The Witch's Dream *(1985), and* Being-in-Dreaming: An Initiation into the Sorcerer's World *(1991). Anthropologist and sorceress, Florinda Donner lives in Los Angeles, California, and Sonora, Mexico.*

ALEXANDER BLAIR-EWART: Can you talk about this living myth of the sorcerer's world that you were drawn into?

FLORINDA DONNER: The myth of the Nagual is a myth, but a myth that is being relived over and over again. You see, the myth that exists is the myth that there is the Nagual and that he has his troop of apprentices and sorcerers. I was an apprentice of Castaneda who was an apprentice of don Juan. I am one of the "sisters" who were actually of the women of Florinda, and she gave me her name. So, in that sense, it is a living myth.

ABE: The myth of the Nagual is that there is an unbroken lineage from the ancient Toltecs right down to modern times. Can I get you to talk about what the pattern of the myth actually is?

FLORINDA D: Well, there is no pattern to the myth. That's why the whole thing is so baffling and so difficult. When I first got involved with these people my main quest, my main aberration, which I came to call it later, was that I wanted to have some rules and regulations about what the hell it is I had to do. There were none. There is no blueprint, because each new group has to find their own way to deal with this idea of trying to break the barriers of perception. The only way we can break the barriers of perception, according to don Juan, is to cultivate energy. Our energy is already deployed in the world to present the idea of self—what we are and who we want to be perceived as. Don Juan says 90% of our energy is deployed in doing that and therefore nothing new can come to us. There's nothing open to us, because no matter how "egoless" we are, or we pretend to be, or we want to believe we are, we are not. Even with, let's say, "enlightened" people, or gurus that I have met—at one time Carlos Castaneda was going around trying to meet gurus—the ego of those people was gigantic in terms of how they wanted to be perceived in the world. And that's, according to don Juan, exactly what kills us. Nothing is open to us anymore.

ABE: A real Nagual, a real seer, wouldn't care how the world perceives them, particularly, would they?

FLORINDA D: No, they don't. But they still have to fight it. Castaneda has been at this for thirty years. I've been at this for over twenty years, and it's ongoing; it doesn't stop.

ABE: You use the language of the warrior. What's the nature of the battle? What are you fighting?

FLORINDA D: The self. It's not even the self; it's an idea of the self, because if we really get below the surface, we don't know what it is. But it is possible to curtail this idea, this bombastic idea we have of the self. Because whether it's a negative idea or a positive idea doesn't really matter. The energy employed to sustain that idea is the same.

ABE: There's tremendous emphasis in this tradition on overcoming what is called self-importance.

FLORINDA D: That's the main battle, to shut off our internal dialogue. Because even if we are alone, we are still constantly talking to ourselves.

That internal dialogue never stops. And what does the internal dialogue do? It always justifies itself, no matter what. We replay things, events, what we could have said or could have done, what we feel or don't feel. The emphasis is always on "me." We're constantly spouting this mantra—"me... me ...me"—silently or verbally.

ABE: So, an opening emerges when. . .

FLORINDA D: When that dialogue shuts off. Automatically. We don't have to do anything. And the reason people reject Castaneda as not true is because it's too simple. But its sheer simplicity makes it the hardest thing there is to do. There are about six people in our world engaged in the same pursuit. And the difficulty we all have is in totally shutting off that internal dialogue. It's fine if we're not threatened. But when certain buttons are pushed, our reactions are so ingrained in us that it's so easy to fall back on automatic pilot. You see, there's one great exercise that don Juan prescribes—the idea of recapitulation. The idea is that you recapitulate your life, basically. But it's not a psychological recapitulation. You want to bring back to yourself the energy you left in all the interactions you've had with people throughout your life. You start from the present moment and you go backwards in time. But if you really do a good recapitulation, you discover, by the time you are three or four years old, that you have learned all your reactions already. Then we become more sophisticated, we can hide them better. But basically the pattern has already been established of how we're going to interact with the world and with our fellow human beings.

ABE: So the human being travels the path of the "Tonal," or the world of the social person. But this other world, this other opening, is something that has apparently always been there.

FLORINDA D: Yes, it's always there. Nobody really wants to tap into it, or people think they want to tap into it, but as don Juan pointed out, the seeker is usually involved in something false, because a person who seeks already knows what he's seeking. The disappointment that so many people who are "seekers" have with Castaneda is they have already made up their mind how things should be. So they're not open.

ABE: My version of that is that I'm interested in self-realization, not self-improvement. I'm not concerned with whether or not what I turn out to be in the process of realization is something nice and spiritual and acceptable, because it's going to contain elements of madness as well as everything else.

FLORINDA D: Exactly.

ABE: But this is a very deeply disturbing idea for most people.

FLORINDA D: It is, definitely. You see, we believe in this idea that we are basically energetic beings. Don Juan said everything hinges on how much energy we have. Even to fight the idea of the self requires an enormous amount of energy. And we move always to the easiest path. We go back to what we know, even we who have been involved in this for so long. It would be a lot easier just to say, "Oh, to hell with it, I'm just going to indulge a little bit." But the thing is, that little bit of indulging would plunge you right back to point zero again.

ABE: Except for one thing that we both know, Florinda, which is this: that once you pass a certain point within yourself, if you have reached that silence, I believe, even for one moment, if it's real...

FLORINDA D: ...you can't stop it. Exactly. But to reach this moment of silence you need the energy. You can reach what don Juan calls this momentary pause, this cubic centimeter of chance, and you can "stop the world" immediately. If a critical mass of people could arrive at that feeling or at that knowledge, we could really change things in the world. The reason nothing can change is because we're not willing to change ourselves, whether because of our attachment to political dogma, economic or social issues, whatever. What the hell is the whole thing with the rain forest and the environment at the moment? How can we expect someone to change if we're not willing to change ourselves? The change is phony; it is a restructuring or replaying of the pieces. Basically we are predatory beings, you see. That hasn't changed in us. We could use that predatory energy to alter our course, but we're not willing to change ourselves.

ABE: Now, in the myth, the individual seer and/or Nagual is selected by providence, the unknown, the ineffable.

FLORINDA D: Yes. Carlos has been "tapped" energetically. In terms of energetic configuration some people are energetically different. They call

Carlos a three-pronged Nagual; don Juan was a four-pronged Nagual. So what does that really entail? Basically, they have more energy than the rest of the group, and that's something very curious. Why the hell him, or why, for instance, are always the men Naguals? We have women Naguals in the lineage, but the men have more energy, the ones that have been selected so far at least. They're not better. There were people in don Juan's world who were infinitely more spiritual, better prepared, men of greater knowledge, and it didn't make any difference. It is not that Carlos is more or less than somebody else. It's just that he has that energy to lead.

ABE: And he can give of that energy, too, give somebody a boost.

FLORINDA D: We draw from that energy, yes. But it is more that he has the energy, if nothing else, *not* to become what the world presents. For instance, the worldly goodies that have been presented to Castaneda are unbelievable. But he has never wavered from his path. If I had been put in that position for that many years, I could not honestly say that I would have been so impeccable. And you see, for that you need energy. That's when you need whoever is then the leader of the group to point out that way. If somebody else who didn't have the energy had been the Nagual, he would have succumbed.

ABE: Can a Nagual succumb and then recover?

FLORINDA D: No. There is no chance.

ABE: Why is that?

FLORINDA D: Go back to the myth. The Eagle flies in a straight line. It doesn't turn around,

ABE: So, the Nagual works in different ways to fulfill the unfolding of the myth.

FLORINDA D: Don Juan had more people behind him. Energetically he had a larger mass, so he could practically pluck you out and put you someplace. Carlos will not do that. For him, whoever he is working with— there are six of us—it's a matter of decision. That's all. Our decision is all that counts, nothing else. He will not cajole us; he will not beg; he will not tell us what to do. We have to know. Having been exposed to this for so long, having been with don Juan, any way that we can try to walk on this path has to be enough for him.

ABE: Different Naguals work in different ways. I've heard Castaneda described as the Nagual of stalkers.

FLORINDA D: Yes, but I would say... I don't know... he's a dreamer.

ABE: Yes, that emerges, too. Could you talk about dreaming?

FLORINDA D: What is this idea of dreaming, dreaming and being awake? It's a different state. It's not that you're zonked out. No, you are totally normal and coherent, but something in you plays energetically on a different level.

ABE: There's something in your eyes, too, something in your eyes that is able to learn to look at two worlds simultaneously.

FLORINDA D: Exactly. And again the idea is that you have collapsed the barrier of perception. Whatever we perceive has been defined for us by the social order. Intellectually we are willing to accept that perception is culturally defined, but we will not accept it on any other level. But it's absurd, because it exists on another level. And I can only say, because I've been involved with these people—and certainly I'm also in the world—that it is possible to see on those two levels, and to be totally coherent and impeccable in both.

ABE: In the book *Being-in-Dreaming* you talk about how women are actually enslaved by their attachment to the sexuality of men.

FLORINDA D: Definitely. First of all, to me, one of the most shocking things which I denied and refused to believe for quite some time was this idea of the fog created by sexual intercourse. They went even further to explain that basically what goes on is that when we have sexual intercourse, when the male ejaculates, not only do we get the semen, but in that moment of energetic outburst, what really happens is that what don Juan calls "energetic worms" or filaments are passed into the woman. And those filaments stay in the body for a long time. From a biological point of view, those filaments ensure that the male returns to the same female and takes care of the offspring. The male will, at a totally energetic level, recognize that it is his offspring by their filaments.

ABE: What is the exchange of energy in sexual intercourse?

FLORINDA D: She feeds the man energetically. Don Juan believes that women are the cornerstone for perpetuating the human species. The bulk of that energy comes from the woman, not only to gestate, to give birth, and nourish her offspring, but also to ensure the male's place in the whole process.

ABE: So, the woman is enslaved, then, by this fog. How does she release herself?

FLORINDA D: If we talk about it from a biological point of view, is she enslaved? The sorcerers say yes, in the sense that she always views herself through the male. She has no option. I used to be excruciatingly mad about this whole discussion. I used to go over and over it with them, especially because this was in the early seventies when the women's movement was at its peak. And I said, "No, women have come a long way. Look at what they have accomplished," and they said, "No, they haven't accomplished anything." They said that for women to be liberated sexually, in a way, enslaved them even more, because suddenly they were feeding energetically not just one male, but many males. They were not prudes, and they were not interested in morality. They were only interested in energy.

ABE: That's interesting.

FLORINDA D: So, for them, it was absurd, and don Juan foresaw in the seventies what is happening now. He said that women were going to dive down on their noses, were going to be weakened. And they are. The few women I've talked to at my lectures and during the writing of my books agree. I thought I would have a great deal of difficulty with this subject, but especially women who have gone through the process of having multiple lovers said they were exhausted and they didn't know why.

ABE: So we are talking about something beyond the sexual.

FLORINDA D: Beyond the sexual aspect, the female womb ensures that the woman is the one who is closest to the spirit in this process of approaching knowledge as "being-in-dreaming." The man cones upward, and by the sheer definition of the cone, it comes to a finite end. He strives because he is not close to the spirit, or whatever we want to call that great energetic force out there. According to the sorcerers, the woman is exactly the opposite. The cone is upside down. They have a direct link with it because the womb for the sorcerer is not just an organ of reproduction; it is an organ for dreams, a second brain.

ABE: Or heart.

FLORINDA D: Or heart. And it does apprehend knowledge directly. Yet we have never been allowed to define what knowledge is in our society or in any society. And when women do create or help to formulate a body of knowledge, it has to be done in male terms. Let's say a woman does research. If she does not abide by the rules already established by the male consensus, she won't be published. She can deviate slightly, but always within that same matrix. It is not allowed for women to do anything else.

ABE: So the sorceress is removed from the hypnotism of all of that.

FLORINDA D: On the social level, yes. It's very interesting that you mention the idea of hypnotism, because don Juan always said that when psychology produced Mesmer and Freud we were too passive. We are mesmeric beings. We never really developed that other path.

ABE: Yes. The path of energy.

FLORINDA D: And this would never have happened to us if Freud hadn't attained the upper hand.

ABE: Well, he's lost it now.

FLORINDA D: No, not really, because who knows how many generations it takes to change something so deeply ingrained? He may be discredited intellectually, but people who don't even know who Freud is still talk in those terms. It's part of our language, our culture.

ABE: Yes, I know. It's very frustrating dealing with people who approach the whole of reality from this hackneyed psychological viewpoint.

FLORINDA D: Yes. And they don't even know where it comes from. It's part of our cultural baggage.

ABE: So the sorceress is freed from this condition.

FLORINDA D: Well, free in the sense that once you see that the social order really is an agreement, then at least you are more cautious in accepting it. People say, "Oh, but look how different life is from your grandmother's or mother's time." I say that it's not. It's only different in degree. But nothing is fundamentally different. If I would have lived my life the way it had been established for me—yes, I was more educated, I had a better chance—I still would have ended up the same way many do: married, frustrated, with children that by now I would probably hate, or who would hate me.

ABE: What occurs now that you've realized that there is that thralldom and you begin to free yourself from it? What is it that opens up to perception?

FLORINDA D: Everything. First of all, in your dreams you can "see." For instance, my work is done in dreaming.

ABE: Now you're using the word dreaming in a very specific sense as understood in this tradition. Can you talk about what dreaming actually is?

FLORINDA D: In the traditional sense, when we fall asleep, as soon as we start entering a dream, in that moment when we're half awake and half asleep, we know from Castaneda's work that the assemblage point flutters, it starts shifting, and what the sorcerer wants to do is that he wants to use that natural shift to move into other realms. And for that we need an exquisite energy. We need an extraordinary amount of energy because we want to be conscious of that moment and use it without waking up.

ABE: Yes, a very high accomplishment.

FLORINDA D: For me, it's very easy to enter, to use it. The thing is, I had no control at that time—although I have now—over when it was going to happen. But I could enter into this state of what they would call the "second attention" or "dreaming awake." And you can reach different levels. What happens is that in that dreaming state eventually you have the same control you have in your daily life. And that's exactly what the sorcerers do.

ABE: So you are now able to exist in another reality?

FLORINDA D: Well, I don't really know. You see, we don't have the language to talk about it, except in known terms. So in a weird way, when I ask myself, Do I exist in another reality? I have to say yes and no, because it is all one reality. There is no difference. Let's say there are different layers, like an onion. But it's all the same. So how am I going to talk about it? In metaphors? Our metaphors are already so defined by what we already know.

ABE: Yes, the problem of language.

FLORINDA D: But it is as real as any other reality. What is reality? It is, again, a consensus, and it all hinges on energy.

ABE: That's right. But it also hinges on something called "Intent."

FLORINDA D: Exactly. "Intent" is out there, it's this force. Don Juan was not interested in religion, but in a weird way maybe "Intent" is exactly what we call God, the supreme being, the one force, the Spirit. You see, each culture knows what it is. Don Juan said you don't beg for it, you ask. And in order to ask for it, you need energy. Not only do you need energy to hook yourself onto it, but you want to stay hooked.

ABE: This idea of "Intent" is easy to talk about, but it's actually quite a complex operation, isn't it?

FLORINDA D: Yes, exactly, very complex. For don Juan and his people, sorcery is an abstraction, and it is based on this idea of expanding the limits of perception. For them, our choices in life are limited by the social order. We have boundless options, but by accepting these choices, of course, we set a limit to our limitless possibilities.

ABE: And yet the human being seems...

FLORINDA D: ...constantly to be searching for that which has been lost or caged in by the social order. They put blinds on us the moment we are born. Look at the way we coerce the child to perceive the way we perceive.

ABE: Yes, the transmission of culture.

FLORINDA D: It's the most perfect example. Children truly perceive more, obviously, a great deal more. But they have to make some order out of that chaos, and we, of course, are the perennial teachers of what is proper to perceive within our group. And if they don't abide by that, my god, we shoot them with drugs, or lock them up in therapy with psychiatrists.

ABE: There have been these traditions, which have existed for a long, long time, and now in the last twenty or thirty years in particular we start to hear about them. Why did Castaneda write his books?

FLORINDA D: Writing those books was a sorceric task that don Juan impressed upon him. For our mentality as the Western ape, as don Juan always called us, we have to be hooked first intellectually, because that's how our whole being works.

ABE: So, the knowledge is made available to millions of people, and people become hooked by it. And does that mean that the tradition has now begun to proliferate itself in that way, also?

FLORINDA D: I don't know. If I go by Castaneda's mail, which he doesn't read, I would say yes. But I open letters from time to time, and they're mad, they're crackpots most of them. Some of them are very, very serious inquiries, but most of them are just truly cracked people. *[laughter]* Like, "I am the new Nagual," or "I have been visited by you in dreams."

ABE: Well, there are many levels to that, as you know. But I think that the whole Castanedan reality has actually affected the mass collective consciousness of, particularly, North America.

FLORINDA D: It is as you say. The work is out there. There's a great many people reading it. And some people are truly very serious about it.

ABE: Some of them are people who are non-Natives who have become involved in Native spirituality. And in a way, the work that has come from your group has had a tremendous quickening effect on Native spiritualities all over this continent, who have found a track back into their traditions.

FLORINDA D: You see, the whole point of don Juan was that you don't go back, because we get caught again in the myth and the rituals. Don Juan said that originally a ritual is only to hook your attention. Once your attention is hooked, you drop it. As the apes that we are, we of course are very comforted by the ritual. People that truly transcend a certain knowledge do it by exactly getting out of it. Yet the rest of the mass is mesmerized by the ritual.

ABE: Castaneda describes you as the new seers. What does this mean for you?

FLORINDA D: The new seers? For the women, it is very important, this idea that the womb is not just an organ of reproduction. In order to activate this, our intent has to be different. In order to change our intent, we go back again to energy. You see, we don't really know what it means to use the womb as an organ for being, an organ of light, of intuition. For us, intuition really is something that has already been defined. There is no real intuition anymore because we intuit with our brains. Don Juan was interested in women, and people always ask, "How come there's always so many women? Do you have orgies?" He said, "No, it's because the male doesn't have the womb. He needs that magical "womb power." *[laughter]* It's very important, you see.

ABE: Let me ask some technical questions there, if I may, on behalf of our female readers. Does the womb have to be fully functioning? I mean, if a woman had her tubes tied, would her womb still work?

FLORINDA D: Yes, as long as she doesn't have a hysterectomy.

ABE: So long as the womb isn't removed.

FLORINDA D: Yes. The only thing is you need to summon that intent. I was talking to some women a month ago, and they were all in goddess groups. Every month they go into the forest; they go up to Sequoia or someplace and they groove in the forest, among the trees, and oh, they have a great time hanging out, debating, making rituals in the river. And I said to them, "But what the fuck are you doing? You go back home, and then you are the same assholes you were before. You open your legs whenever the master says, 'I need you.'" And they were shocked. I mean, they quite disliked me because they don't like to hear that. They said, "But we felt so good for three days." And I said, "What's the point of feeling good for three days if your life continues the same way?" What are we resting from? Why don't we change? The idea of these rituals and even going back to the Native beliefs—well, it didn't even work back then, on one level. We *were* conquered.

ABE: So it's something that has to live now in a completely authentic way.

FLORINDA D: It has to be fluid, and the practitioner has to be fluid to accept these changes. Even within us, things are changing constantly, and we're so comfortable in a certain groove until something blasts us out of it. And we resent it. But we have to be fluid, and only energy will give us that fluidity.

ABE: How do you accumulate energy?

FLORINDA D: To start off with, at least at the beginning, it was don Juan's idea that the best energy that we have is our sexual energy. It's the only energy that we really have, and most of our sexual energy is squandered.

ABE: Is it the same for men and women both?

FLORINDA D: Of course it's the same for men and women. The only difference is that with women you see that energetically the woman takes on the burden of feeding the man through her energetic filaments. So, in that sense, it's worse for women, and for the man, too, because the man is hooked. Energetically he is hooked, no matter what. And we have all kinds of psychological explanations for this to do with the people we've had affairs with, or our obsession with certain relationships, or whatever. You see, we have this gray barrage of psychological description, but what really is going on is on a totally different level, a level that we don't want to talk about because it's not part of our cultural kit.

ABE: So the primary way of accumulating energy is to be celebate?

FLORINDA D: Well, it's very difficult, but it would be a good start.

ABE: If a person was called to this path, that is if they got "hooked," how would they know that they had been hooked by a tradition and not just by some damn obsession?

FLORINDA D: You will know that something has changed because you will feel it energetically. And you know that you are not part of the social agreement. You see, if you let something go, something in you will know.

ABE: These books that you and others have written are affecting a change in the way people perceive themselves.

FLORINDA D: Yes. Basically the goal is realizing how we perceive the world and ourselves, and breaking those parameters of perception. But we don't want to focus on the "I." We want to be a witness. Because everything in our society is filtered through the "I," through the "me," we are incapable of telling a story or recounting an event without making ourselves the main protagonist. You see, don Juan was interested in letting the event unfold itself, and then it becomes infinitely richer, because then it opens up. And even in the world, as an exercise, just become a witness. Stop being the protagonist and it's amazing what opens up.

ABE: Now, on this long path, one of the things that's described in the literature is that the person, the seer and the Nagual, everybody, will reach a period of despondency, where they're sure it's going to fail. And the reason I raise this is because I have a sense that this feeling is actually being shared by many people now.

FLORINDA D: I'm going to add to your depression. [laughter] It is true. Something in us knows, and that's why there's the urgency with don Juan. The imperative from the point of view of Nature is the perpetuation of the species, and we are no longer interested. We are interested in evolution, because evolution is an equal, if not a greater, imperative than procreation. If we don't evolve, if we don't mutate into something different, we are truly going to blast ourselves out of this planet, I think irredeemably. We have destroyed our resources. Whether we have fifty or a hundred more years in terms of time, as a planet, is immaterial. It doesn't really matter. We as a species are doomed. And in that sense, evolution is our only way out. And as don Juan stresses, evolution is in the hands of women, not of men.

ABE: So, as a male, what do I do? I just sit here and wait for women to save the world?

FLORINDA D: Yes and no. You see, the man has to relinquish his power, and he's not going to do it, not peacefully. I'm not saying that, you know, you're beating your chest, saying, "I will not relinquish my power!" No, it's much more insidious than that. For instance, here are these sensitive men who have been in men's groups, trying to come to terms with their spirituality, and who have moved into a place of total agreement with their wives, or the female they are with... but not quite. There are certain things they will not relinquish because it's too threatening. This whole idea of the men's movement originally started out as a truly spiritual movement. But something in the male is threatened. There is this fear of relinquishing something that will have to be relinquished for us as a species to go on. We certainly know that the female has to be given time for something to evolve. For instance, for us to become erect, when the vagina had to change position, well, who had to adapt? The males. The penis had to grow larger. Well, the female again needs time. And the male has to give her that time. From one point of view the male has to give the female time for the womb to try to switch into its secondary function. There have to be enough females who have that time so that something will change in the womb. They have to dream a new possibility. Don Juan said our evolution is Intent. You see, that leap from the large crawling reptiles to flying creatures, this idea of wings, was *intended*. It was an act of Intent.

ABE: That's very interesting. So you feel that women all over the world currently, sisterhoods of different kinds, are intending a new human future?

FLORINDA D: They're not aware of it although some women, I think, are.

ABE: And the man is now going to take a backseat in the evolution of the species?

FLORINDA D: Not a backseat, really. Again, those are words that suggest a positive/negative kind of connotation. No. It's more that you have to provide the time.

ABE: How can the man do that? Talk about that functionally.

FLORINDA D: You see, we women are relegated to the status of second-class citizens. No matter what power we attain, we still don't have any real power. We don't decide anything. And even for us to talk in little groups is almost like banging against a huge iron door, because whoever decides, whoever's in power, is not going to relinquish this for the hell of it. Do you think for a moment those men in Washington or Ottawa are going to even listen to what we're saying? Not in the least. But some kinds of pockets have to be found for something new to develop. Otherwise we're doomed. And in terms of this idea of saving the planet, the environment, well, all we are really thinking is that we as a species will not survive. The Earth will certainly survive; it might go into some kind of horrendous winter, but eventually it will come out of it. But we as a species will not survive.

and then the white buffalo woman began to sing

JEWEL

in conversation with
ALEXANDER BLAIR-EWART

Jewel Kilcher from Homer, Alaska, won a part scholarship to Michigan's Interlochen Arts Academy where the people of Homer continue to support her. She won a full scholarship for her senior year. A spring-break visit to her mother in San Diego caused her to fall in love with the sunshine state where she subsequently moved. At eighteen years of age she found herself living in a Volkswagen van and surviving on the small proceeds from a once-a-week coffee house singing performance at the Inner Change Coffee House in Pacific Beach. The range of her voice and the emotional and spiritual complexity of her songs is already a legend. At the time of this conversation her recording Jewel Pieces of You *on Atlantic is gathering momentum. She tours incessantly. She has much to say.*

ALEXANDER BLAIR-EWART: Was there contact with Native American Indian culture there in Alaska, or is that something that's also evolved through your journey?

JEWEL: I was adopted in the Indian way by a family when I was fourteen. My mother was always spiritually guided, a woman of integrity, very wise, and has always had the strength to listen to herself and her heart. And to be raised around a woman like that was a great learning. She would listen to her dreams and be fascinated by them and in awe of them, and try to understand them. So I was raised with a sense of magic, and also a very deep appreciation and love for the Indian way.

ABE: I don't know if you can talk about it, but I take it that you were invited into Native spirituality beyond the level that most people experience.

JEWEL: I don't feel I was particularly singled out, or anything. But my heart craved that kind of spirituality and I wanted to understand it, and I was given an opportunity to participate in dances or drum circles. I've carried medicine bags with me since I was very young.

ABE: There is a very real sense of you as being deeply connected to this North American land.

JEWEL: To be separate from what is sacred to me, is like being suffocated. I was raised in Alaska. My father was raised with the land. I don't think he's a very, say, religious person, in that sense, or very self-consciously spiritual. And so I was raised with a great respect for the land, how to work with it and understand it, and listen to the porcupine sound and hear the calling trees. And my mother is a very intensely spiritual woman, and so I was fortunate enough to be raised in a very nurturing environment. My personal world wasn't very pretty, emotionally, and that caused me to depend on and have faith in the spiritual.

ABE: When you were adopted in the Native way at fourteen, was that like a small family?

JEWEL: It was a group, a gathering, a talking circle, and I was adopted by one uncle, which meant that my family was large because there was my uncle and his brother and all the other adopted people. I remember there was a lot of fuss there because all the wives were worried their husbands liked me. So, I didn't fit in very well. *[laughter]* Anyway, in the talking circle I was paralyzed, shy, couldn't think of things to say, anything real. I'd written my whole life and was verbally speechless. I was only able to express myself when I wrote. My uncles took me up on a mountain and walked with me and told me of the White Buffalo Woman, and said that I had a gift to give to the world, and that I first had to learn... Do you know the story of White Buffalo Woman?

ABE: I don't think I do.

JEWEL: You know the white buffalo that was recently born?

ABE: Tell me about the white buffalo.

JEWEL: I'll see if I can remember the story well. I'm terrible for details. I sort of get a feeling from the story. Buffalo woman carried the pipe to the first American Indians, and she was beautiful, silvery, almost like a ghost with long hair. And she danced across the meadow to two young braves, and she said, "I have something to give, Who will take it?" And the more arrogant one who thought she was very beautiful and had not the most pure intentions, went more aggressively for her, and the other stayed back. And she knew by this that he was not the one. That it was the one with the humility. And my uncles said that it was in Buffalo Woman's wisdom to see the difference between them, and that this was something I needed to learn. I needed to learn to speak from my heart more. It was very hard for me. I remember going up on a mountain by myself and trying to say anything to the wind, and I couldn't. I made a very conscious effort to learn to speak honestly, of my heart. And not to rely too heavily on clever. I was deeply into philosophy at the time. I believe Einstein said, "Sell your cleverness and buy bewilderment." *[laughter]*

ABE: What kind of philosophy were you into at that time?

JEWEL: I read a lot of Kant and Plato, Dostoevsky, many other people. that's when I realized that none of us are taught to think. And it's also when I started believing that contradiction was the root of all evil. *[laughter]* That's the problem with reason. So around that time one of my teachers took me aside and he said, "Jewel, why are you telling everybody when they contradict themselves?" I was making terrible enemies at school, as you can imagine, in tenth grade, causing quite a ruckus, calling teachers hypocrites. *[laughter]* And I said, "Because I want to bring about change." And he said, "Well then, wouldn't you want to do it through the most efficient means? And I said, "Well, yes." And he said, "Well then you should do like a positive virus would, where you enter slowly and take them over." And I like that. I really appreciate that thought, and it's something I've really taken to heart. It gives me much patience.

ABE: What does philosophy mean to you?

JEWEL: A train of thought, I think, it means less to me now that it used to. I like it, though, it taught me you could read anything and find profound meanings in it. Like, we had a second grade class reading *The Velveteen Rabbit,* and by the end of it these little second graders were asking, "Just because Mommy and Daddy love me, does it make me real?" That's a killer, you know. I mean, most adults don't even take the book that far. And I like philosophy because it taught me to look at things, even if you were reading meaning into it that wasn't implied, that's fine. Get out of what you can. And it taught me to layer my writing.

ABE: So you read a lot. Who do you especially like to read?

JEWEL: I'd say especially I like to read Pablo Neruda. I love his poetry. Another South American poet, whom I haven't been able to find another book on, her name is Giaconda Belli. I love the South American poets, fiery, passionate, full of revolution and love and lust and... ah!

ABE: Have you read any of Octavio Paz?

JEWEL: I have, I love Octavio Paz. I understand Neruda's style more than I understand Octavio Paz. I could write like Bob Dylan, but I could never write like Harry Nilsson, not because one is better than the other, but it's the way I work in certain ways. And Octavio Paz I just stare at and go, "How does he do that?" It's beyond my ability to even understand the order, and it's beautiful.

ABE: So, is there a favorite Neruda poem?

JEWEL: "Your Breast Is Enough" is probably one of my favorites.

ABE: In the song "Pieces of You," (and I would like to include the words to it here so that our readers will understand what we are talking about), you seem to be taking a strongly anti-racist anti-bigot point of view, you feel like you've really made a stand about that. And I was just wondering what's informed that for you.

She's an ugly girl, does it make you want to kill her?
She's an ugly girl, do you want to kick her in her face?
She's an ugly girl, she doesn't pose a threat
She's an ugly girl, does that make you feel safe?
Ugly girl, ugly girl, do you hate her
'Cause she's pieces of you?
She's a pretty girl, does she make you think nasty thoughts
She's a pretty girl, do you want to tie her down?
She's a pretty girl, do you call her a bitch?
She's a pretty girl, did she sleep with your whole town?
Pretty girl, pretty girl, do you hate her
'Cause she's pieces of you?
You say he's a faggot, does it make you want to hurt him?
You say he's a faggot, do you want to bash in his brain?
You say he's a faggot, does he make you sick to your stomach?
You say he's a faggot, are you afraid you're just the same?
Faggot, Faggot, do you hate him
'Cause he's pieces of you?
You say he's a Jew, does it mean that he's tight?
You say he's a Jew, do you want to hurt his kids tonight?
You say he's a Jew, he'll never wear that funny hat again,
You say he's a Jew, as though being born were a sin.
Oh Jew, oh Jew, do you hate him
'Cause he's pieces of you?

JEWEL: I never perceive myself as making stands. I see myself as going through my life learning and growing. And outwardly expressing what phase I'm at. So, it's not as though I mean to talk against racism. I think that it's obvious, what racism is. Perhaps I take it for granted. I was fortunate enough to be raised around parents that were not prejudiced. I did have black boyfriends and my dad was ecstatic that he'd raised a daughter that wasn't afraid, you know. I believe in embracing our differences. I'm not so much a strong feminist as I'm a strong humanist.

ABE: When you're doing your songs do you feel like the audience is in total agreement with you on for instance that racist issue? Or do you feel there are other ripples, there, other undercurrents.

JEWEL: I think there are always undercurrents. I don't believe there's *the* truth. I believe that one of the reasons that people come to performances is to gather things to themselves, to add to their own knowing. I think ultimately we know what's right in ourself. Reality is relative to our inner integrity. I had a girl come to a show in Vancouver and say, "I love that song 'Pieces of You.'" But then she said "I was looking around the room and I thought, yeah, but that's only half the truth. I mean it's not the truth. And what if people really think that the only reason racism exists is because other ethnic groups are pieces of you?" And I'm like, "I'm no prophet. I'm just saying that often we spend so much energy looking at others, and we have to look at ourselves once in a while." And it's not like "Pieces of You" is going to be a consistent theory. I don't believe there is any such thing.

ABE: There are Angels in your songs. So if I ask, What is an Angel? What does that mean for you?

JEWEL: What is an Angel? I'm very shy talking about it.

ABE: I know, because Angels are often described as being very powerful and therefore very shy, very sensitive. So, I'm aware that there's a certain crassness in getting you to talk about angels. *[laughter]* This is an interview so I have to do this.

JEWEL: I do believe we are assisted. I do believe we are loved beyond our ability to even understand. And I do believe we have Angels.

ABE: From listening to some of your brilliant raconteuring, about your wild adventures, I guess that you must believe that you're protected.

JEWEL: Not in the sense that I believe that I am somehow special, or chosen, or any of those words. I do believe, though, that we are all divine by nature. I do believe that Angels whisper in our ears asking us to remember our royal heritage. And I am infinitely supported. If you ask for what your heart desires, if you know you are God, then the universe will respond to you. I believe that we are supported. When I feel very lonely, or very scared that I am too young, too inexperienced, or too weak to handle some things, I imagine the support of everything that is around me. It's immense, and sacred. Women come up to me and say, "I used to really be into Angels, but now that they've become so popular I'm not really into them anymore." And I think we should always have the courage to love what moves us and not to move on unless it uninspires us. But to move on prematurely is sort of cowardly.

ABE: I have a sense that you're very ecologically concerned as well. That really comes through. Is that the Alaska experience?

JEWEL: It is the experience for me of what is sacred. I was raised with a sense of sacredness around me, of God around me in the beauty, in simplicity. And I felt close to that, I felt close to my own spirit. And so, I suppose I'm not concerned ecologically to the extent that I see kids here worrying about the pollution, although of course that concerns me. I'm more concerned about how separate we are from what is sacred, and how hollow we become when away from what is natural.

ABE: That in itself is very interesting because what I hear you having just said to me is that you're not a resource ecologist, that you don't see the planet as, you know, if we look after it we're always going to have plenty of wood to burn, or build houses with, or that we're going to have clean water. But that there's more to it than that.

JEWEL: I feel that it's a learning, on many levels. I feel that it's all one process. It's kind of beautiful when I step back far enough and watch, that we're learning to care for our planet. We're learning to embrace the American Indian tradition and marry the sacred gifts of each culture. And I think it's exciting and I feel like it will work itself out. I don't feel too afraid concerning that.

ABE: At some point you decided maybe that you were going to go for the music totally, rather than going to university. Or is that something that's still open for you?

JEWEL: I didn't know what I was going into. I knew I didn't want to go to school. School was hard for me. I would have appreciated a mentorship. In that sense it was how I personally learned better, an apprenticeship, sort of... but there's nothing like that in our societies today. So it was a hard time. I've always felt so restless, so pushed to do something, and had no idea what it was. I was like a bird needing to fly south. I just didn't know which direction south was. It was very unsettling until I ended up with my mother in San Diego. And then there were the waitressing jobs and the like. It was a very hard time for me. It nearly killed me. I wanted to check out again from this lifetime, you know. I was horribly scared. I didn't know how to make this world work. It seemed so foreign and unsupportive.

ABE: How old were you at the time that happened?

JEWEL: Eighteen. And I really didn't know if I was up to it, to sacrifice your pride and health just for a roof. I'm capable of so much more, and I didn't know how to do it. But I also had this strong sense of, damn, it, I don't want to come and get to this point again for nothing. I want to figure it out. So at least I had this very strong drive of, well I don't want to die and so I'm going to figure this out, damn it. And that's when I really became willing to drop out of society, to die if that's what it took, to do what I love, and to do what my heart wants. And it was hard to figure out, well what the hell do I want? I started singing just to make money. I never thought of a record deal or anything. And I just prayed in my van every night that by me living my dream somehow people would remember theirs. And that's what I've been fortunate enough to accomplish.

ABE: So you're kind of on a mission, aren't you?

JEWEL: I wouldn't say I'm on a mission any more than you are, or any more than a housewife is. It's just that I feel purpose in what I'm doing. My life feels filled with purpose, and that's very beautiful, and I wish for people's lives to be filled with that as well. And I like that now there's no weight on the contradiction. I love that. I love that we're North and South, and I just think it's the best thing. I'm very naive, of course. And these writers put in the papers, "She's naive," as though it were some discovery. And, like, "I'm twenty-one!" *[laughter]* It's no big discovery. I'm also wise in some ways. I'm also very girlish and very womanly in others. And I enjoy being all those for people on stage because it's not often we get to see that. It's usually a very singular persona that we see in an entertainer or a hero, very consistent. I'm very sweet, but I cuss, and those are all things that change and come and grow, and I don't mind being that in front of people. I enjoy being able to be spiritual and very real, and functioning. I enjoy doing that for people because it does bring freedom into people's lives.

ABE: I think part of what goes on in this culture, though, is that instead of people saying, "Look, Jewel, I'm cynical because of what's happened in my life, and you're not. Tell me, how do you manage to stay not cynical?" I mean, they say you're naive, which means you're not cynical...

JEWEL: Isn't that a pisser? *[laughter]* Like, give me some credit. I think you have to work to stay innocent. I don't think you lose innocence. I do believe you have to work to stay innocent, and to stay optimistic. It's a choice.

ABE: Well the choice is that you don't develop a fixed image about yourself. And I think this is true for everyone, if the public person gets to grab all your other moments, you're in trouble.

JEWEL: Yeah, oh, definitely. That's very clear for me.

ABE: And I don't know if there's any way that you can actually be prepared in advance to be a public person...

JEWEL: It also depends on what skills you've been given to understand. I mean, a lot of us just aren't given any skills for understanding the energies involved and what those energies can become. I'm so ahead of most musicians, and that's not because of me. It's because I've had people around me to teach me that there are energies, and to learn how to separate and differentiate.

ABE: It seems to me that what we are talking about here is beautifully epitomized in your song or poem "I'm Sensitive" and I am wondering if I can get you to recite it.

JEWEL: You really want me to do that?

ABE: Yes! Yes, please.

JEWEL: Okay. Well it goes...
I was thinking that I might fly today

Just to disprove all the things that you say
It doesn't take a talent to be mean
Your words can crush things that are unseen
So please be careful with me, I'm sensitive
And I'd like to stay that way.
You always tell me that it's impossible
To be respected and be a girl.
Why's it gotta be so complicated?
Why you gotta tell me if I'm hated?
So please be careful with me, I'm sensitive
And I'd like to stay that way.
I was thinking that it might do some good
If we robbed the cynics and took all their food.
That way what they believe will have taken place
And we can give to people who have some faith.
So please be careful with me, I'm sensitive
And I'd like to stay that way.
I have this theory that if we're told we're bad
Then that's the only idea we'll ever have.
But maybe if we're surrounded in beauty
Some day we will become what we see
'Cause anyone can start a conflict.
It's harder yet to disregard it.
I'd rather see the world from another angle.
We are everyday Angels
Be careful with me 'cause I'd like to stay that way.

ABE: There's a struggle that we all have. Because the brutality of society is saying, "Why don't you grow a rhinoceros skin." Many people find that to be the easiest thing to do. But how to stay sensitive, how to stay open, how to stay truly alive. How do you stay sensitive?

JEWEL: It's a process and it's also a need and when I grow sad it's just when I feel separate from the sacred. And I'm able to go longer and longer distances away from my mountain. I'm learning to bring my mountain with me, so to speak. Mountain meaning just what I associate with what is sacred to me. And I make sure to pray in the mornings and in the evenings, and in my thoughts remember myself. And each day just grow and learn new ways of doing it, and try to remember that I am, I already am.

ABE: In some respects you can be seen as a blossoming of the sixties. And I'm wondering, what do the sixties mean to you?

JEWEL: Well, I wasn't raised around hippies until later in my life. But they didn't carry the same weight that I think... I'm not very aware of what went on, to tell you the truth. I was raised in Alaska, and it never really hit, you know. I was raised a bit isolated from it, although I understand the basic principles, and all the stories you hear. So I guess I feel like a couple different things. I feel like kids want the sixties again, and so there's a strong resurgence. If music were to reflect a social consciousness, a climate of opinion of a society, I think it does. I think the early sixties really reflected where people were at with sexuality. It was, like, "Oh my god—Elvis!" you know. And the later sixties really reflected the social change that was going on.

ABE: How would you characterize the decades since the sixties?

JEWEL: Well I think the eighties reflected the sleep. The nineties reflected "Okay, I've been raised in cities. I feel fucked up and I feel hollow, and I don't know what the hell to do. I'm going to kill myself." And then now all of that is reaching a new stage. It's turning around and going, "Okay, what do I do about it?" And I think when people felt the most meaning of any of those generations was in the sixties and seventies. And so they want to return to that.

ABE: So are the nineties and beyond going to be a sixties replay, a nostalgic revival, or are there differences?

JEWEL: There are some fundamental changes, I think. This might seem very naive of me to say, but I don't feel like there's really any "us" and "them" anymore. And I feel like it's just "us" now, people trying to do the best they can with what they've been given, and there are no lines to be drawn in that sense. And also to start doing it without drugs. I feel like the sixties were ahead of their time, in a sense. I mean they prepared ground, so nothing is ahead of its time, but I feel like it is coming back around in even more beautiful and more accessible and more grounded ways.

ABE: Earlier you were talking about reincarnation without actually naming it. And I was just wondering what does reincarnation mean to you, and do you have a sense of other times, other places?

JEWEL: Yes. I believe the purpose of the soul is to experience, to gather experience and emotions, and to be all things. I believe compassionate people have been many things, and thus are compassionate.

ABE: So I'm wondering what your other ancestry is like, if I can lure you out to talk about it.

JEWEL: I do, but I don't really feel like going into it too deeply, just out of its newness to me.

ABE: It's a tricky thing to talk about, anyway.

JEWEL: Out of a loyalty to myself, when things are new I'm careful.

ABE: I'm with you all the way. So without getting too specific about current new reincarnation realizations, would I be right in thinking that your Native experience...?

JEWEL: Yeah, I sense a lot of North American Indian, and many other experiences inside this, but I wouldn't even know how to start to single one out. I have a sense of great strength, as well as great pain, you know, a wide spectrum of experience in other times.

ABE: Does it show itself in your creativity in some way?

JEWEL: Yeah it does a lot, I am aware of my writing being from something else. I write of things that, not only are imaginary, but are something beyond that, thinking of other times, other experiences.

ABE: Do you have any memory of when this other time awareness began for you in this life?

JEWEL: As a child, before I knew my name, I remembered being conscious of myself again in my body, and standing at the bottom of the stairwell in the basement, and inside myself I could feel the physical space as though it were a large cool space inside of me, likened to a thick old stone walled cathedral, cool. In my head were these colors. And my mom was yelling at the top of the stairs, "Jewel, how'd you get there?" And I went, "Are you

Jewel?" And all those colors, speaking to them. "How'd you get there, Jewel, c'mon up." And I must have been very young, and I remember going, "Yeah, I'm Jewel." And that was what Jewel was, was the colors in my head. And that has led me my whole life, and I've always had an awareness of my feet when I was little and going, "How close they are to my nose." *[laughter]* And then in five years going, "My, they're further now." How funny that this body carries me around. I've always had a certain sense of that.

ABE: I think almost everyone has their version of that. But somehow because of the way we live we forget these important things, and in the process forget who we are. I've asked a lot of people this inane childish question, "When did you first know you were you?" An amazing number of people have a spiritual experience in that first moment of self-recognition.

JEWEL: That's true, and it is true also that so many of us forget, or don't even get a chance to ever remember how whole we really are. They tell us that we are fallen, that's just what breaks my heart, that people really believe their skin is dirty. It breaks my heart. They believe they're alone. I used to believe I was alone. It's a horrible thing to believe. It really is uncomfortable to be so confused by yourself, to never even be taught how to think of yourself, much less of another, to feel that separate from your skin, to feel as though somebody had to die for something you did wrong. It's all very strange to me.

ABE: Were you brought up as a traditional Christian?

JEWEL: No, I wasn't. I see it in people. Plus, it's a very strong belief in us, perhaps genetically the belief is passed on. I was raised Mormon, which is a pretty benevolent religion. There's no hell.

ABE: I'm with you that it's genetic by now. After two thousand years...

JEWEL: Yeah, and it's intense. And it's just so in our society, it really is. "I'm only human." I hate that saying! I'm only human, as if it were some excuse to do something wrong. I don't get it. *[laughter]* What a strange way to, say, have compassion for me. And also, to be raised away from anything that's real, anything that's spiritual or sacred, not to be taught about how to think about yourself so that you have to go to a therapist to understand, to be intimate with yourself. And no wonder people do drugs so much, or drink martinis before bedtime. Because it's hard. There is a hole in us.

ABE: There's an outpouring of energy that comes from you, and then there's a collective energy that comes from the audience, and it flows backs into you, and then you have to transmute that energy. So there's probably a marked difference in each place afterwards with the energy that you've received, too. And I'm wondering, what do you do with that energy? How does that work through you?

JEWEL: I'm learning. It's very overwhelming. I'm extremely sensitive, and to pour yourself out, as I do, not only during my show—that the end of my day, and I've had a full day of press and people pulling at you, you know, and little sleep—and then at the end of the day you do a show where you empty yourself utterly, and fill yourself with people's hopes and dreams, sicknesses and fantasies. All the energies, balanced and unbalanced. And so, in learning to transmute them, I've learned certain things, like, to dance in the mornings in a spiral to bring things out of myself. Things like that. But it's a learning process, and it's what I am here to do, and I have no doubt that I will learn to do it better. Also learning just to realize that sometimes I cry and it's not because of me. It's just their energies in me.

ABE: You had a deep reaction, a response as so many of us did to the Kurt Cobain suicide. You have a song which is like an ode to Kurt Cobain. And I remember wanting to learn the words of that as you were singing it.

JEWEL: It's one of my favorites. I love it as a poem.
Your mother's child.
But night lays you down
Hair aflame, wild look in your eyes
Naked belly to the ground
Forest fire nibbles at your veins
Crawls up your arm
Runs away with your mind
And burns dry thoughts like leaves
Amen.
Eyes stare up but something's in the way
In the Bible only Angels have wings
And the rest must wait to be saved.
A dry tongue

Screams at the sky
But the wind just breathes words in
As a strange bird tries to fly
Amen.
Pieces of us die every day
As though our flesh were hell
Such injustice, as children we are told
That from God we fell.
Where are my Angels?
Where's my golden one?
Where's my hope
Now that my heroes have gone?
Some are being beaten
Some are being born
And some can't tell
The difference anymore
Amen
Hallelujah
Hallelujah....

ABE: There it is again, the awareness invoked by real poetry. That says so much to me. I think that we all need to open ourselves to try and understand this new generation, in their own terms.

JEWEL: He was the spokesperson for that nineties generation, that "I feel fucked up" generation, and he let it consume him, as you can as a young artist. Like, for me, my first paintings were so dark. And you can easily get caught up in that your whole life, or you can make a choice and go, "Wow, that could just kill me." I feel like he was so helpful just showing people, you know—the hero for the heroless? And it showed a lot, I think, where a generation was, or is. And I think it also shows the product of being told that you're ugly—so you act ugly, or you feel ugly. The song was not so much for him as much as for the suicide following he had.

ABE: Do you think that suicide following has dissolved now?

JEWEL: Probably, yeah.

ABE: And here you are, you're twenty-one years old, and so you are a member of that nineties generation. Generation—what does that mean anymore? Things are blurry in one way. But in another way they're very definitive. Do you have any thoughts about where your generation is moving to? What kind of world are they trying to bring into being?

JEWEL: Well, say when a person dies that you love, you go through phases—shock, denial, anger, grief, and then finally acceptance, i.e., how am I going to deal with this? I feel like this generation, we're kind of like doing that in our evolution. I think it's an exciting time to be alive. I think we're at the phase where we're like, okay, we have a lot of things that have gone before, we've been able to learn a lot. We've been able to enjoy the benefits and the excesses and the wisdom of those who have gone before us. And I feel that it's a great time to be alive. I think people are waking. I think it's an accelerated time. I think invention is accelerated. I think things will start to be more and more inventive.

ABE: It's hard to be young right now, and I agree that its all in the learning from one generation to another and hopefully that goes both ways, but you also have to ignore the past and do something new that belongs to the unique and present time.

JEWEL: Yeah, so I'm excited. I'm excited about my generation. I hope my excitement spreads to other people. I think there's a great hopelessness that plagues us, and it really doesn't need to be. I think it's a pretty darn nice time to be alive and to be thinking. We've a lot of luxuries afforded us, and more than enough skills to handle the problems we have. And most importantly, I feel that today we're learning. You know, I don't know personally how to solve the pollution problems. I don't know personally how to solve the political problems. I just know how to, in my own life, make a change for myself, my own little personal sit-in, as it were. And it's affected people so greatly, I never would have thought. I like that. I think it is a time for kids to take a stand, in that sense, and make their lives real and sacred to them, and not expecting somebody else to do it for them, and getting mad that nobody else is.

ABE: So you feel that if people can get in any way connected to the sacred, whatever that means to them...

JEWEL: Yeah, indeed. Learning to integrate and not...

ABE: ...disintegrate.

JEWEL: Yeah. *[laughter]* To integrate the spirituality, it's a hard task, to be spiritual in a profession, or any kind of work, to balance the two, to balance the intellect which is so fun and which by itself can be incredibly unbalanced. The same with just spirituality, you know. To be spiritual, to do what people did in caves and on top of mountains, but in this life, in this world. It's a great thing.

ABE: When you were thinking about having this conversation, you must have had thoughts about it. What was it that you were wanting to say that I didn't ask you about?

JEWEL: I think the saddest thing that happened to me as a child was that I believed somebody else could know me better than I could know myself. I learned to mistrust my own inner voice, and I was told it was selfish. And it caused me to lose hope. I sincerely wish for people not to lose hope. I hear kids saying that they're not going to have any kids in the future, because they don't want to bring anybody into this world. And I think that's sad. At all costs, bring love in.

note to
the reader

AS WE HAVE SEEN, no one in this book is attempting the kind of definitive absolutism that limits the "old paradigms." These thinkers are not confined to an absolute good or an absolute evil, or any kind of final definitive description of reality. But they are attempting to create paradigms or models that illustrate the fluxy universe that we're *actually* experiencing. This allows for an outlook that is ethically creative and responsive to change rather than fearfully resisting it. This outlook is called Holism.

The conversations in this book represent samplings of alternative paradigms which for the sake of discussion can be grouped under the heading "New Spiritual Paradigm(s)." Since we know that paradigms are suspect, we are not trying to actually acquire one, but rather to participate in an act of creativity.

There are many more people in this book than would seem apparent from the list of foregoing conversations. We need to acknowledge the contributions of other thinkers not directly mentioned in this book and currents of thought which cannot be attributed to any single individual.

A vast global movement of thought and creativity in many disciplines and cultural forms stands in the background of the issues explored in these pages. The people in the conversations are all involved in this global movement towards a new world culture. For those readers who want a deeper understanding of the coherence and essential unity underlying the subjects explored in these conversations, I offer this analysis, which must itself be considered only as a general outline.

analysis

THE MOST OFTEN HEARD WORD in the areas of new thought, particularly during the last decade, is the word "Paradigm," from the Greek *paradeigma*, conceptual model, which is associated with *mimesis* or mimicry. For many people this term has become a buzzword. This ubiquitous word well describes a wide variety of theoretical efforts being made to create a model of reality capable of describing the complex issues inherent in the new Universe and global situation. At the same time, these new paradigm theories are provoking the sweeping changes which are now redefining the whole world.

The fact is that at no time in history has humanity lived without a paradigm. History itself is a paradigm. The old cultural paradigms were exclusively patriarchal, and often racist and genocidal (which is reason enough in itself for them to change). In the Judeo-Christian West there are two visible paradigms in the Bible. The one at the beginning of the Old Testament tells us that "In the beginning God created the Heavens and the Earth." Everything else follows from this, including the creation of Adam and Eve as innocent beings.

The god invites Adam to fill the blank spaces in the paradigm by inviting him to give names to every other creature and thing that this god has created. In this god's paradigm, Adam and Eve are supposed to avoid "eating the fruit" of the tree of knowledge of good and evil. They listen instead to Lucifer and they eat the fruit and lose their innocence, or wake up from their ignorance, depending on how you choose to interpret the paradigm. This act of disobedience/freedom results in a truly awesome "paradigm shift," and Adam and Eve, having committed the Original Sin of changing the paradigm, are driven from the garden of innocence: Eden.

For almost two thousand years in the West, history revolved around the attempt to square reality with this paradigm of the fall of humanity into original sin and the attempt to be redeemed from the fall by the intervention of Jesus Christ.

This is a paradigm of nostalgia saturated in guilt, longing for a past perfect: the sentimental theology of other worldly romanticism; the dangerously idealized politics of archaism, longing for a distant age. As time passed, this state of perfection was projected into the future as the "second coming." History becomes progress; the future becomes futurism.

The paradigm in the New Testament is much more metaphysical, abstract, and mysterious. It begins: "In the beginning was the Word (Logos) and the Word (Logos) was with God and the Word (Logos) was God." So here the god is the Logos. In the philosophy of the early Greeks from whom this word comes, and in particular Heraclitis, the Logos is simultaneously Spirit Fire and Mind Fire; Kosmic Ideation or intelligence. In his philosophy of flux and change, Heraclitis described how this living Being, which is the universe, continues to evolve and change. Creativity and order arise spontaneously out of the cosmos-making forces and energies, the ideations that are inherent to life itself. In the more adventurous schools of modern theology, the Logos considered in this way is identified with the fiery explosion or big bang at the beginning of the "Standard Model/Paradigm" of astrophysics.

The Heraclitian idea that even "god" is changing has become one of the seminal ideas of the twentieth century through astrophysics, quantum mechanics, and various other twentieth-century disciplines. We're discovering that, in fact, the Universe is extremely fluxy, that it is changing all the time. No sooner do we emerge with a paradigm of insights into how life operates, which we think is definitive within current reality theory, than we discover something new, and have to change the paradigm or discard it altogether. There is this fluxy quality to both consciousness and to phenomena.

The challenge in this never-ending change encourages us creatively to continue in the attempt to develop a "unified field theory" to illustrate the human experience within the Universe in such a way that we can feel sanely at home within it. We are, of course, undeniably here. Whether we feel at home or alienated in the world is determined by our paradigm of reality. We believe that we need paradigms, but it goes deeper still than that: we are paradigm creators by nature, even though we don't always know this. Our essential nature is that we can transform how we conceive our essential nature. We are self-paradigming beings.

All creation myths from all times and peoples of the world are paradigms. Calling them myths in no way minimizes their importance or meaning for as long as they last. And there's the rub. Just as the first paradigm of Eden was shattered by the knowledge of good and evil, so, too, any paradigm can be shattered by greater knowledge, or by its failure to make sense of the experience of life. Experience, knowledge, and the perceived meaning of human existence are the ultimate quality control for paradigms.

As Martin Heidegger has made so clear, every disclosure (in this case paradigm) is also a concealing. The dominant paradigm of our time is the Technological Paradigm which discloses nature, the world, and the Universe to us in a specific way which Heidegger calls "enframing."

To understand disclosing and concealing, you could say, for instance, that the Gnomes (nature spirits) disclose the temperamental qualities of the Earth but conceal the biochemical analysis, which in turn conceals the Gnomes. Or that psychoanalysis discloses the contents of the mind but conceals the neural networks, and the biochemical magnetic workings of the brain/mind complex, which in turn conceals the purely intuitive activities of the mind. Or, again, that the rules of grammar disclose the structure of language but conceal the free-form poetry, which in turn conceals the rules of grammar.

Every way of disclosing a reality to ourselves conceals the other aspects and possibilities inherent in that reality. This is essentially what Thomas Kuhn deals with in the book *The Structure of Scientific Revolutions*, which started all this talk about "paradigms" and "paradigm shifts" in the first place. He describes what he calls a paradigm cycle like this: Paradigm–Anomoly–Crisis–Revolution–Acceptance–Paradigm. Basically, one monoparadigm turns into another.

In this case, all you end up doing is replacing one "disclosure" and "concealing" setup for another. Of course the really intelligent thing to do is always to acknowledge that that's what you are doing and to preserve a thoughtfully open mind to all possibilities for disclosure in everything. This sounds very unattractive to people and organizations who want their version of reality to also give them a lot of power and influence. A good definition of fascism would be "monoparadigmatic thinking," which obviously isn't Thinking at all in the true sense of the word.

In technoscience, the view is that each paradigm shift is a step towards a true unified field theory, a way of viewing the world that comprehends everything that we can experience. The danger is obvious. The day we find a unified field theory that explains — enframes — absolutely everything, it will spell the end of human creativity. This final enframing will conceal innumerable creative and spiritual possibilities that we can't even imagine yet.

All that we will be able to do is further refine the user-friendly technologies and environmentally friendly forms of production, with justice and fairplay for all, etc. In TOE (theory of everything) or GUTS (grand unified theories), it is imagination itself that will come to an end. The positive side of this possibility however is that people will eventually come to the conclusion that the final truth isn't that compelling after all. And that, as Neitzsche put it, "Art is more important than the Truth."

Paradigms, as we understand them in the West, philosophically and scientifically rather than theologically, go back to Aristotle, Plato, and the early Greeks. Against this background of thought, we have developed different ways of perceiving the nature of reality. The "scientific method," which came into its own during the Enlightenment through Descartes and Newton, amongst others, offered the illusion of absolute certainty. That certainty is gone now into the "uncertainty principle." The fluxy nature of the Universe is here to stay. The implications of how this modifies culture are still sinking in.

Paradigm creation must always concern itself with the question of human freedom and the meaning of the Earth as a Whole. At best, a really good paradigm is a good approximation always open to adaptation and change. There is no model of reality that is able to speak to all of our experience; no model that contains the dramatic "All," the life of the Whole. Life is not a paradigm.

Enframing conceals everything that is outside the purview of technology by implicitly and blatantly denying that anything that cannot be disclosed by technology can possibly exist. This leaves humanity with a "world picture" but no awareness of "Being and beings." This is the danger of technology, which of course is not just hardware and software, but an all-engulfing way of disclosing/perceiving and concealing reality.

Technology implicitly denies that it is merely one possible paradigm amongst many. It regards itself and its methods of knowing things as decisive. Part of its all-engulfing nature is displayed in its readiness to absorb all other ways of perceiving as information. The seduction of the technological paradigm is that it produces the illusion that information about life is life. Or to put it bluntly, that life is information. And that there will be only one truth — the technoscientific truth. Ergo monoparadigmatic technological thinking is fascism. Neitzsche made this very clear by saying that the will to power had passed over into technology.

Technology has produced the information age with its arrogant thoughtlessness. Gathering and processing all possible information about the world and then exploiting the information and the world as a usable resource is not a particularly enlightened approach to life, as the ecological crisis so distressingly illustrates. The information age is the age of the cybernetic man who exists as a mass of quantifiable information which includes everything from his DNA genotype to his psychological profile and data image. Yet nowhere in all of this information is his freedom as a being to be found. It is man's potential to transform the human condition, his real being, that is ultimately enframed and concealed by the technological paradigm.

At the risk of sounding pessimistic and even apocalyptic, when all experience and knowledge is enframed (defined) by technology, it will be impossible to create or implement any public, spiritual, cultural, or economic initiative that is not predetermined in its final form by the structures of technoculture. This would represent a new dark age which might last for an awfully long time.

The technological paradigm sees everything and everyone as a usable and reusable resource. It is the mentality of utility applied willy-nilly to the whole world. There is a totalitarianism implicit in all of this to which it behooves us to be alert. The new world order, as it emerges everywhere by technological means at the disposal of the new world state, raises the issue of human freedom as never before. This oppressive new economic technological world order enforces a predetermined future upon all humanity. We are already in the post-democratic age. Electorates in all the countries that still carry on the media-manipulated ritual of elections know that national governments no longer decide anything of real importance.

It's easy for us to believe thoughtlessly that technology is simply advanced machines, equipment, silicon chips, and microcircuitry. What is less obvious about technology is that it's actually a way of looking at the world that has deep spiritual and psychological significance. It defines everything as usable information and resource. Thus technology conceals every other level of meaning and reality.

For example, the technological mentality becomes visible in instrumental ecology. We are told that the reason why we should save the rain forest is because it contains genetic information that could help us to heal illness in the future, and that if we cut down the rain forest before we've gotten hold of this information, we'll lose out. Or, again, that forests are much more economically valuable as eco-tourist resources than as lumber. That's technology posing as ecology.

An actual ecological understanding of the rain forest says that the rain forest is a part of the whole natural world order, and that it has the right to be there. Not only does it have the right to be there, but it also has the right to be allowed to be what it is. Now this doesn't mean that humans can't at the same time find medicines and other things helpful to us in it. But we need to recognize that that isn't why the rain forest is there. It is part of an amazingly complex awareness organism called the Biosphere. Its context and being will always be greater than any definition that we can give to it. It has multiple meanings and will always unfold in human awareness as even more meaning. But all of these meanings that we give to it will never arrive at a final meaning for the rain forest. It will always mean more than we can comprehend. Regardless of how much information we gather about it. But it's virtually impossible for technology-driven culture to see the rain forest or anything else in this light — which is in the light and presence of free being.

The monoparadigm thinking of technology invades culture, psychology, and education in the form of "everything can be improved, made more efficient, effective, and competitive." Everything and everyone can be streamlined, downsized. Global reality has been defined in advance as the field for economic and technological competition. All other considerations are subordinated to this.

Technology implicitly denies the spiritual being of the human being who has the right to remain open to her own possibilities for self-definition in which human evolution can unfold within a free, democratic world culture or a recognition of the real complexity and potential variety of the individual's being or experience. Anything that can't be translated and represented as definable and useable information has no value and thus does not actually exist.

All of life and every individual is to be diagnosed, assessed, and improved as quickly as possible. Compelled to "get with the program!" If they can't be improved, then they can be dismissed as technopeasants, rejected from culture altogether, marginalized to become a welfare burden and then demonized. This is a political sensibility expressing itself through and as technology. The issues involved in all this are complex beyond any known religious or political ideology.

I have no desire to add new insults to the language, but the real meaning of the term "technopeasant" should refer to a person who knows only the technological way of being and understanding the world. When such a person is in a position of power, a better term for her would be "technofascist." This mentality insists that the future is going to demand economically viable technological solutions for every need, problem, and crisis. In this paradigm, all aspects of life are subordinated to the profit motive focused in technological systems.

This narrow way of organizing life not only conceals the human being's spiritual nature, but keeps it out of sight by substituting databases for reality. Of course, by the time that we're all perfectly efficient, functioning entities within a mobilized, competitive, technologically advanced society, we will all *be* technology, too, in the age of the cybernetic man who lives in the various cyberspaces of the new information economy and entertainment technology.

It is not that technology necessarily has an essential enigmatic nature beyond the comprehension of human beings. But it is the use to which technology is put by those who command it. Even though the nature of technology raises profound spiritual questions, its immediate and obvious impact is much more a global, ecological, economic, and political problem. As a spiritual question, we must ask how technology seduces individuals into defining themselves in exclusively technological terms. The extent to which those who command it are already defined by it and thus incapable of thinking beyond it will become a burning geopolitical issue.

The political and economic propaganda being used to sell us the future "new world order" smacks of utopianism. We're being told that through the new world order, through GATT, through free trade, by breaking down economic barriers, the whole world is going to join together in a glorious future "global economy" in which there will be free-market democracy, civil rights, and prosperity for all. A new and better world in which all wars will have been brought to an end — after all, there will be no need for them.

Doesn't this all have a rather familiar ring to it? Haven't we heard this half a dozen times already in the last couple hundred years? At both the French and American revolutions? Didn't we hear it in China before Mao Tse-tung's revolution? Didn't we hear this in Moscow sometime around 1917 before the Bolshevik revolution? Didn't we hear this at the Nuremberg rallies in Germany in the thirties? Haven't we heard this all over the world during the last century? And where have these utopian dreams always led? To war, disappointment, and disaster, of course, because these are simply the monoparadigmatic lies that power elites tell in order to come to power or to retain power.

The corporate takeover and merger frenzy that has characterized the last few decades is escalating on a global scale. The new global corporate State and, in particular, America, as NAFTA, the new Europe, Russia, the Middle East, Africa, and Asia are locked in a mighty economic war of world domination. The general agreement on trade and tariffs, GATT, is an economic panzer thrust on many fronts at the remaining economically non-aligned sovereign nations. The global battleground for this world war is technoeconomics with human populations defined as resources. Whether defined as sources of technoscientific expertise, competitive production quotas, yet-to-be developed marketplaces or consumers, human beings have been assigned a very specific role in the new world order.

This emerging monolithic world government has many ways of rationalizing itself as the solution to the world's problems. But we should not forget that most of these problems are the result of the clash of economic and military imperialism in the first place. The imposition of rigid structures upon life is not order but oppression. The carriers of the old paradigms, like the carriers of terminal viruses, are in the process of destroying themselves, each other, and the Earth. In the emerging new world order chaos reigns. It is to this stark reality that we are beginning to awaken. Every monoparadigm generates Chaos.

There is the immediate problem of spreading chaos in the ecological crisis, the collapse of sovereign states, the chaos in the monetary debt system planetwide. The spreading destruction of culture and community. This chaos is both local and planetary, involving all humanity and life, in the rush of precipitous and radical change. A new consciousness of chaos has imbued new paradigm thinking with the fire of urgency. The need is urgent that we create a new planetary cosmos capable of integrating the chaos that has arisen over the last century.

The whole idea that order emerges from chaos and overcomes chaos is something that has had mythic and metaphysical meaning through most of humanity's history. "And darkness was upon the face of the deep (Chaos) and God said, 'Let there be Light (Cosmos).'" In the modern world this chaos–cosmos paradigm suffers from two fatal flaws. It has lost its relevance and it is not global.

It wasn't until this century, particularly through the exploration of quantum mechanics and astrophysics, that a rethinking of chaos–cosmos theory began. The cosmos of astrophysics begins with the most chaotic event imaginable, namely the "Big Bang," which by all accounts is still banging. Chaos and cosmos have come into focus as observable technoscientific phenomena. Not that we can actually draw metaphysical meaning from scientific discoveries alone. But I mention this here because astro-quantum physics has been *sounding* increasingly metaphysical all during this century.

Originally, in ancient Egyptian, Persian, and Hindu culture, and in classical Greece, chaos was understood as everything to do with the raw life that is found in the "primordial ocean": out of raw life order emerges. This has been symbolically represented as a point in a circle, and that point defines the circle, and the circle defines the point. This too was the symbol of the individual spirit, so that both cosmos and chaos are ahistorically predefined. We don't believe this anymore. There is no ahistorical predefined truth that remains true as such for all time and all beings.

In the ancient and classical world, chaos was identified with the element water in a world comprising four elements: fire, air, water, and earth. The water element was also the fertilizing element—the fecund germinating source of new life. By symbolic analogy and extension, the waters of metaphysical space come to symbolize the womb of the Earth. This symbolism is actualized in the sacred waters of the Nile or the Ganges, as they flow through the immediate Earth, revitalizing and nourishing all of life.

In the West we have the myth known as the flood, in which a god, punishing humanity for disordered behavior, inundated the earth with chaotic water. But he allowed that point in the circle to remain, which was Noah and the Ark, which was the seed vessel of order and life. At the moment when the waters begin to subside, Noah released a dove that flew over the waters and returned with an olive branch, showing him that chaos had subsided and that cosmos had begun to reestablish itself in the growth of life. This allegory could also be taken as a mythic description of the end of an ice age or of cosmogenesis. Cultures the world over contain identical chaos–cosmos myths.

In the twentieth century, chaos isn't just the result of quantum, mechanical, and astrophysical observations of black holes in space, supernovas, and eccentric subatomic particles. Or the big bang. Chaos is also what went on in the two world wars; chaos is the atom bomb falling on Hiroshima and Nagasaki, nuclear testing, and all the global conflict and terrorism both private- and state-sponsored. The media are essentially reporting chaos from all over the planet.

Chaos is what is going on in the streets of the inner cities. The homeless have no civil rights in a society that likes to think of itself as "the free world." And in order to enlarge the scope of "free-market democracy" society blithely ignores civil rights in China and all over the so-called third world. The media-fostered illusion is that "free-market democracy" can achieve civil rights there when it won't achieve them here. Here being the European community and North America. We continue to grapple with the relationship between corporate state-driven social chaos and global injustice. This issue can only be resolved on a global scale and we see little evidence of this as yet.

It has long been obvious that if authentic global democracy is to be accomplished, it will be in overcoming the various fundamentalisms and dictatorships still holding so much of humanity hostage. But these regressions are themselves being taken prisoner by the new economic world order. The final phase in the establishment of global democracy will mean the overcoming of free-market democracy as a front for the continuing global power struggle. Or what seems more likely, the power struggle will end in a decisive victory for a monolithic world government. Then the task will be to spiritualize, democratize, and transform the global state from within. It is imperative that we begin this now.

One of the characteristics of the mass emotional climate of the twentieth century is cynicism, which is repressed paranoia, and the will to power. The paranoia is understandable in a world becoming increasingly cruel. (Or should we say rather that the shocking new awareness of global reality induces paranoia?) Amid this "cosmopolitan new world order" there is a growing ethnic backlash in the form of wars of national independence: Bosnia Herzegovina, Africa, South America, the breakaway republics of the former Soviet Union. A new world order of escalating violence becomes the new world disorder. Orwell's newspeak and doublethink on CNN reporting that America ("the best country in the world") is an erupting volcano of violence with its Los Angeles riots, Waco, Oklahoma City—the "killing culture." The cosmos of escalating chaos. Still, cynicism, the mask of revenge and power, is not a particularly creative response to paranoia.

An older culture/paradigm would say a god was punishing us or was shaking down false gods, false idols and images, before establishing a new messianic age. Which would be a new paradigm, exactly like the old paradigm, only more so. Many Gaia-conscious people believe that the Spirit of the Earth is in the process of correcting the ecological imbalance of the world through cataclysmic Earth changes. She is doing this in order to reestablish an archaic world of econaturalism. The Gaians are trying to make the rest of us aware that it's our current aberrated and antinature cosmos that is the cause of the chaos.

As we strive to make sense of this chaos we find ourselves compelled to imagine a new cosmos that has the creative scope and elegant complexity to gather all of this chaos together, a new order, a new dynamic harmony, out of the expanded creative possibilities that go with this enlarged chaos. But it can't be an idealistic, simplistic, ideological solution.

The upshot is that any monoparadigm, whether metaphysical, scientific, technological, religious, cultural, or economic, generates oppressive chaos and destroys community. The entire ideological approach to reality has lost all credibility. History seen in this light is the narrative of the imposition of ignorance upon life. Instead of seeking to understand the whole, power elites have been attempting to violently impose rigid ideological structures of control upon fluid natural dynamic order. We begin now to learn that this natural dynamic order is infinitely more complex and better adapted to maintain its own balance than anything we might try to impose upon it.

It certainly is not my intention here to naively celebrate the "end of ideology" as if its mere apparent demise represented some automatic gain on the part of humanity. The collapse of ideology is initially disempowering to the people within the State. The loss of clearly defined political positions makes it harder for people to organize the defense of civil rights and economic justice. Besides, what is closer to the truth is that ideological technology and ideological free-market democracy are setting up an ideological dictatorship. This too must end before we can claim the end of ideology.

The question is: What is to replace ideology as a way of dealing with the issues surrounding Ecology, Spirituality, Global Humanity, and Technology? As evidenced by all of these thinkers in conversation, we have begun to open our minds and senses to the actuality of the whole of life understood as a vast living organism. We call this Ecology. It is ecological awareness that spells the real end of ideology and monoparadigms. The human race is either going to learn the reality of the Earth or perish. If all goes well we will soon enter the post-technological ecological world.

As we can see, paradigms are not merely models of reality in our heads. Paradigms go much deeper than that. Dr. Jean Houston says, "Myth is the DNA of the psyche," meaning that our whole spiritual and psychological conditioning is mythic in origin. She also speaks of this time as being the time of the uncoding or unraveling of these mythic structures within us. Indeed many people recognize this uncoding experience and many more people have been undergoing it unconsciously. It means release from the deepest layers of cultural conditioning.

What is at issue here is security and power. Throughout our long history of organized societies, beginning with the change (paradigm shift) from hunting and gathering to organized agriculture, the issue has been security. Security of adequate food, shelter, and clothing are legitimate human needs. But something has gone badly wrong in our relationship with security, and thus in our relationship to everything else.

The essence of materialism and godism is the inversion or internalization of external security needs. The demand for a secured subjective existence. What is valid as a physical survival need has been internalized into the awareness field of human consciousness. This sets up the unhealthy illusion of a permanent and fixed subjective person, a separate self who is, of necessity, isolated and alienated from other subjective persons and life. Cultures made up of separate selves are competitive, power-driven hierarchies, in which the most powerful come out on top. The evolution of democracy has been the attempt to temper and reduce the injustices produced by this pathology of power.

The fixed separate self is a psychological monoparadigm. A self composed of layers of coding. On the surface, for example, the monoparadigm of technology and beneath that the monoparadigm of a religion, and beneath that layers of mythic monoparadigms and so on. A kind of fossil record of revealing and concealing. These are the coding or DNA of the fixed subjective psyche, the separate self. The uncoding of this fixed psyche is one of the central psychological events of our time. Regardless of whether the separate self enters willingly into its own destruction or not, it is still being affected by the loss of supporting cultural context, and the loss of certainty about the nature of reality. We call the separate self "I." This is the source of the stress and anxiety about which we hear so much. This, too, is the psychological reaction to what is meant by the statement "God is dead."

The historical, metaphysical, and theological foundations of the fixed subjective psyche have to do with god-making.

The god or spirit outside time is the god outside the natural rhythms of nature. The separate self is a faithful mirror of this god. Thus time itself is devalued and with it the whole ecological Earth of living time. This has developed as the notion of a securely fixed and static all-powerful god and a fixed concept of the essential spiritual nature of human beings. The separate god is the archetype of the separate self.

The idea of a permanent soul or higher self outside time leads the human being to devalue this world as a temporary way station to a higher world. At best, merely a stage in evolution or progress. And this is just as true of the one life on Earth only of judeo-christian-islamic belief, as it is of those who believe in reincarnation, or even materialism. This obsession leads to religious and ideological fanaticism and thus unnatural violence.

These beliefs spring from an obsession with security. The desire to establish security in realms where security is not only unhealthy but impossible can only be described as obsession. The demand for spiritual, psychological, and emotional security is absurd. Psychologism, too, with its therapy myth of "total integration" posits a permanent subject who must establish psychological security. The secure psyche is a sick psyche. Secured emotions are autism. The fundamentally unchanging subjective identity is a nexus of neurosis leading directly to senility and social chaos. And this is the source of the atomization of community and the destruction of the Earth.

With the advent of obsessive security came the internalized invention of evil as a fixed entity representing every aspect of life that could not be secured. This internal and thus external chaos was set over as the shadow against the fixed god representing the light of absolute control. This split has become encoded deep into the secure psyche so that humanity is conditioned to be the scene of the struggle between the opposites of good and evil. But this, too, in the final analysis is merely a paradigm.

The "shadow" (psychological chaos) of which we hear so much in contemporary cultural and psychological discourse represents the recognition that we have developed a terminally rigid and life-denying attitude towards ourselves and the rest of nature. We are evolving into bigger, more complex, and creative people as we reinclude the fragmented and disenfranchised aspects of our nature. This means overcoming the "light" and "dark" split at the core of the separate self. And its god-devil obsession.

The individual who unravels or decodes this paradigm is beyond good and evil, in the old sense. But far from producing cultural and individual fragmentation, this process results in a deepened harmony of being and an enhanced appreciation of the sacredness of all life. A re-membering of the self into the Whole. From this arises a new inclusive ethic dedicated to sustaining the Whole and overcoming fragmentation and dominance in every area of culture.

The central characteristic of our time is the collapse of this age-old paradigm of good and evil and the subjective psyche produced by it. Technology, which is neutral in this sense, moves into the vacuum as absolute control without any need to posit an ethical dilemma. Through data processing and electronic networking it produces the illusion that integrated information about life is an integrated life, requiring no essential spiritual or psychological change in the separate self. This is the metaphysical danger of technology that it fulfills the needs of the fixed psyche for absolute security. The desire to live outside the natural world and its rhythms of time. This outlook is appearing as the notion that humanity is now transcending the organic world altogether and in the process of entering a silicon-based cyberspace — life as information and electronic experience.

Any being or thing that can exist at all must of necessity exist in, and as, time. All that truly lives is the scene and source of the constant change that characterizes ecological spiritual life. We are these spiritual beings, awareness organisms, who are living time. As are all other beings who are born and die on Earth. If we live before birth and after birth, it is as living time that we must do so. Therefore our life on Earth in the natural rhythms of time is our spiritual life. If we fail to awaken to the Earth as the spiritual home of global humanity, then how can we possibly experience any state at all in an authentic spiritual way? To insist upon a fixed and permanent spiritual self or a deity outside time is to fall into a dangerous illusion, failing altogether to comprehend the nature of living spirit which is the Whole of life.

If we only read this and do not think it through, then it is easy to overlook what a radical, foundation-shifting movement this is. In fact, it is the end of ideological foundationalism itself. Throughout the long millenia of world thought, and particularly in the thought life of the West, we have been describing our place in the Universe as it *should be*. The Universe of Plato is the Universe as it should be. The same is true of judaism, islam, buddhism, and hinduism. You should be saved in one case, you should be enlightened in the other; paradoxically they are totally different things that come to the same thing, namely an otherworldly *meta-should-be*.

Some new spirituality theorists argue that the spirit of cosmos within chaos is directly inspiring the new spirituality. This notion is called the Anthropic Principle, and even though there are several versions of it, they all agree that because we have awareness we must have been essentially intended from the beginning of the big bang. The evidence used to support this notion is that the laws that govern the universe and ecology are just too non-accidental to actually be accidental. So it must follow that there is an anthropomorphic deity after all. And a predefined human spiritual essence. This is old paradigm thinking exploiting astrophysics and biology and presenting itself as a new spiritual philosophy. A technotheological version of "In the beginning God created the Heavens and the Earth."

It is exactly now in the development of this new world situation that nontechnical visions of the future take on supreme importance. Humanity is challenged to reinvent freedom and democracy in this new technological economic world order. Real freedom is a spiritual awareness capable of free imagination, which is what makes a culture of real freedom possible. No human being can be assigned an essential nature by another. The capacity to envision the future with realistic enthusiasm and joy, because you are going to be directly and freely involved in its fulfillment.

When are we going to reach a collective state of technological sophistication where we are quickly able to discriminate between good technology and bad technology? And evolve a democratic politics of decision making in this area? What is the difference between good technology and bad technology?

We already know that nuclear bombs and power stations along with weapons of mass destruction are bad technology. So, too, are gasoline- and diesel-consuming internal combustion machines, destructive chemicals, etc. Good technology is solar power, recycling, chemical-free agriculture, and so on.

We can safely say that bad technology is ecologically hostile and that good technology is ecologically friendly. But does the issue end here or is there more to it? The human being is an awareness organism evolving as an integral part of the whole ecological rhythmic complexity of the timely Earth. Human time is not technological time. Yet technology presents itself everywhere as "time saving" when its actual impact is to speed life up until it makes human time impossible. In this way it subverts human presence, scatters human presence and community into the speeded-up world of technotime. This is a politics of oppression and dominance, slyly wearing the mask of progress. "What shall it benefit a man if he quickly gain all the data and lose his human presence?"

The question really is: When are we going to reach a stage of democracy when we are able to choose the technologies that become integrated into our everyday lives, rather than passively allowing them to be imposed upon us?

We have grown fatalistic. Many of us feel that there is nothing we can do to change any of this, that it doesn't include us as free decision makers, that we've got nothing to say about it. We're told that the age of television and VCR, as we know it, is over and we must now get ready to embrace the age of CD-ROM, interactive media, and virtual reality. We do not yet have the democratic means to exercise any freedom of choice about having our lives radically changed and predetermined by these culture-altering innovations.

We're able to protest when an agricultural agency agrees with a pharmaceutical giant to put new hormones or drugs into cows to increase milk or beef production. We react to the irradiation of our food, and chemical additives. And these dubious things don't come to pass when enough people say, "We don't want our food affected in this way." We seem, however, unable to bring the same kind of overall health-protection attitudes towards the larger cultural impact of technology as a worldview.

Technology is very obviously here to stay, at least until it's finished with us or we're finished with it, *as we inevitably one day will be.* In the same way as we had the Middle Ages, the Renaissance, the Enlightenment, then the Industrial Revolution, technology is a central characteristic of this age. Not that there is anything simple about the characteristic of an age. We're now in the third phase of the Industrial Revolution, which is the current phase of world technological society. But because of the all-engulfing monoparadigmatic nature of technology, it presents a special danger in that it circumvents the possibility of its own overcoming. As a mentality, it intends the rest of history to become the endless history of technology itself.

These other futures must inevitably presuppose the inclusion of technology, but a technology at the service of human freedom and not the other way around, as is the case at present. In order for technology to be at the service of human freedom, human beings need to have a lot more in mind than simply the production of more technology. The attempt to compress the human experience into exclusively economic technological terms is generating fatally explosive pressures at every level of existence. The technological domination of global reality, and its culture-determining nature, has already placed it beyond having to answer to what it has denounced as backward-looking fear, prejudice, and merely religious condemnation. But it must be made to answer Humanity and the Earth.

In the twentieth century we have become quite expert at fighting off many forms of traditional oppressions in the name of progress. What we face in technology and the new world economy is a form of overwhelming oppression that calls itself progress, even as it serves both traditional and new power elites.

THE FIRST PRINCIPLE of the new paradigm is the Whole, also called Holism. As Fritjof Capra would put it, "the shift from the parts to the whole... and a shift towards the network as a central metaphor." This means that every life-form and every energy form are connected. This becomes so ridiculously obvious after even a moment's reflection that we wonder why it took so long for this to become accepted wisdom.

In the older paradigms, all of the parts are isolated areas of specialized expertise. These isolated disciplines could not talk to each other; there were no bridges or networks. An example of how this change is being recognized is in the environmental reports which now must precede the building of, for instance, a dam or hydroelectric complex. Still, the old paradigm thinkers in the corporate and government sectors continue to resist holistic thinking, primarily because it tends to make thoughtless exploitation difficult.

Moving from the parts to the whole and recognizing the network is another way of acknowledging that for everything that we disclose, we also conceal something else. It is what we allow to remain concealed when we build that dam, that comes back to haunt us in the form of degraded environment and extinct salmon. It is the single strategy of the bottom line in corporate and industrial downsizing that conceals the burned-out executives and workers — the wrecked lives, the tyranny of redundancy and fear-ridden employment, the social chaos.

By the same token, the Whole is a multifocal spiritual reality, a constantly changing, flowing presence. The ground of human freedom. Presence within presence. And not as was previously indoctrinated into humanity by way of an all-powerful god outside the Whole. Neither is it a supreme guiding spirit within the Whole, but separate from it. Or as the cliché has it, "a ghost in the machine." We have gone to great lengths in the last few centuries to protect religious freedom, through the separation of church and state, and having religious freedom *enshrined* within the constitution. But, in actuality, what does this kind of freedom amount to? When all it means is that the individual is free to choose from a selection of theo-monoparadigms. All of these essentially predefine and fix the spiritual essence of man's being. And in various ways, both subtle and obvious, actually deny the real spiritual freedom of the individual.

The spiritual reality of the Whole confirms itself in the endless array of spiritual awareness states of which human beings are naturally capable. These awareness states involve presence within presence outside the narrow band of experience defined by consensus reality. The so-called supernatural is the product of an equally narrow band of experience defined by spiritual, mystical, religious, and psychic-consensus supernaturalism. Nostalgic mysticism of the variety found in most traditions involves the repetition of past modes of spiritual experience. It is the very fact that these "higher" or transpersonal experiences fit into the old patterns that confirms them as genuine spiritual experiences.

This entire traditional approach to spiritual, mystical, religious, and psychic experience and the validation of these experiences is called into question. After millenia of these traditions, humanity remains in its current condition. Indeed it is apparent that these conflicting traditions are responsible for the current state of humanity and the world. In our time spiritual liberation means liberation from both materialism and these old forms of supersensual and supernatural experience. This is why both traditional and new age supernaturalism and magical thinking have a fascinating past but no future. The notion of a spiritual life or experience somehow separate from any aspect of the Whole has come to an end.

The Whole as the central metaphor for our time has begun to become visible to the majority of people as Ecology. Even though everyone now knows this word and has some understanding of what it means, it is obvious that we still have a long way to go. Currently Ecology is in a

David-and-Goliath struggle with the old paradigm establishments all over the world. A handful of important concessions have been wrung from governments and the transnational corporations, who are still able to move environmentally destructive industries to areas of the world with lax or nonexistent environmental protection laws.

In spite of all the green hype, we have barely begun to face the implications of Wholeism as ecological reality. So how far does Ecology go? How much of life does it include? All of it. We are in the process of awakening to an ecological awareness that includes the spiritual, mental, psychological, sexual, emotional, and physical. And all of this is summed up in the terms Ecology, Gaia, and Biosphere. And so we are discovering and developing an ecology of consciousness.

If humanity is to survive and flourish into a future counted in millions of years rather than decades, we will have to learn to live ecologically. This will mean that all paradigms and ideologies will be abandoned in favor of the only paradigm that counts: the reality of the laws of nature in all their enigmatic wholeism. A new age of creativity will begin in which human beings will include the understanding of these ecological laws in everything that is created. Geopolitical reality is in the process of going through a renewal as an eco-geopolitical consciousness. "Workers of the world unite!" could easily turn into "Ecologists of the world unite!"

Try to imagine economic ecology where the flow of money and goods is perfectly attuned to the biosphere and the real survival needs of communities. Where these communities are designed to eliminate the use of automobiles and fossil fuels. And the community itself is a large extended family. Where social institutions and civil order are self-policing. Does this sound utopian? Perhaps, until you realize that you will consume less, own less. But on the other hand, you will worry less and be free from economic anxiety and social alienation. Does this sound like state communism? Perhaps, until you remember that state communism was a monoparadigmatic ideology that was imposed upon both nature and society. And failed for precisely this reason as a capitalist free-market democracy is bound to fail for exactly the same reason.

Captain Paul Watson put it like this: "The most important thing is to serve the earth, and to take a biocentric viewpoint, not an anthropocentric viewpoint of things. I think this is the only salvation for the earth, which involves a complete revolution in consciousness, economically, spiritually, politically, and culturally. Everything has to be shifted from an anthropocentric to a biocentric point of view. If that happens, then I think there is real hope for our species and for the earth."

If humanity can even begin to meet this challenge and accomplish something new in world culture, it could also begin to free us from the dread of extinction.

This is our new world thought putting the biosphere at the center of our understanding of reality. Seeing, from a survival point of view, that humans are simply one species among many. That we are to become the caretakers of the Earth without domesticating it. And that it behooves us to abandon the Darwinian image of ourselves as the dominant predator. This will also mean overcoming the various forms of predation which exist within cultures, such as economic exploitation, the violation of human rights, and crimes against humanity.

When I spoke to the wise woman, Oh Shinnah, she said this: "I think that the Earth is the healer. If we really get ourselves concerned and involved in solving the problems of ecology, all those other things will go away, because we're all working for the same purpose, and that purpose is the survival of our species and all other species, and the Earth itself. I think that transcends any color, any race, any religion, and that's the way out."

It is apparent that most of what passes for modern civilization is really a composite mixture of old metaphysical paradigms. From the mystical side these will continue to be combined, refined, and synthesized into an increasingly complex spectrum of consciousness and psychospiritual paradigms. From the secular side we have increasingly complex information databases being synthesized into instruments of economic and social engineering.

These two apparently distinct paradigms have been infiltrating each other for some time in, for instance, "new age management techniques," and in all the ways that the interior of the human being is understood in psychotechnical terms such as "reprogramming the software of the subconscious mind." And "personal spiritual power" as a path to power in the world and over others. In this way, a culture based upon pathological power urges continues to perpetuate itself as the hierarchy of selfishness, exploitation, and injustice. Yet we are also on our way to an actual new age which involves the going beyond all of these past patterns.

Indeed, even what we understand by the terms "humanity," "womankind," "mankind," "individual" will pass away in a new global era. Ecological awareness will determine the real context for a new Earth life. And the combination of these four realities will be decisive: Ecology, Spirituality, New Humanity, and Technology.

What we now understand by the terms "Spirit" and "Spirituality" will emerge in a completely new sense of the sacred. Free of romantic otherworldly nostalgia and hierarchical mysticism that has characterized the spiritual life of the past. It seems likely that many people will remain attached to the fragments of old ways and old-culture forms for generations to come. And they should be free to do so. With the world all around them changing beyond all recognition.

Of all the possible scenarios of the future, how can we be so sure of these four things: Ecology, Spirituality, New Humanity, and Technology? Our very survival depends upon their realization as an integrated Whole. And because we have come to the end of all our yesterdays, this is the other future.

As we learn under the specter of extinction to do justice to the biosphere, to learn its language, the laws of ecology, we may come to an appreciation of what it means to be an awareness organism — an awareness organism present and continuing all presences. And so to do justice to all creatures including all human beings everywhere. We ourselves are the Earth and more than earth. Yet of this we cannot be sure until we arrive upon the Earth for the first time. To discover the spiritual meaning of the Earth and so to discover the spiritual meaning of ourselves.

glossary

akashic records: from the sanskrit word "akasha", the master records (said to exist in the astral plane) of everything that has occurred since the beginning of the universe.

alembic: anything that refines or purifies.

antigen: a protein, toxin, or other substance of high molecular weight, to which the body reacts by producing antibodies.

biofacture: the creation of living organisms or tissue.

dark matter: also known as "missing mass;" matter that is postulated to exist to explain the rotational motion of the Milky Way Galaxy and other galaxies, to explain the motions of galaxies in clusters, and, in certain cosmological theories, to achieve the critical density of matter in the universe that is just sufficient to close the universe.

deep ecology: a type of ecology which includes the recognition of the Earth as a sacred being.

depth development: an exploration into the deepest unconscious layers of the self for the purpose of psycho-spiritual healing.

entelechy: in Aristotelian philosophy, the actualization of potentiality or of essence; in vitalism, the inherent force which controls and directs the activities and development of a living being.

eschatology: the branch of theology, or doctrines, dealing with death, resurrection, judgement, and immortality.

Gaia: from Greek mythology, a goddess who is the personification of the Earth; the Gaia hypothesis, proposed by James Lovelock, regards the Earth as a self-regulating, living organism.

genome: the genetic endowment of a species.

gnostic: pertaining to knowledge.

Gnosticism: the belief in salvation or liberation through esoteric knowledge; often associated with the idea that the spiritual world is to be regarded as good, and the material world as evil.

Götterdämmerung: the total, usually violent, collapse of a society, regime, institution, etc.

illuminati: term first used in 15th century Europe to signify adepts, specifically those who were in direct communication with a higher source. It was associated with various occult sects and secret orders, including the Rosicrucians and the Freemasons.

jump phenomenon: a quantum leap in development unaccounted for by the laws of natural science.

kundalini: a psycho-spiritual energy said to reside sleeping within the body, and which is aroused either through spiritual discipline or spontaneously to bring new states of consciousness, including mystical illumination.

millenarian: a person who believes in the coming of the millenium (a thousand-year period of peace and prosperity expected to occur immediately before the end of the world).

morphic field: a field responsible for the organization of structure and patterned activity of a self-organizing system.

morphogenetic field: an energetic field containing an active, innate memory that plays a causal role in the coming into being of form; i.e., DNA is a form, and its morphogenetic field determines its structure.

mutagenic: pertaining to substances which are capable of noticably increasing the frequency of mutation.

myelinated memory: memory dependent upon and connected to the structure and viability of the central nervous system.

panentheism: the doctrine that God includes the world as a part though not the whole of his being.

pantheism: a doctrine that the universe conceived of as a whole is God; the doctrine that there is no God outside the combined forces and laws that are manifested in the universe.

planetarization: the impulse towards global awareness.

psycholytic: pertaining to hallucinogenic or psychedelic drugs.

quickening: the awakening of spiritual awareness and energy, leading to an escalation of psychological transformation; culminating in the experience of the liberated self.

scientism: a belief system which regards natural science as the only valid source of authority.

super-saturated solutions (supersaturation): the condition existing in a solution when it contains more of a dissolved substance than is needed to cause saturation.

transpersonal psychology: a movement that studies phenomena thought to go beyond the limits of the individual person. They include awe, ecstasy, mystical experiences, and other altered states of consciousness.

ungulate: referring to an animal that has hoofs.

yoga: system of spiritual discipline and liberation from the senses; the search for the mystery of the universe undertaken as a search for one's true self; **bhakti yoga:** the path of devotion; **jnana yoga:** the path of knowledge or wisdom; **karma yoga:** the path of selfless service; **hatha yoga:** the path of the purification of the body through physical exercise.

Zeitgeist: the spirit of the age.

index

"global economy," 313
global village, 150
glossolalia, 62
Gnomes, 309
Gnosticism,
    and the shadow, 107,
    shortcomings of, 108
    Stalin member of cult, 245
God,
    a communicating, 99
    alive in Nature, 130
    all comes from, 101
    and St. Paul, 94
    and the notion of sin, 10
    both immanent and transcendent, 130
    is "Intent," 282
    is Nature, 130
    Old Testament, 106
    saviors of, 252
    -seeded primates, 252
    the mind of, 102
    was within Jesus, 88, 93
"God, guru and self are one," 202
"God is dead. God is dead," 109, 318
"God preserve me from Jungians," 164
god(s),
    anthropomorphic, 320
    as patterns and paradigms, 236
    -ism, 317
    is the Logos, 308
    outside time, 318
    partnership with the, 239
    /self, 247
    shaking down false, 315
    the separate, 318
Goddess Remembered, 127, 136
goddess,
    god/ as infinite nature, 126
    history of goddess tradition, 136
    of chaos, Tiamat, 106
    re-emergence of, 8, 179, 183, 184
    the Greek, 185
    tradition of the, 127, 128
Goddesses in Everywoman, 183, 184, 185, 187

Gods in Everyman, 187
Gombe, 48, 49, 50, 51, 53, 56, 59
Gonzales, Raphael, 133
Goodall, Jane, 48
Gore, Al, 177
Gospel of Thomas, 108
Götterdämmerung, 106
government, monolithic world, 314, 316
grace, 90,
    St. Paul's gift of, 94
grandfather, importance of, 170, 174
Grant, George, 243
Great Horned Goddess, paleolithic religion of, 63
Great Mother, 107, 174
Great Pyramid, the, 75
Greece, classical, 314
Greeks,
    ancient, 238, 239, 310
    mythology, 185
Greenpeace, 34, 38-39, 40
Grof, Stanislov, 199
growth, steady state, 105, 240
Guatemala, 208
guides, 227
Gulf War, 168
Gurdjieff, G. I., 30
guru(s),
    and ego, 274
    -consciousness, 201
    essential?, 202
GUTS (grand unified theories), 309
"hall of records," 84
hallucinagenic imagery, 62
Harpur, Tom, 86-102
hashish, 71
Hasidism, 132
healing,
    cancer, 16
    shamans and, 70
    the planet, 146
Heaven,
    and Gnosticism, 108
    flesh of, 32
    Kingdom of, 88
    linked to Earth by world ash tree, 187

ecological criteria applied to, 10
the beast as image of, 107
revolution,
anti-industrial, 187
French and American, 313
in consciousness, 40, 324
industrial, 107, 321
of cellular consciousness, 11
Russian, 245, 313
Reykjavik, 36-37
Rig Vedas, 69, 249
Ring of Power, The, 187
Ring of the Nebilung, 187
rituals,
and sacredness, 130
"hook" our attention, 284
in the Craft, 128
in *The Odyssey*, 239
multi-cultural/racial, 133
must be fluid, 285
Roman Empire, 61, 112
Rowan, John, 174-75, 176
Rumi, 24
Russia, 313
sacred,
a new sense of the, 326
art and the Sphinx, 83
Christian site, Druidic site, 6
conflicts about what is, 136
definition of, 130
dream, 145
living Earth, 128
lodge, 147
separation from the, 295
the "Word" as, 7
wheel, 145
witness, 145
Sacred Sexuality, 190, 191, 192
Sahara Desert, 63
Sai Baba, Swami, 15, 20
salvation, search for, 108
samadhi, 194
Samhain, 133
San Diego, 296
San Francisco, 186
sangha, 203

Sao Paolo, 248
satsang, 203
schizophrenia,
and mystical experience, 215
disease of the human condition, 107
Schneerson, Rabbi, 92
Schumacher, 4
Schwartzkopf, General Norman, 168
"scientific method," 310
scientism, 235
Scotland, 41, 167
Search For The Beloved, The, 234, 247
Sea Shepherd, 36, 37, 38, 39, 47
Sea Shepherd Conservation Society, 34, 38
Sea Shepherd guidelines for operation, 37, 38
Seattle, 46
"second attention," 281
"second coming," 308
second law of thermodynamics, 4
security,
demand for, 318
relationship with, 317
"seer(s)," 261, 268, 274, 275
self,
a metaphorical dagger, 272
fighting an idea of the, 274
losing the fixed, 265-66, 267, 271
luminous, 269
overcoming the split in, 319
patterns of the, 270
stalking the, 272
the separate, 318
self-importance, 263, 265, 274
Sequoia, 284
Serengeti plains, 49
Serpent In The Sky, 74
sexuality,
energy during conception, 272
holistic, 196
lack of, 15
of primates, 62
psilocybin and arousal, 62-63
sacred, 191
spiritual breakthough in, 191